D0394176

Stealing from a Deep Place

Brian Hall

STEALING
FROM A
DEEP PLACE

TRAVELS IN
SOUTHEASTERN
EUROPE

Hill and Wang / NEW YORK

A division of Farrar, Straus and Giroux

Copyright © 1988 by Brian Hall
All rights reserved
Printed in the United States of America
First edition, 1988
Designed by Cynthia Krupat

"Creatures of Land and Water" was originally published
in From the Hungarian Revolution: A Collection of Poems,
edited by David Ray, copyright © 1966 by Cornell University.
Reprinted by permission of Cornell University Press.
The excerpt from The Truth That Killed by Georgi Markov,
copyright © 1983 by Annabel Markov, is reprinted by
permission of Ticknor & Fields, a Houghton Mifflin Company

Library of Congress Cataloging-in-Publication Data
Hall, Brian.
Stealing from a deep place: travels in southeastern Europe /
Brian Hall.—1st ed.
1. Europe, Eastern—Description and travel.   2. Hall, Brian.
I. Title.
DJK18.H34 1988   914.97'7043—dc19   88-4711

For Zsóka,
who surprised me by liking it;
with love

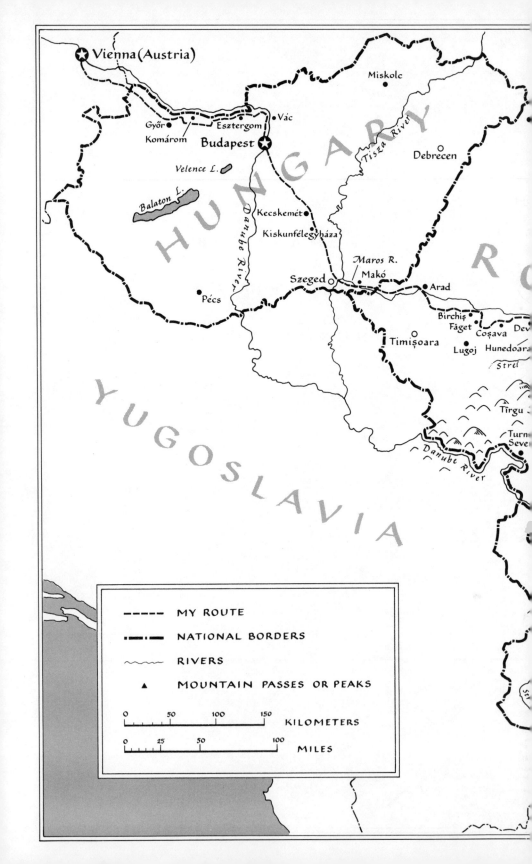

Vienna (Austria)

Miskolc

Győr
Komárom
Esztergom
Vác
Budapest

HUNGARY

Velence L.

Balaton L.

Danube River

Kecskemét
Kiskunfélegyháza

Tisza River

Debrecen

Maros R.
Makó
Szeged
Arad
Birchiş
Făget
Coşava
Dev

Pécs

Timişoara
Lugoj
Hunedoara
Strei

Tîrgu

Turn
Seve

YUGOSLAVIA

Danube River

MY ROUTE
NATIONAL BORDERS
RIVERS
▲ MOUNTAIN PASSES OR PEAKS

0   50   100   150   KILOMETERS

0   25   50   100   MILES

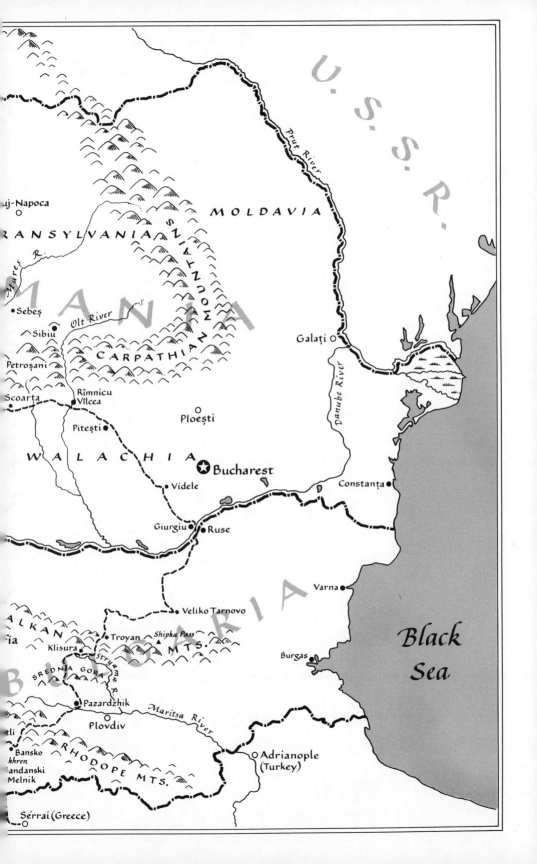

CREATURES OF LAND AND WATER

I draw on my diving gear,
My blanket, and sink down.
My net of language drifts back up, behind me.
Far down, leaves yield their damp shadows wide open
To my hands' ripples in the darkness.

Down there, behind closed shells,
Treasures have lain, blinded, for a thousand years.
When I swim past, mother-of-pearl flares
Fire through the dumb lips.

My hands tremble, as I lift up
The jewels of that night.
Hurry, hurry, string them on sentences
(God whispers to me).

I carry them back toward the light, these riches
I stole from a deep place.
It's no use. One word, and the whole fire
Falls to gray ashes, and the pearls scatter
Back into the sea.

—TIBOR TOLLÁS,
in prison at Vác, Hungary, 1954
Translated by James Wright

ROMANIA

POSTA ROMANA

ON MY LAST MORNING in Hungary, I went out to buy food. There was a little supermarket a block down the main street from the hotel, with stencils of bottles and loaves of bread in the long windows. I wandered up and down the aisles, trying to calculate how much food I would be able to fit into my rucksack and the panniers on my bicycle.

I had to buy things that would last for days, squeezed into the bottoms of bags. I picked up a kilo of rice immediately. Several soup mixes. Bouillon cubes. I lingered in front of a stack of flat cans, deciphering their contents from the faded, misstamped labels. I took four cans of some pork spread and four more cans of mackerel parts. There were other cans whose contents I could not even guess at, so I took along two, out of curiosity. Crackers. Bars of chocolate. At the back of the store, a big loaf of Hungarian white bread. Five apples from a beat-up crate. I picked up a couple of pears and walked with them for a minute or two, then decided they were too old to travel and returned them. More crackers. I hefted the basket. I wasn't used to carrying more than two days' worth of food—I was supposed to bike with all of this? I still needed cheese; I *had* to have cheese. What kind would last best? I looked, and found a stack of pasteurized, processed cheese, in round cardboard containers. I took two precious wheels, each divided into six foil-wrapped wedges. Just like Kraft—processing, foil wrapping: a little bit of America in the heart of Central Europe.

I dumped the wheels in the basket and headed for the checkout line.

The receptionist in the lobby of the hotel laughed when she saw me struggling with the bag through the door.

"Food?" she asked gaily.

"Yes, food."

"Oh boy." The rotund brunette used informal English with zest. "Oh boy. How much you got?"

"Enough for about eight days. If I eat light. If I can just find bread there, then I can stretch it out to two weeks."

"But, Brian—why you go there?" she asked, with a broad smile, in a coaxing voice. "Nobody want to go there. Don't you know that? Rumania is terrible. Terrible! You got smarts, you go by Yugoslavia. Don't hafta buy food for Yugoslavia."

We had talked about this the night before. It had been substantially the same conversation that I had already had two dozen times in Hungary. I reached for the easy excuse: "I've got mail to pick up in Romania." I used the modern name, with the *o*, which the Hungarians scrupulously avoided. "If I want my mail, I have to go."

She snorted. "Make the mail go forward. Write the post and tell them." She was afraid I didn't believe her. "They do it. Really."

"I know they will. But—" But but but. "But I want to see Romania, anyway, no matter what everybody says. I'm interested." She shook her head. "It can't be as bad as all that." Can it? I thought.

She continued to shake her head. "Oh, it is." She scowled in genuine horror. "It is."

When I cycled out of Makó, with the heavy rucksack on my back, the sun was already past the meridian. I could not suppress a feeling of nervousness. The Hungarians' advice to me about Romania over the past two weeks had been simple and unanimous: "Don't go." I knew they had reasons to dislike the Romanians, or, as they insisted, the R*u*manians; so I knew that their advice was untrustworthy. But I had listened to some of it—I had bought food. And I heartily wished that I had not heard the rest, especially the tales of danger, of thieves and knives in the Carpathians. I tried to forget the warnings, but the harder I tried, of course, the less I succeeded.

I rounded a curve between ash trees. Guard towers, fences, and the steel curls of barbed wire slid into view—the fortified border of Romania. This was the line that had been drawn in 1920, in the Treaty of Trianon. The treaty had detached a substantial fraction of Hungary and given it to Romania. Between two Warsaw Pact allies, the line looked more secure, more xenophobic, than the border between Hungary and Austria. A soldier holding a submachine gun watched my approach from the edge of the trees.

·

The Romanian customs officials kept all of us waiting for two hours while they ostentatiously did nothing. The wind of the morning had died down, and the bright autumn weather had become beautiful for cycling. Sitting on the curbstone, watching the sun slide toward the trees, I indulged in fantasies of revenge.

The traffic was exceptionally light. Perhaps it was always light at this border. One automobile, one van, and I were waiting. The drivers and passengers smoked and stared patiently into space.

There were two officials that I could see, a fat one who remained inside most of the time, coming out at rare intervals only to refuse to look at passports and to repeat his order to wait, and a thin one who sat in a shoddily hammered-together wooden box with the sign PASSPORTS depended from the windowsill, who also refused to take passports. The fat one managed to look imperious, and whenever he appeared, I and one or two others would follow him like subjects begging favors, holding our passports out as offerings, until he disappeared again. The thin one only looked persecuted. He wanted just to be left in peace, to be allowed to sit in his box and look out, making irritable tongue-clicking noises at regular intervals. I felt as if I were back home, trying to renew a license at the Massachusetts Registry of Motor Vehicles.

I had gone into the building twice, unasked. Each time I had discovered the fat man sitting, with his feet on his desk and his hands behind his head, watching a soccer match on television. He turned to me each time, keeping his feet on the desk, and told me in English not to worry, that I had to wait, that he would process the passports when he could get to it. He had a shiny face, glassy black eyes, and a halo of black curls as waxy as doll's hair. His words implied that he had other things to do, while he wanted me, in fact, to see that he had nothing else to do. The joy of the job, his imperturbable glassy-eyed stare told me, is not that I can make you wait because I am so busy but that I can make you wait for no other reason than that I want to make you wait. And the more obvious our relationship, the better.

The fat man chose, at last, to put his feet down and look at our passports. He had us gather around him, and he assumed a harried expression. As I handed him my papers, I was chagrined to realize that I felt grateful to him.

At length, the six passports were given to the thin man, and he flattened them on the sill, clicked his tongue unhappily, and stamped them, one by one. Halfway through, he stopped and sighed. There was a pause. It appeared for a moment that he would be unable to continue. But then he rolled his eyes, sighed again, and stamped the remaining three. He handed everything back to the fat man and returned to picking his nose.

The inspection of the van took some time. A great amount of food was revealed in the stacks of boxes inside. Although it was perfectly legal to carry in food, the driver looked sheepish at this uncovering of his personal hoard. The fat man rummaged around for a while and then decided that he wanted to look under a metal plate in the floor of the van, so the driver and his companion had to unload all the boxes onto the asphalt. The fat man stood immobile, with his arms crossed, and watched them work. I inferred that this was their punishment for bringing in so much food.

Once the van was empty, it turned out that the fat man didn't have the wrench necessary to remove the plate. Neither did the driver. Much time was spent looking for a wrench. After some banging and struggling, they managed to detach one side of the plate, and the fat man pried it up two inches in order to peer in. Then the thin man came out of his box and peered in. Then a third man, whom we hadn't seen before, a short man in a medallioned uniform, was brought out, and he peered in. The fat man and the short man discussed what they were seeing at great length. The thin man stared into space. The driver stood among his scattered boxes and maintained a pliant, innocent expression. The sun was behind the trees.

Finally, the fat man turned to me. Behind him, the driver began the long job of reloading his van. Now that the process was over, he looked angry. The driver of the automobile had gone back to sleep.

The fat man had me disgorge the complete contents of my panniers. He squeezed my sleeping bag so hard I was afraid he was going to burst a seam. He examined my camping stove for nearly a minute (it was a Swedish Primus stove, and it bore a slight resemblance to a bomb). Looking through my books, he said, "You got a Bible, mister?"

"No."

"Are you sure you don't got a Bible, mister?" He flipped through *Absalom, Absalom*.

"Yes, I'm sure."

"It's very bad to bring a Bible into Romania, mister. *Very* bad. You get in big trouble." He fanned an Ibsen. "You *sure* you don't got a Bible?"

He said everything with a fixed, empty smile, the black eyes shining and unreadable. I interpreted his attitude as cheerful malice. When he saw the food, he gave me a bright, quizzical look. "Hey, lots of food! You got lots of food, too?"

"Some," I said. I was afraid he might take it from me.

"Why you bring food into Romania? We got lots of food here. Not necessary!" This statement was the best indication I had yet received that what the Hungarians had told me was correct.

The fat man observed, "Hey, that's a nice bike! Is that your personal bike?"

"Yes."

"How much it cost?"

"About $200."

An explosion of spittle: "What?! But that's expensive!" He wiped his chin.

"They're all like that," I said. "Or more."

"You are rich? You must be rich. What job?"

I never knew how to answer that question. My responses, though true enough, were always different.

"I paint houses."

"You paint houses! And you are rich?!"

I hesitated. Compared to most Romanians, I *was* rich, in a way: I had freedom of movement, a prestigious education, and citizenship in the richest country in the world. I certainly didn't want to tell the man that I was poor. At the same time, it was an aggressive question, and I didn't feel like acknowledging, on this sunny and pleasant afternoon, that I was a capitalist pig—especially since most of what I owned was sitting on the bike next to me. So, with a feeling of irony, I said, "No. I'm not rich."

He nodded his head slightly, and the omnipresent smile widened into what was now, unmistakably, an expression of malice. "Ahh—it is a lie." And he turned his back to me.

Passport control over, my next duty was to change money. The civilian in the exchange booth was a tall, friendly polyglot with a disarming stoop. After settling on Italian, we talked about what it was like to tour on a bicycle, while I filled out the forms and wrote traveler's checks.

Romanian law required that I change ten dollars into Romanian lei for each day that I would spend in the country. I would have to show the official exchange slips to customs upon leaving Romania. This was the government's way of getting a jump on the black marketeers, who would be offering me better rates as soon as I left the border station. Beyond the ten dollar per diem, I was free to trade on the black market, as long as I felt like risking a fine, or perhaps imprisonment. That was part of the game. Everyone knew the trading went on, most people did it, and every now and then one of those people who are born every minute was hauled in for it. But I was so cheap, I wouldn't even need the black market: I had no intention of spending more than the official ten dollars a day. (Nor did I intend to spend less. Romanian currency, like all the East Bloc currencies, is soft. It does not appear on any foreign markets. As far as the rest of the world is concerned, the Romanian leu is play money. Any bills that I kept with me when I left the country would be good for lighting campfires—nothing else.)

I asked the tall man what had been on my mind since the beginning of our conversation: "Is it true that there are food problems in Romania?"

"The food? Yes." He shot an involuntary glance toward the two customs men, twenty yards away. "Yes. It's very bad now. We are not supposed to say, but it is bad. You have food?"

"Yes."

"Good."

He handed me the receipt with a wad of bills, plus change. Some of the coins were old and heavy: the coins of a country once rich in metals. But the smaller, newer coins were made of aluminum, and they clicked together with the sound of buttons. Play money.

The tall man looked a last time at my bicycle, still disheveled from the customs search. "And you are heading south, through the mountains? Toward Bulgaria?" He shook his head in disbelief. "Then I wish you luck."

⋅

With only an hour and a half of light remaining, I tried to cover some distance. The sunlight slanted in from the west like a blade sharpening itself on the turning earth. I hurried between dug-up potato fields and passed, now and then, through flat, dusty villages.

At the sight of me, children pointed and laughed. In the unfinished fields, squadrons of women worked with hoes and bare hands, moving down the long lines like brown gnomes, bent at the waist. They seemed encumbered by their full, pleated skirts; haloes of dirt and dust shook from their black hair. I saw men in the villages, working on an automobile, hammering together something, or lounging; or in the fields with the women, hoisting the heavier crates or idling by the wagons with the horses. The men wore heavy wool pants and jackets over cardigan sweaters, dark-colored and dirty, and brimless black hats like large skullcaps that flared subtly around the rims—a touch of Chico Marx.

I came up a slight rise and saw white, wooden buildings on the left. The sign said something about a "technic" for an agronomical cooperative. A slender man stood in a square of green, by an open well, and I stopped for water and directions. The bucket that he hauled up out of the depths on a moss-streaked rope was made of vertical wooden slats held together with iron bands—a design that hadn't changed for a thousand years.

The heavier light of evening, washing skin to the color of clean brass, lent weight to every detail. I saw the bright green grass, beaten down and torn around the well, showing patches of black topsoil; I saw the clapboard buildings, yellowing; the fringe of black oaks behind, breathing through green-gold leaves; the rising path of dust that I had twirled up along the road. I looked at the man, in a linen shirt, young, with light-brown skin and a face of sharply defined parts—nose, eyebrows, and Adam's apple. I drank, and the water from the well tasted sweet and full.

The man spoke some French. He told me there was a campground just five kilometers down the road, on the far side of Arad. He was sure that it was open.

I asked him about his work—I wanted to know what a "technic" was, and if it was a cooperative, how was it arranged? But he seemed reluctant to talk about it. He preferred instead to dwell on the beauty of the evening, and the goodness of the water. I had not spoken French since mid-June, and it was a pleasure to stumble over the nasal words again, to start knocking off the rust of months.

But the conversation was over almost as soon as it had begun. A dump truck rumbled into view on the road, and the young man stopped in mid-sentence. He wished me luck on my travels and ran out to hail the truck. The bed of it was crowded with field-workers, mostly women sitting, and the driver nearly passed the man by. But he yelled—exasperated, cajoling—until the truck finally slowed down for him. He grabbed a handle and hoisted himself up. The others made room for him cheerfully, their field tools swaying above their heads like the jostling lances of soldiers. This was the workers' transportation home, and in the unseasonably warm air it seemed to me a congenial way to get back to apartments in Arad. The young man waved to me as the truck accelerated, and the others, looking a little surprised, all waved as well.

I remounted the bike and pedaled through horizontal shafts of dusty light.

The town of Arad announced itself with a ring of enormous gray complexes of apartment blocks. The road widened, and I moved through the ring with my head down. Gradually, the air began to smell bad. I looked around me and saw industrial plants mixed with apartment houses. Smokestacks shot out billows of smog. The evening became suffused with a gray, cancerous light. The road reverted to cobblestones, and the cobblestones were slimy with oil. The walls of the buildings were streaked with black. I felt as if I had stumbled into the pages of *Hard Times*. I had been warned about Romanian towns, but nothing had prepared me for this.

The road surface became more and more uneven, and I was forced to walk the bike. An urgent desire to escape came over me—but I moved along at a snail's pace, slithering on the layer of grime.

Now and then, men asked if I wanted black-market lei. They sidled up to me on the street corners and whispered, with a furtive desire that bordered on the obscene, "Hey—changemoney?" Or, if they thought I was German, they said, *"Geld wechsel?"* Almost everyone motioned for a cigarette. ("Marlboro?" one man asked plaintively, from beneath a Chico Marx hat.) Unfortunately, I hadn't known cigarettes would be in such demand, so I hadn't brought any. I had to shrug, and smile no, and hope that they believed me. No one did.

I was looking for a certain road out of Arad, and I stopped to ask directions. But I got nowhere; communication seemed impossible. My map of Romania was a novelty; it was regarded with some awe. I stood among a group of Romanians on a street corner south of the town center and watched them pass the map from hand to hand, turning it one way and then the other, arguing not only about where I should be going but about where I was now. I repeatedly had to show them Arad's location, but their fingers would wander off again, searching futilely for inspiration.

Arms waved me in opposite directions, and voices began to rise. I remembered a friend's comment, which I have since been unable to verify: "Maps are restricted in Romania; it is not desirable that people know their way too well around the country."

On my way out of the town, at last on the correct road, I was intercepted by a group of children that ran into the street in front of me. "*Sta! Sta! Gumi!*" they cried. They were asking for gum— but I didn't have any of that, either. The two biggest ones, about ten years old, mimed smoking a cigarette. I veered to the other side of the road. The children tried to block my way, but I skirted them, yelling excuses in Italian. One of them got his hands on the back of my bicycle as I passed, but I pedaled hard and broke away. I expected stones to chase me, but nothing was thrown. I felt ashamed: I was escaping from a flock of children with my goods intact.

The sun had set, unseen, behind the smog of Arad. I came out into the countryside again. The air still had an acrid smell, but at least the slime on the road was gone. The moon was new, and the evening would be pitch-dark by six o'clock. Fortunately, European campgrounds are elaborate: there was a good chance that the one I was headed for would have a café, or some kind of lighted place in which I could spend the evening. The man by the well had said five kilometers, but I had already bicycled six or seven. I passed field-workers trudging home, who perhaps had missed the trucks, one or two on rattling old bicycles. I stopped several times to ask about the campground. Each time, I was told that it lay two or three kilometers on, and each time I was assured that it was open. Ten kilometers outside of Arad, I arrived, in total darkness. The campground was closed. The moon, diving after the sun, was a sliver of white on the darkest violet.

I did not relish the idea of camping, hidden off the road somewhere, in darkness. In a few days, there would be enough moonlight to make free camping comfortable, but not now. Some lights shone from the other side of the turnout for the campground, and I headed toward them. It was a motel—an ugly, aluminum-sided affair. I left my bicycle on the concrete porch and went in.

Noise and music poured out from a dingy restaurant at the back of the lobby. Men stood around smoking, looking as if they had nothing to do.

A sign behind the receptionist listed the room prices: as I had been told to expect, the prices for Westerners were four times those for Romanians. I couldn't really afford a room, but now that I was here, I couldn't bear the thought of going out and looking for a place to sleep in the dark. I paid and then carried my bicycle in from the porch. The receptionist saw the bike and started to say something, but I stared her down as I walked past the desk.

The room had what seemed to be cardboard walls, a filthy, damp carpet, and a bed with brownish sheets that had once been white. In the ceiling fixture, three of the four sockets were empty; the fourth socket held a forty-watt bulb. There was barely enough light to read or write by. The customs man had called me rich for owning a bicycle, but ten nights in this hole would cost me more than the price of the bike. I would not come to one of these motels again. Camping in pitch-darkness was better than a damp carpet and the smell of tobacco, the muffled noise of arguments coming up from below. Depressed, I checked the shower and was surprised to feel the water warming up as it splashed between my fingers. I took a very long shower, trying to get my money's worth from that, if from nothing else. The hot water slowly relaxed me.

·

The decision to travel through Eastern Europe had come to me months before, at the end of a sweltering July day in Ravenna, Italy.

I had paid for a night in the Ravenna youth hostel and was sharing dinner with half a dozen other travelers in the hostel's cafeteria. I had been trapped into eating the hostel's food— minimalist spaghetti—because a saint's day in the town had closed all the grocery stores and had caught me completely without supplies. Some of my fellow diners had been similarly surprised.

We were the usual WASPish hodgepodge of hostelers: a linguistics student from Tennessee, an Austrian medical student, two Californians with Eurail passes and brand-new backpacks, and a young Swiss couple. The first two were cyclists like myself, and the three of us, in a leisurely way, were trying to impress each other.

The Tennesseean claimed that he had cycled 250 kilometers in one day. The Austrian was modest for a cyclist, but he owned to some elaborate feats of endurance in the Dolomites, the week before. I couldn't match their stories of speed and strength, but I had one inarguable statistic to my credit: I had been cycling *longer* than either of them. Like the tortoise, I was slow, but my steadiness was hard to beat.

By that time, I had been bicycling for four and a half months. I had landed in England in March 1982, with a lump of money from a Harvard travel fellowship and the determination to make the money last as long as I could possibly stretch it. Six months before, I had completed seventeen straight years of school, and the only thing that had been in my mind on graduation day, from the champagne breakfast (after $40,000, another $2.50) to President Bok's figurative shaking of the aspergillum over our 1,600 heads ("I *wel*come youuu, to the *fell*owship, of *ed*ucated men and women . . ."), my only thought had been "At last." What a long, narrow, musty trail—kindergarten, elementary school, junior-high school, high school, college. I had done well in my studies, and my professors' advice to me was to keep studying, to allow peristalsis to carry me on through graduate school. They were acknowledging the obvious: I had shown an aptitude for nothing so much as being a student.

E. M. Forster once complained that the English public schools developed students' minds but left them with undeveloped hearts. Public-school graduates were prepped to live narrow lives. They may go out into the world with a knowledge of Latin, Forster suggested, but they are woefully unfit to improve or even to understand a world of whose peoples they are not only contemptuous but utterly, imperviously ignorant. Perhaps I now belonged to the fellowship of educated men and women; I had my "Latin": the familiarity with certain books and intellectual currents that was expected of me. I would not embarrass myself in conversations with my peers. But I knew, also, that I had been wasting my time, that I was still a thorough provincial.

So I decided to travel. All I had needed was some money, and a few days before graduation, the secretary of the English Department had called to tell me that I had it. Or at least a good start on it. I put the diploma in a closet, took three jobs, and doubled Harvard's money in six months. I flew out of the United States on the penultimate day of winter 1982.

I had no particular plans. How could I have? I had no idea what I was getting into. And besides, I was running away from plans. The trip itself would have to tell me where to go. I intended to spend at least two years on the road, and that meant the money was tight. With the bike for transportation, a sleeping bag, a camping stove, a tent smaller than a doghouse, and a youth-hostel card, I set my budget at nine dollars a day.

I cycled in the Cotswolds and Wales, pushing myself gradually into shape over a period of four weeks. Welsh roads with 33 percent gradients taxed both my quadriceps and my credulity. I was rained on constantly, snowed on twice, and people told me that England was enjoying its balmiest April in decades. A pink-cheeked girl in a pub north of the Brecon Beacons told me how to predict Welsh weather: "If you can see the Beacons, it's going to rain; if you can't see them—it's raining."

I crossed the Channel and headed south. I stopped to visit an American friend at Évian at the beginning of May, and spent a few days floating around Geneva, counting lovers and going to concerts. Then I pedaled into the Alps and discovered that I loved mountain cycling. I spent three weeks climbing from pass to mountain pass, cycling, in the higher regions, between eight-foot walls of snow on newly scoured roads, where the cars had not yet started to come.

Corsica followed, and then Sardinia. And now, after the snow in England, the temperature reached 105 degrees every day by one o'clock. I learned Italian in the dark, cool bars of Sardinia, between the hours of 1:00 and 7:00. I cycled in the mornings, and as the sun was going down. And I grew lonely. The Sardinians were friendly, but their very friendliness made me feel the barrier between us more acutely; my rudimentary Italian made me long for my native language. I escaped loneliness and the heat by taking a boat to Italy. On my last day in Sardinia, the temperature reached 110 degrees.

From Livorno, I cycled to Spoleto, where a friend was playing in a music festival. I filled up with conversation, over the space of a week, the emptiness that I had been feeling. We talked about people we knew in the United States. Provincial talk. I sneaked into festival performances. I saw Barishnikov showing off at the Spoleto swimming pool. All the rooms in town were filled with festivalgoers—but the weather was fine, and I slept each night on the aqueduct above the town, where thousands of bats kept the air free of insects and jittered and spun in the spotlights, looking like scraps of oiled paper. The festival ended, and I headed north toward Austria, chasing cooler weather. I crossed the Apennines and descended to the Po plain. I bypassed San Marino, because I didn't feel like seeing stamps. But I *did* feel like seeing mosaics, so I arrived, late one morning, in Ravenna.

And all this time I had kept to my budget. I had even undercut it: I was averaging eight dollars a day. Keeping to my budget had meant camping on three nights out of four, cooking my own meals, and strictly rationing my entertainment whenever I was in a city. I was not saving money for its own sake. The cheaper I traveled, the longer I could travel—and I did not want to get off the bike for another year and a half.

Yet, on that hot evening in Ravenna, I was frustrated. Italy in July feels like an occupied country—it arouses thoughts of escape. To where? Virtually all the inhabitants of Western Europe change places in the summer, becoming tourists of other countries. It is during the summer that one grows aware of how small Western Europe is, and how similar are its parts. I knew, sitting in the hostel cafeteria with five other members of the Germanic tribe, all of us, like our ancestors, attracted to the warm, easy life of the Mediterranean, that I was tiring of this tolerant, interconnected world. I wanted something more secretive, more elusive.

The linguist from Tennessee had recently returned from

Eastern Europe. I asked him how he'd liked it, and he answered, "Well, Budapest is a *jewel*."

At that moment, I knew—I would see Budapest. And while I was at it, I would travel in other countries of the East Bloc. Which countries had he seen, I asked the linguist.

Czechoslovakia, Hungary, and Yugoslavia.

Not Romania or Bulgaria?

No. As far as he knew, not many Westerners traveled to those countries. He had an idea that Romania was depressing. He'd heard bad things.

Like what?

Like the roads were in terrible shape for bicycling. And the people were suspicious of foreigners. Afraid.

And Bulgaria?

He knew nothing about Bulgaria. No one at the table did.

And neither did I. So it was settled—I would visit Budapest, the jewel, and then go to Romania and Bulgaria. I would spend the autumn in Eastern Europe. Perhaps I would gather enough material there for a couple of travel pieces. I would gradually work my way south, and reach Greece by Halloween, before the onset of winter.

I left Ravenna and continued north toward the Dolomites.

Then, as usual, I drifted behind my intentions. One day led to another. I found myself at the Salzburg Music Festival. Then, somehow, I promised to meet a college roommate at Freiburg, not realizing how far west the city was. Coming back east, in September, I was trapped by Vienna, where I whiled away the days going to the opera and sampling varietals in the wine cellars. As a result, I did not enter Hungary until October 1, more than a month after I had thought I would. On my third day in Hungary, the weather turned cold and rainy, and I sat at a motel window in Esztergom and wrote worriedly about winter.

When the weather cleared, I cycled around the Danube Bend, where the river takes a great and decisive turn to the south. Following the river, I reached Budapest. My plan was to visit the city for three days. But Budapest, like Vienna, trapped me. I did not think it was a jewel—it was too unkempt for that—but within forty-eight hours I thought of it as a home away from home. I had met someone; I stayed in her apartment. We had our dinners together, and walked around the city, and talked about ourselves. After two weeks, I left, but I had promised to come back.

By then, I was *very* late. Southern Hungary would have to be sacrificed; I took the east road out of Budapest and hurried across the sprawling Hungarian plain. Great clouds of gnats rose from the fens and blew across my path, blackening my front with their bodies; at night, in the restaurants, I scooped them, dead, out of my pockets. Ferries took me across turgid, swampy rivers. Moss hung from the trees, and one scrawny village followed another over the moist, featureless terrain. Soon I was at Makó, near the Romanian border. I booked a room in the hotel for my last night. It was October 21. If winter came early this year, it would strike any day. I prayed for a late winter.

POSTA ROMANA

THE MOTEL RESTAURANT, in the morning, still bore the traces of the night before. Several chairs lay on their backs, and the carpeting was littered with cigarette butts. A woman with an expression of pain ran a vacuum cleaner along the back of the room. She motioned to me to take a seat.

A heavy morning fog pressed against the windows. Except for the woman, who looked at me from time to time and scowled, I was alone. Through the fog, I could see that the parking lot was empty of cars. The crowd in the lobby and the restaurant the night before had left no trace but their cigarettes.

At length, the woman switched off the vacuum cleaner and came up to me reluctantly. She looked as if she had been hoping that I would give up and go away.

"Da?"

"Could I have some breakfast?" I asked in Italian, enunciating carefully. I had had to buy breakfast along with my room.

She shook her head. She hadn't understood.

"Breakfast? Breakfast?"

Nothing.

So much for Italian. I tried French.

Nothing.

What else could I be in here for? I mimed eating.

"Ohhh . . . *Da.*" The woman's shoulders went slack. *"Da. Micul dejun."* She fixed me with listless, defeated eyes. I wondered if this was what the Countess in *Justine* had looked like, after the Count had been draining blood out of her. The woman muttered something with a questioning inflection. Now it was my turn not to understand. She turned away and disappeared into the kitchen. I sat by the window, at a loss.

I had made the mistake in Vienna of not buying a Romanian dictionary, and I could have kicked myself for it now. I had not wanted to take on the extra weight any earlier than I needed to. But when I looked for a dictionary in Budapest, I'd gradually realized that there were no books about Romania to be found anywhere in the city. I had asked at the bookstores up and down Váci Street, and the booksellers had sniffed, or snorted—they'd let it be known that they hardly considered Rumanian to be a living language.

So I did not know the language, and I had no means of learning it—a new situation for me. Cheerful friends in the West had assured me that my knowledge of Italian would enable me to communicate in Romania, as Romanian is a Latin language. I would ask my questions in Italian, their predictions ran, the answer would come back in Romanian, and we both would have a vague idea of what we had just said to one another. I was encouraged in my optimism when I glanced through a Romanian magazine at the embassy in Vienna and saw how similar to Italian it appeared on the printed page. True, I couldn't really read it, but I felt that I almost could. I should have allowed that little warning bell to sound. Because now that I was confronted with the spoken article, I could already tell that the procedure recommended by my friends was not going to work. I could not understand more than a tiny fraction of what was said to me. Whether this was a reflection on the quality of my Italian or on the quality of my friends' advice, I could not decide.

In Sardinia, when I had only begun to pick up Italian, I had discovered the frustration of being unable to speak about complex things, of being confined always to colorless formulations like "That is not good" or "This is better than that." Now, in Romania, I was beginning to realize how much worse it was to be incapable even of the homely, pragmatic phrases. I was growing appreciative of the simple effectiveness of questions like "Which is the road to Zăbrani?" and "When can I get my passport back?"

Fortunately, I did happen to know about a dozen words of Romanian—most of them, not surprisingly, having to do with either traveling or eating. Exactly where I learned them I can no longer remember, but I was glad they had come along for the ride. They were:

da	yes
nu	no
vă rog	please
mulţumesc	thank you
cu plăcere	you're welcome
unde	where
este	is
pîine	bread
apă	water
lapte	milk
vin	wine
bere	beer
poşta	post office
drum bun	bon voyage
fumatul oprit	no smoking

(The last I had learned in the waiting room of the Romanian embassy in Vienna, while I was breezily flipping through a magazine and congratulating myself on knowing Italian——the words had been printed in foot-high letters on the wall. All the Romanians in the waiting room had been smoking.)

And now, thanks to the woman with pernicious anemia, I could add a new word:

micul dejun	breakfast

Still, it was not a list to warm the heart of an adventurer.

The woman reappeared with a dish and dropped it in front of me. Three slices of a fatty sausage, half a green pepper, and a slab of bread. Considering the stories about the food, this was better than I had expected.

"*Cafeá? Limonată? Apă?*" she asked.

"*Cafeá, vă rog.*" My first Romanian sentence.

While I picked at the sausage, chewing hard on the gristle, I unfolded my chintzy tourist-office road map of Romania, which looked as if someone had drawn it with a crayon. I had to figure out where I was going now. I couldn't really postpone the decisions any longer.

Romania is divided, geographically and culturally, into three main regions. The principal dividing line is provided rather decisively by the Carpathian Mountains, which enter the country from the north, proceed approximately to the center, take a sharp right turn, and exit in the southwest. The huge northwest region enclosed by this curve—fully half the country—is called by the Romanians *Ardeal*; the Hungarians, who lost the area in 1920 at Trianon, call it *Erdely*, while Americans know it by the Latinate word "Transylvania," which means "beyond the forest"—a twelfth-century word suitably evoking removal, since the area served as a fortified outpost for the Hungarian nation after A.D. 1003. The region has a few valleys but consists mainly of rolling highlands, historically inaccessible, not because of their size, which is small, but because of their forests, which until recently were nearly impenetrable.

The southern region of Romania, between the lower Carpathians and the Danube, is named Walachia, and the Romanians who live there are called Vlachs, or Walachs (although "Vlach" is also the common historical word for *any* ethnic Romanian). The word "Walach" is related to "Welsh"—both stem from the Gothic word for foreigner. (The Goths invaded the Danube basin in the third century and immediately complained about all the foreigners living there.) Within the past century, the Romanians have decided that the terms "Walach" and "Vlach" are derogatory. They prefer to let the river Olt divide Walachia into Oltenia, on the west, and Muntenia, which means "mountainland," on the east. (The last choice of name is odd, since Muntenia is flat.) The inhabitants are thus called Oltenians and Muntenians. These terms, however, are rarely heard outside Romania.

Moldavia is the third region, and it lies in the northeast, between the upper Carpathians and the river Prut. Moldavia was the last of the regions to gain inhabitants, these being Transylvanian Vlachs who crossed the Carpathians in the Middle Ages, and it has remained the most sparsely populated and primitive of the regions. From Moldavia has come the liveliest and richest folk art, and in it survive the best-preserved villages and monasteries. Postcards, posters, advertisements for Romania—these are usually photographs of Moldavia. The stunning wooden villages with the distinctive rooflines, like groups of pointed witches' hats, are Moldavian.

Unfortunately, Moldavia was the one region that I wasn't going to see at all. Time was the problem, as it had been ever since I had agreed to rendezvous in Freiburg without knowing where Freiburg was. I had entered Romania from the west, in southern Transylvania, and would be exiting south, out of Walachia, by crossing the Danube into Bulgaria. I didn't even have time to see northern Transylvania, another subject for the brochures. If I biked so far out of my way as to reach Moldavia, I risked not only getting snowed on but running out of food and starving to death—if the rumors about the food situation were true.

So I would have to remain in southern Transylvania, working eastward through the foothills above the Carpathians and then cutting through one of the river valleys to the Walachian plain. I traced the bright, clumsily drawn routes on the map with a finger. I could continue to Deva, turn south into the Strei Valley, and cross into Walachia at Petroşani. From there, south to Tîrgu Jiu and east to my mail stop in Piteşti, then south again to the border crossing at Giurgiu. Fine.

The woman appeared with the coffee and plopped it in front of me, right on the map.

"Uh . . . *Mulţumesc.*"

She turned away. I immediately knew, from the look of the stuff, that I had made a mistake in asking for it. The liquid was muddy, green-brown, and more than half sediment. I sipped it. A lukewarm mixture of dark grains, much worse than chicory—it tasted like sour dirt. Of course. If they didn't have bread, why should they have coffee?

I left it. I wrapped up the last piece of sausage and a quarter of the green pepper and put them in my knapsack. For lunch. I was afraid to waste anything. These scraps might be the only Romanian food I would see all day. I felt as if I were heading into a disaster area.

The vacuum cleaner whooshed into life again as I went out the door.

.

Looking for a place to eat lunch, I came into a village shaded by plane and plum trees. Tumbledown houses of one and two stories centered around an open square of packed dirt, where hens stepped nervously around each other and two or three mongrels slept in the patches of sunlight. The two grocery stores (in Romania, as in Italy, they are called *alimentari*) were closed and dark. I looked through the windows and saw empty shelves. The public fountain at the edge of the square was dry and choked with dust. By the time I had gotten someone to understand that I needed water, a crowd of children had gathered around me, asking for gum and cigarettes. Adults began to mix with the children, and they offered to change money. Dozens of questions were thrown at me, but I could not understand them.

My bottle was returned, filled with water, and I headed out of the village. I would have liked to sit on a bench in the square, among the sleeping dogs and the circling hens, watching the village life while I ate, but I couldn't be comfortable at the center of a crowd. It had been happening all morning—each time I had stopped in a village, people had immediately gathered around me. The expressions on their faces, as they had deluged me with queries, had been a mixture of wonder and guile—wonder at my beard (Romanian men, I was learning, were mostly clean-shaven); wonder at my ten-speed bike, my touring helmet; guile at the thought of my dollars, my blue jeans, my cigarettes. And the clamor of questions had never stopped, even after it had become clear that I couldn't understand.

The road was in sorry shape. I dodged potholes as large as kitchen sinks, now and then ones much larger. There were potholes in which the bicycle and I could have lain, side by side. A mile outside the village, just where the road curved into the foothills, I stopped to eat. I got out the sausage and the green pepper from that morning and tore off a piece of the Hungarian bread. I opened a tin of ham spread, and a smell of salt and preservatives came into the air. There was no place to sit, so I ate standing up, leaning against a guardrail.

A tractor carrying two farmhands went by. I think I nodded a greeting. Thirty yards past me, the tractor suddenly stopped and the two men jumped out. They were dark, sweat-begrimed, and muscular. They came toward me, yelling and waving their arms. I stopped chewing on the bread and looked at them, alarmed. They kept coming. They were big. In the four glowering eyes I could read, I felt sure, a murderous intent. There was no one else around, no house in sight.

The Hungarians had warned me repeatedly about physical violence in Romania, and I had not listened. They had told me to buy a knife to protect myself, and I had scoffed. Now all their stories came rushing back to me. Only a lingering sense of the indignity of panic prevented me from jumping on my bike and trying to escape. (A disinclination to look like a fool has no doubt prevented many a fool from saving himself.)

When they were about six yards away, the two men stopped. They began to stamp on the road surface, slapping their great farmer's boots down, cursing. Then one of them went to the side of the road and broke a stick away from the brambles. With the stick, he picked up the bloody carcasses of two snakes. He flung them, one after the other, into the bushes. The man with the stick turned to me and said "*Vipera!*" He encircled his eyes with his fingers to mean "keep an eye out." The vipers had been crawling in my direction. The Hungarians had warned me about the vipers, too. But they hadn't told me that the Romanians would protect me from them.

The men didn't give me a second glance. They wiped their hands on their pants and jumped back onto the tractor. The engine snorted to life, and they took off. I can't recall now whether I remembered to thank them or not, but I was probably too dumbfounded to think of it.

.

Perhaps I should explain why the opinions of the Hungarians keep intruding.

When I decided in Ravenna to travel in the East Bloc, I knew only a little about Hungary and practically nothing about Romania or Bulgaria. So over the next couple of months I would venture, now and then, into a public library and read whatever I could find on the subjects. I read about the President and First Party Secretary of Romania, a man named Nicolae Ceauşescu (pronounced "Chow-*sheh*-scoo"), who had become leader in 1965. Ceauşescu was a nationalist who expounded, with some force, the 200-year-old idea (among Romanians) that he and his people were the direct descendants of the Romans. (It was Ceauşescu who changed the country's name, in 1965, from Rumania to Romania.) The Romans, under Trajan, conquered what is now Transylvania and Oltenia in A.D. 106, and pursued a vigorous colonization policy there for the next century and a half. The new Roman province was called Dacia, after the Dacians, a Thracian people who had inhabited it before the Romans came. After the Roman conquest, the Latinized colonists of Dacia and the conquered Dacians, in all likelihood, intermarried and formed a Daco-Roman population. It was from the Daco-Romans that Ceauşescu and his countrymen claimed descent, and they pointed to their Latinate language—so striking in a region of Slavic and Uralic tongues—as proof. Ceauşescu used this racial theory as a rallying cry to arouse nationalist feelings against the Hungarians and the Russians. The Western governments valued Ceauşescu, because in developing his nationalist ideas, he had pursued an independent foreign policy for the past eighteen years that had, on occasion, embarrassed the Soviet Union. In the English-language books, the word that kept coming up to describe him was "maverick."

Unfortunately, the commentary centered almost exclusively

on foreign policy and didn't tell me much about the internal
situation in Romania. For that kind of information, I had to rely
on the opinions of other travelers—an unreliable source if there
ever was one. And in this case, it was especially unreliable, because
only the Hungarians seemed to hold strong opinions about
Romania.

I received my first warning in Montagnana, Italy, just a few
days after I had left Ravenna. I was having dinner with a friend
from college, and I happened to mention that I would be cycling
through Romania. A look of horror came over his face, and he
burst out with a passion that took me completely by surprise: "But
you can't want to travel there! The Romanians are genetically
impoverished—too much in-breeding! They're all stupid, and they
have hair growing out of their ears!" I laughed. But he leaned
toward me and hissed, "I mean it! I wouldn't go there if I were
you!" Much later, after I had returned to the United States, I
would learn that my friend's mother was a Magyar.*

As soon as I entered Hungary, the stories mushroomed. Every
country has bad things to say about its neighbors, and the closer
you get to the Balkans, the more vicious the insults grow. Hungary
and Romania have been enemies for nearly a thousand years—the
length of time that they have been fighting for ownership of
Transylvania. And the Romanians' theory concerning their Daco-
Roman descent is caught up in this dispute, since Transylvania
formed the heart of ancient Dacia.

The Hungarian King Stephen I (St. István) consolidated
Magyar control of Transylvania in A.D. 1003, and set up the area
as a wide frontier post, to protect Hungary's eastern flank from
tribes of Russian-steppe riffraff and—as it would later develop—
the Ottoman Turks. Romanians claim that the invading Hungarians subjected a population of Transylvanians: the Daco-Romans/
Vlachs, who had survived eight centuries of barbarian depredations

* "Magyar" is the Hungarians' word for themselves and their culture. Today, the terms
"Hungarian" and "Magyar" are practically interchangeable, but historically, "Magyar" has
been used to refer to the ethnic group and "Hungarian" to refer to inhabitants of Hungary,
whether Magyar or not. This was once a crucial distinction—at the end of Maria Theresa's
reign, for example, less than 40 percent of the inhabitants of Hungary were Magyar.

by taking refuge in the heavily forested hills. For their part, Hungarians maintain that the region was virtually empty when they found it, depopulated by the centuries of invasions, and that the Vlach shepherds and other mentally deficient serfs moved back into Transylvania from havens in northern Greece beginning in the thirteenth century. (To this they add that Dacia under the Romans was transformed into an enormous penal colony, and that the Romanians, if anything, are the descendants of criminals and perverts from all over the Roman Empire.)

Regardless of how the Hungarians found Transylvania in 1003, by the 1400s there was a substantial population of Vlach serfs living under Magyar rule. And the Vlach element, aided by immigration and the Turkish depopulation of Hungary, grew faster than the Magyar element. By the beginning of the eighteenth century, the Vlachs, now calling themselves Rumanians, comprised a majority of the Transylvanian population. At the end of World War I, the Allied powers, following the principle of national self-determination (and keeping in mind that the Hungarians had been on the losing side of the war), detached Transylvania from Hungary and handed it to Romania.

Unfortunately, although the majority of the population of Transylvania *as a whole* is Romanian, there are areas deep inside the region—along the frontier line that King Stephen established nine centuries before—that still have heavy Magyar majorities. Slightly over 2 million Magyars live in Romania (the Romanians say 1½ million, the Hungarians say 3 million—Balkan countries have a talent for juggling statistics); the government in Bucharest treats them with all the hatred that it feels for Hungary, and for the memory of Hungary's own repressive rule in Transylvania. It has closed Magyar schools; it bars Magyars from positions of authority, and grants them only the most menial and degrading jobs; it forbids the import of books about Magyar culture and religion; it harasses the Magyars' Roman Catholic faith (most Romanians are Orthodox). The Hungarians, enraged by a defeat at the hands of a people they consider to be inferior to them, look on the plight of their erstwhile countrymen, many of them relatives, with an anger and a sense of injustice that borders on hysteria.

Knowing this, I knew that I couldn't trust what the Hungarians told me. But one can hear only so many times that one is a stupid fool before one begins to believe it. During my stay in Budapest, some of the stories began to stick. After three weeks' listening to Hungarian opinion, I approached the Romanian border with a certain feeling of dread. I hadn't bought a knife, because I considered advice like that always to be foolish—I hadn't the faintest idea how to handle a knife. But I *had* bought food. And when two muscle-bound men hopped off their tractor, in the middle of nowhere, and came at me yelling, I very nearly scrambled onto my bike and fled, abandoning my food, my knapsack, and my helmet to what I believed were homicidal Vlachs.

I know, in writing this account, that I had better not let my friend in Budapest see it. She would never forgive me.

.

Turning south into the foothills of the Transylvanian Alps, I rose slowly out of the plain around Arad and felt as if I were shedding successive layers of unpleasant clothing. Soon the flatlands were a film of brown, increasingly hidden by bushes and outcroppings in the undulating terrain.

The road became scenic, as I discovered with surprise that it was deep autumn in the Carpathians. I had thought autumn had come and gone while I was on the enormous Hungarian plain, where trees had been as rare as radio towers. Now, suddenly, I found myself in woods as impossibly colorful as those of a New England fall. The bushes fell away as the road wound deeper into the hills, and I cycled between forest floors shaded and hushed like cathedral naves. Most of the trees were beech, with a few ashes and rheumatoid oaks. The air was warm and still under an almost violet sky. I kept moving upward, between canopies of orange and yellow, with the smell of leaf mold in my nostrils. I felt comforted and peaceful.

I passed another cyclist, a local man on a three-speed rustbox. We exchanged smiles. He had a gap-toothed, goofy grin and an appealing face. Elated by the beautiful scenery, I suddenly felt I had to ignore our language barrier. I turned in my seat and spoke to him; he smiled wider and nodded. I mentioned the fine weather, the pastoral beauty of our route, the strenuous cycling among the hills—I became rhapsodic. Pedaling serenely, he continued to nod and to smile. With his round, fleshy face and mouth made for smiling, he reminded me of Peter Potamus, the friendly hippo in the old Hanna-Barbera cartoon.

I waved goodbye. But although he hadn't said anything, Peter was determined, now that I had spoken to him, to keep up with me. His bicycle was in terrible shape, and I had overtaken him at a good clip, so it must have required a good deal of exertion on his part to follow me. Yet even on the steepest hills, each time I glanced around, he would be right there, and he would flash me the same happy, silly grin. I slowed down a bit to make it more comfortable for him. The only sounds were his breathing and the creaking of his bicycle. He never lost his smile. He never spoke. I began to wonder if perhaps Peter was a simpleton.

In a dell, we came to a hamlet of three or four farm buildings, built of fieldstones painted white. I turned to Peter, and said, *"Vă rog—apă? Unde este apă?"*

He dismounted immediately and led me around one of the buildings, to an open well. It was the kind of well I would see throughout Romania, looking, to my industrialized sensibility, like a primitive contraption for pumping oil. The high, sun-bleached arm, from which the rope and bucket dangled, was an old, dressed tree trunk fixed with a spike to a wooden fulcrum. By pulling the rope down, hand over hand, one lowered the bucket into the well, and then the counterweight, on the short end of the trunk, helped lift the full bucket up from the depths. The motion of the hands and the trunk—a flash of palms and the wood bending slowly down and up—made a graceful ritual. Many of these wells in Romania had been supplanted by the crank-and-drum variety (such as the one outside the agronomical cooperative), which were easier to maintain but less striking in appearance. There was something fragile and solemn about the older wells, thrusting their spindly, bowed backs, not quite vertical, thirty feet into the air. Out on the empty plains, they were the simplest of steeples.

While I was drinking and Peter looked on, two boys came out of the nearest building and ran up to me. But they did not yell

"Gumi, gumi!" Instead, they regarded me silently for a while, and then the older one asked me what must have been "Where are you from?" They were grave, good-looking boys, about twelve and nine years old.

"America," I said, expecting a pair of blank faces. "I'm an American."

They bolted into the house, like startled deer, yelling, "An American! An American!" I almost thought it was panic. But presently they reappeared, tugging behind them their father and mother. The parents were small—the father wore a black vest, a Chico Marx hat, and baggy brown pants; the mother was encased in the usual windings of half a dozen skirts and shawls. The family stood around me in a semicircle, the children wide-eyed, the parents faintly amused. I still held the dripping wooden cup in my hand. I felt as if I were about to hold a press conference.

The boys asked if they could see an American dollar. I fished through my emergency funds and handed them a twenty. They touched it and viewed it reverently, the way one might handle a magic wand. The father had laughed at his boys' request, but he took the bill, too, and examined it grimly for many seconds. He turned it over and back again, staring as if there were something printed there that he had to decipher. The mother didn't even want to touch it; her self-deprecating laugh signified that the money was too important to be entrusted to her hands.

Next the boys wanted to see my electronic watch. They were sure I had an electronic watch. They were wrong. My windup Timex, with a cracked crystal and a broken wristband, was an unspeakable disappointment to them. Even their father's watch was better than *that.*

The boys didn't ask about my foodstuffs, but I suspected they were curious, so I broke off for each of them a square of chocolate, which they accepted with delight. Then, in a rare moment of insight, I dug out and distributed some tablets of Dextro-Energen (quick-energy sugar pills for cyclists and other weirdos). I was hoping that the scientific, plastic-packaged look of the stuff would make them think "American," and "professional cyclist's food," or some such nonsense. They were suitably impressed.

More questions followed, of the what-hometown, which-family, where-to, how-long, how-far, and why-on-earth variety. We were largely discouraged by the dearth of common words between us, but the family's curiosity drove them on. I could understand about a third of their questions, after many repetitions; they understood none of mine. I think I was trying harder than they were. I asked one question several times, in Italian and French: Was the farm their own? I had read that the land in the high country was still privately owned. But the father misunderstood; he told me what was on the farm, not who owned it—a cow (the boys said *"nguuuu"*), two pigs (the boys said *"screeeee"*), a goat (*"ne-ne, ne-ne"*), and two dozen hens (*"bok-bok-bok"*); three and a half hectares of fodder and grain. But it had to be his; no state would be stupid enough to take ownership of farms that small.

The father treated the boys with a gentleness that appealed to me, asking them earnestly how they had liked the chocolate, urging them to ask something else, touching them lightly on the shoulder as he spoke. The mother, hirsute and thick-bodied, brought out a rough deal chair for me. The father squatted on his heels beneath an oak at the corner of his house. Peter lounged against the well wall and explored his hair with a happy expression. I was poured a mug of new red wine, which tasted like hard cider: tart, sharp, and effervescent. A mug of milk followed, with bits of cream and yellow flecks of fat floating on its surface. Then a slab of bread with honey; the honey was clear and colorless, tasting marvelously of flowers and thorny bushes, and smelling of the woods.

With the sun darkening against the trees, the boys returning gradually from their curiosity to horseplay, Peter the mild fool leaning against a well that raised its arm to heaven, and the woman bringing to me, out of the white stone cottage, the classic libations—wine, milk, and honey—everything slipped into a feeling of rightness. The ugliness of Arad and the motel, the customs men, the children begging for things that I didn't own—everything was forgotten. The only world that mattered was the dell, the shower of yellow leaves, the white stone and the peaked roofs of wooden tiles.

Then the moment passed. The meal was over; the block of sunlight on the cottage wall rose above the door. Beyond the gesture of hospitality, which the family performed so well, there was no reason for me to remain, nor desire that I should. In any case, Romanian law forbade my staying there after sundown. Peter had not spoken from his post by the well, but when I got on my bike, he immediately did the same. We left together, waving and thanking. The road became steep, and he slowed down. The trees fell away from the road as we came to the crest of a ridge. The yellow, red, and green flowed out in swells all around us. I wanted to cover several miles, so finally I pulled away from him. I turned and waved a last time as I rounded a hilltop, and he was a small figure against the brilliant colors, sitting stiffly, smiling. Then I lost him.

Hamlet followed hamlet, and the road twisted up, into fir trees, between blueberry bushes picked clean of their fruit. The evening sun flowed caramel-gold over the long straight streets of the hillside villages. For a moment, the gold lit from behind a rumbling, teetering wagonload of hay, bringing Monet to mind. The wagon driver directed me to an artesian well for my camping water, declaring it the best in the region. It bubbled from a pipe and smelled strongly of sulphur. On the far side of Birchiş, the road abruptly lost its pavement, then quickly dissolved into a narrow, rocky lane. I passed a Gypsy encampment just as the sun was setting. Three catlike dogs came screaming up to the road, but kept their teeth to themselves. The men and boys of the camp called out, as the Gypsies always do, for me to stop, but I pushed on. I remember the camp as a scene of pastoral squalor in the highest degree. The dogs were mangy and quarrelsome, the two horses thin and dispirited; horse manure and empty cans littered the ground; old clothes and discolored blankets fluttered in the wind from tree branches and low bushes; filthy, torn plastic sheets made up most of the walls of the shacks; and garbage of all sorts lay, like crusted snow, in the creases of the earth.

OUT OF THE DARKEST BLUE came the sound of hooves, the slap of reins. I was instantly wide awake. I zipped open the top of the tent and sat up. The trees around me were black, and the glimmering light of dawn had not yet gathered at one side of the sky. From the road, thirty yards away, I caught a flicker of movement. A creaking of trees in the wind drifted along the ground—but there was no wind.

I got out of the tent and threw on some clothes. I picked my way through the spruce trees, toward the road. A black shape crossed the opening in the trees. I hung back, in the shadows, where I could not be seen.

The shape of a wagon passed by, groaning over the rocks. The horse slipped in the dew on the uneven ground. The silhouette of a boy sat on the perch, chin tucked, toes curled around the footrest; a tree branch to beat the horse with curved up and out beside him like a black fountain, frozen. The wagon was piled high with shadows, outlines of rough and worn-out necessities. Two men followed, leading a horse mounted with sacks. Then women, trailing their skirts in the wet dirt, and accompanying their movement with a labial, tuneful muttering. Another man, wearing theatrical spurs. A woman, and a child whining mechanically, like a dog. Now and then, louder words by the men floating up and down the line. Twenty people in the darkness, heading east.

It was six o'clock. The Gypsies were on the move.

I stood still. The mongrels came last, gliding with the furtiveness of weasels from side to side of the lane, their tails permanently down. They didn't smell me, about which I was very glad. When it was totally silent again, the eastern edge of the sky was aquamarine.

I had seen no bears, no wolves, no vipers that night. There were probably few of the first, and none of the second any longer in the Carpathians, despite what the Hungarians had said. The wolves used to kill people, but more importantly, they used to kill sheep—and they were hunted as pests, for rewards. The bears were not as dangerous, or as disruptive, as the wolves. The Gypsies used to catch and tame the bears, pull out their teeth and claws, and teach them to "dance" by forcing them to walk on hot metal sheets while they fiddled a certain tune. Bears are as intelligent as dogs, and after several repetitions of this, the bear would "dance," from the memory of exquisite pain, whenever the tune was played. And so the bear would perform for the *gadjé*—the sedentary village folk, whom the Gypsies despised. The *gadjé* never lost their fascination for dancing bears, and they would applaud in delight while the Gypsy women moved in the crowd and deftly picked their pockets. Who could blame the Gypsies for despising such rubes?

But the bears were gone now, and the Gypsies had long since run out of gullible villagers. Their rackets had worked when Europe was large, when they could flee one outraged town in the direction of another, unsuspecting one. There had been no such thing, in either the fourteenth century or the nineteenth, as a country with guard towers and fences all the way around it. In modern Romania, the Gypsies were trapped, and the system was waiting for them. Ceauşescu's government had made it clear that they would have to learn, sooner or later, how to be socialist citizens.

Sunlight flamed the tips of the spruce trees as I rolled up my tent and stuffed it in with the sleeping bag. I carried the bike out to the dirt road and pointed it after the Gypsies. There was little chance that I would catch up with them. The bike, on this rocky, sandy path, would be even slower than the Gypsies' wooden, springless wagons. I started off, the line of tree shadows pointing toward me like the planted spears of a line of defense.

The road grew worse, and I progressed that morning at a crawl. Then a spoke broke, and I spent an hour in the shade of a sycamore, with the bike on its back and the rear wheel in pieces. I reached Făget just before noon and realized I had gone only eighteen kilometers.

Făget was a large, bustling village, on the important road from Lugoj to Deva. Yet none of the streets was paved, and the village seemed to be drowning in dust. The sand at the main crossroads came up to my ankles. Bicycles do not work under those conditions, and I pushed the thing, slipping and sliding, from one corner to the next. People stopped and stared.

"Changemoney?"

"*Nu— vă rog.*"

"Hey—Marlboro?"

"*Scusi— ma non fumo.*"

They walked next to me, and I kept pushing. They tried to catch my eye and spoke encouragingly. I was willing to talk, but they didn't want talk. I couldn't help them. Eventually, they peeled off. I got water from a fountain at the railway station. I pushed some more.

I saw, for the first time, an *alimentari* that was open, and I went in. But in the forty-watt gloom inside, the shelves were nearly empty. I asked for bread, but the sharp-faced woman behind the counter shook her head. At her back, on the plain wooden shelves, were a few old tubes of mustard, label-less jars filled with a dark, greasy compound, and a set of small cardboard boxes (salt?), each fronted with a drawing of a smiling child. There was nothing else.

The pavement came back on the far side of Făget. Now there was a headwind, but I made better progress. Under a cloudless sky, I followed a line of poplars—supple trees, holding their arms high and swaying—for several miles.

The village of Coşava had a pretty square, with benches bolted down between clipped bushes and a modern sculpture pretending to be the center of attention. No one accosted me at first, and I risked sitting in the square to eat my lunch. I had barely begun, when a very small man with fly-blown, graying hair trotted up to me and spoke excitedly in German:

"This is great! This is great! I can't believe this! Where are you coming from?"

"Uh . . . America—"

"America?! I can't believe that! Incredible! Tell me, what would you like?"

"Excuse me?"

"Don't you want anything? Some food, perhaps? Something to drink? Come, I'll get you a beer."

Whenever I am trying to get my bearings, I tend to repeat people. So I said, "A beer?"

"What, you don't like beer? Fine! I can get you something else. What would you like? Chocolate?" The man never stopped moving. He walked to one end of the bench and back, clapped his hands, waved his arms when he spoke to me.

"Chocolate?" I said, watching him go from side to side. He placed his hands on his lower back and leaned far backward, stretching. Then he tipped forward and paced, bent over. He repeated both motions.

If he knew where to get food, I was interested. But I wanted to figure out how strange he was first.

He poked at the bike. "Amazing. Just amazing." He pointed to things. "Sleeping bag, tire pump, water bottle, bags, hey—dirty clothes, here, in the net—great, great! Very smart. I have done this, too, you know."

"Oh?"

"I used to go 200 kilometers a day, 250." He started to touch his toes, very rapidly. "I stretched out like this, first. Then I went everywhere: 260, 70 kilometers a day. I have gone by bicycle all over these mountains. I was born in Szaszsebes."

Szaszsebes. The Hungarian name for Sebeş. Now I knew why he spoke good German. The man was a Magyar.

"I don't do it anymore, because my back is no good. Now I walk instead. The bicycle"—he waggled a finger admonishingly—"too much bending." He bent over and touched his toes again.

"No, this kind of bending is good! But that other kind"—he shook his head—"*szönyü*—horrible."

He was the first Magyar I had met in Romania. When the new border was drawn between Hungary and Romania in 1920, the area around the Arad district was so intermixed that the ethnologists at the Paris Conference had despaired of finding a dividing line. Arad itself was one-third Magyar. But now, in 1982, I had met no Magyars, heard no Hungarian. Did that mean there were fewer of them? Had they moved to cities with old Hungarian majorities, like Kolozsvár? Had they been moved by the authorities? Perhaps they were still here in southern Transylvania, only hidden. The Hungarians in Budapest had told me that the Magyars in Transylvania were afraid to go out in the streets, that they only looked out through cracks in their shutters.

How true was any of this? Here was someone to ask.

"You're a Magyar," I said.

He gave me a quick look. "Yes."

But it would never get beyond that. As I stood up, a couple of other men were walking toward us. They were not at all menacing. It looked as if they had noticed my bicycle from across the street and were coming out of curiosity.

But the little man whipped around and said to them, "Get back! Get back!" He placed himself between the men and my bike.

The two men smiled. They appeared to recognize the Magyar. They spoke to him in Romanian.

"Stay away!" the Magyar yelled, in German. "Don't touch it!" He looked over his shoulder at me and said urgently, "Let's go."

Two or three others were approaching, from the opposite direction. They, too, seemed to be just curious, attracted by the bike and the excited little man. One of them called out a question to me, in Romanian. Something about where I was headed.

But the Magyar stopped me from answering. "Don't talk to these pigs," he said. And then to them: "Get away! Stand back!" And then something vituperative in Romanian.

Everyone seemed to know the man. They were not surprised at his behavior. They came closer, to see the bike. One of them reached out a hand; he was about to speak.

But the Magyar jumped and pushed him back violently. He bellowed now in Romanian, a long string of abuse, then the German word *schwein*. The man who was pushed tried to retreat and bumped into another man; there was a confusion of arms. Another Romanian tried to hold the Magyar down, but he squirmed out of his grasp and swung wildly at the man's face. The spectators on the opposite side of the ring—we were in a ring now, the Magyar and I—kept smiling. Apparently none of this, not even the punching, was unusual. But the smiles showed a measure of exasperation. The Romanians might lose their tempers at some point.

The Magyar turned to me, grabbed my arm roughly. He said in a loud voice, "Let's go, let's go! They'll steal something." And to the Romanians—"Leave him alone!" I thought he was going to add, "He's mine!" Then suddenly he dropped my arm and flew behind me, barreling into another Romanian. "Get back!" The Romanian almost fell over, and a look of real anger came over his face.

The situation had ceased to make any sense to me, and I wanted no part of it. I jammed my lunch hurriedly into my knapsack, grabbed the bike, and excused myself, to no one in particular. I stepped away from the center. To my relief, the ring broke for me. The Romanians were more interested in the little man now than in a foreign cyclist. I feared the Magyar would grab me from behind, but he didn't. I kept walking, without looking back. The sounds of cursing retreated. I could hear the Magyar's rasping voice and the basso shouts of the Romanians. At the edge of the square, I climbed on the bike and pedaled out of Coşava.

Two kilometers down the road, I stopped again to eat lunch at a road marker, where I could sit against the stone and be out of the wind. Two boys showed up while I was eating and pestered me for cigarettes. I was not entirely kind to them, and I felt bad about it afterward.

EVENING, AND I AM LOOKING for a campground, although I don't expect to find one open. Every evening it has been the same routine: in directing me to the nearby grounds, my interlocutors insist that no matter what has been true of all the other campgrounds, *this* place, at least, is open. And so I follow their directions, optimistic in spite of myself. I bicycle three times as far as everyone tells me I have to, and when I arrive I find that the campground is closed. In fact, it has been closed for weeks—there are drifts of dirt on the porches of the bungalows, the office windows are boarded up, and the chain-link fence gates are swung shut and locked. Sometimes a maintenance man still lives there, and he comes out from the back of the boarded-up office and tells me to move on.

So it is evening, and I tell myself I am looking for a campground, but I am really looking for a hotel. A Romanian woman with a cow yelled at me this morning, and I don't feel like hiding again tonight. I want to sleep legally, for the first time in four nights. The road is straight, flat, and boring, and my back is sore; I am going to take the first lodging that comes my way, no matter how sleazy it is.

I come into the village of Scoarţa. The road passes straight between ditches and low walls topped with red tile. Slopes of more red tile glower from behind the walls: roofs. A goat tied to a gate eats out of a pail of garbage. There will be no hotel in such a small place.

From up ahead comes the sound of cheering, and a hubbub of voices. A large wood-and-canvas awning looms on my right, and I see a crowd of people, perhaps two hundred, seated at long tables beneath and around the temporary shelter. Three Gypsy musicians stand at the front, near the road, and draw a wild, swirling dance out of a violin, a clarinet, and an accordion. An electric amplifier sits at their feet and contributes distortion to the music. A few of the men are singing boisterously and clapping their hands. All the people have on their best clothes. I haven't yet spotted the figure in white, but I know this is a wedding.

I smell the wedding food. Oh, God—paprika and sour cream, cabbage and the oily scent of grilling meat. The smells drift across the road like a siren song, and I slow the bike. I am ravenous. All I have to look forward to for dinner is more rice-and-vegetable stew. Except for fishhead soup and a cube of pork fat, I have dined on nothing but that for days now.

I can't control myself. I brake to a stop a few feet from the awning. There is a gap in the garden wall, and everyone can see me. I put an indecisive expression on my face. I try to look as if I am lost. I glance in every direction except straight at the wedding. I feel ashamed of what I am doing, but I cannot force myself to get back on the bike. The food smells too good. There is food in there that I haven't eaten in a long time. I know that the wedding celebrants will invite me in if I give them just half a chance.

Out of the corner of my eye, I can see all two hundred faces turned toward me. The hubbub has increased to a roar. Fingers are pointing. You'd think I were fifteen feet tall and fluorescent lime-green. Perhaps I am the first touring cyclist any of these people have ever seen. I stand my ground.

A wiry man vaults across the ditch between the road and the tent and hands me a bottle of beer. A smile like a shard of china cracks his face. I try to look surprised, and feel guiltier as I take the bottle, but my stomach roots me to the spot. By the time I have sipped twice, there are close to sixty people crowding around the bike, swelling in and out, swaying into each other, gesticulating, smiling, and poking at my panniers and my sleeping bag. I pick out the groom by the extra luster of his clothes and the deference which is paid to him; he looms close and tries to grab my hand, but he is carried away by the crowd. He squeezes back again, and a swell of people push him suddenly into me; the two of us almost go over. But the crush of people on all sides keeps us on our feet. The groom shouts to me over the noise, and I can smell the wine on his breath; he gestures over the heads of the people to the tables. The invitation. A whoop of excitement goes up as I lift my bicycle and carry it off the road, over the ditch, and into the feasting area. I cannot help feeling, through the guilt, like an important man—the wedding guests behave as if I have done them an immense favor, as if I have made the wedding worthwhile, by deigning to eat their food. Me—a lonely, hungry vagabond. The code of hospitality can be terribly seductive. One must not presume—and I have presumed.

Ah well. A man approaches me who speaks rudimentary English and offers his services as translator. He has an eagle's nose, a wide black mustache, and a gold canine tooth. He seems eager to please. He leads me to a table at the edge of the awning and I sit down. The food comes at me from all directions. The three women sitting across from me push plates under my nose; people farther down the table crane their necks to look at me and hand up baskets of bread and a tureen of soup. There are spiced meat rolls, grilled red sausages, cabbage stuffed with rice and mutton and covered with sour cream, marinated peppers, pork ribs with mayonnaise, cornmeal mush, and fizzy red wine in gallon jugs. The soup is lemony-sour, with lots of black pepper, and the bread is fresh. Nearly a dozen people in the nearby seats keep a constant watch on me to make sure that I am both happy and gluttonous. Beyond the simplest inquiries about my origins, they ask no questions; this is a time for celebration, not for base curiosity. I am the stranger, the wanderer whom they have brought to their table, as is right. That is all they want to know.

My translator's name is Miţicu. He sits to my right and does little more than ply me with wine and *tsuica*, and tell me the names

of the dishes. The red sausages—*mititei*. The stuffed cabbage—
sarmale. The corn mush—*mamaliga*.

People all around me are stuffing their faces. I imagine all
this good food is as rare for them as it is for me. Miţicu is downing
sarmale balls at the rate of one a minute. The three women across
the table dispatch plates of grilled sausage with American-football-
player gusto.

Miţicu is drinking, too, and his English gets steadily worse as
a spot of red appears on his nose and spreads outward, like a rose
blooming. By the time the rose has taken over his mustache, he
speaks to me most of the time in Romanian. Unfortunately, my
ability to grasp Romanian gets no better as I knock back glasses
of wine, and soon Miţicu and I can hardly understand each other.
I keep forgetting the Romanian name for the plum alcohol, and
poor Miţicu has to repeat it to me every couple of minutes. Perhaps
because he is getting tired of saying *tsuica* over and over again, he
introduces me to a stronger version of plum spirits. *Rachia*, he
calls it. I think of the Greek plum alcohol, which the Cretans, at
least, call *ratchi*; then I think of the Bulgarian *slivova*, also made
of plums, and nicknamed *rakiya*; then *slivova* reminds me of *slivovitz*,
which is the Yugoslavs' favorite drink. The Balkan peninsula must
be lousy with plum trees, I think, as I quaff a glass of *rachia*; the
liquid goes down like a blade. Yow. That's the same stuff, all right.
I remember the taste from when I was in Greece, four years ago.
The Cretans call it *schnapps* if they think you are German, which
is virtually all the time. Miţicu pours me another.

The bride walks over to our table and greets me. She is young,
perhaps twenty years old. Chestnut hair falls around a noble, Latin
face. I can't help noticing that she is the most attractive thing I
have seen in a long time. Ogling, I tell myself not to ogle. A more
sober part of my brain reminds me that traditional Romanian
fathers just might shoot guests who make passes at daughters on
their wedding days. Fortunately, the bride has better things to do,
and she leaves before I can compromise my safety.

Miţicu leans over and yells above the music that we are
celebrating not only a wedding but a housewarming as well. The

house at our backs has just been built, he says—the bride and groom will sleep in it for the first time tonight. Heh, heh, heh. Thus Miţicu. I turn to look. I try to admire their new house, but it is ugly. Like so much of modern Romania, it has too many straight lines and hard, concrete edges. It sits in its pile of torn-up earth and sand as if it has no place there, as if—like Dorothy's farmhouse—it has just fallen out of the sky and killed someone.

A man leans over at the corner of the new house and gets sick on a pile of sand. Whoo, boy. We're having some fun now. More and more guests are dancing. The bride and groom—an extraordinarily handsome pair, I think, deep in my cups—leap about, arm crooked in arm. Dozens of pairs follow them. In my present condition, I haven't a prayer of figuring out the steps, but it is an energetic dance. The older men sweat and look, through their wide and heartfelt smiles, as if they might drop dead soon. The women have less to prove and don't overdo themselves so seriously. A woman across the table turns and suggests I dance. I decline as firmly as politeness allows. I am an incredible square. All I know how to do is waltz. Gypsies don't play waltzes.

The light is growing purple. Lamps are being lit now under the canvas awning. The musicians play furiously on, indifferent to exhaustion. The bride and groom are seated again at the center table—he talking with his friends, she with hers. Other couples still dance in a frenzy of motion, almost desperate, it seems, to deplete their energy until they can collapse, half unconscious, into waiting chairs. The celebration will be going on far into the night.

But the time has come for me to go. Blackness is minutes away. The moon will be hidden by the clouds. I haul Miţicu off the girl he is flirting with and ask him the distance to the nearest hotel. As usual, there is an unbelievable amount of discussion on this. Fingers point every way except straight up. Finally, a consensus is reached, and I don't like it: seventeen kilometers east. Five kilometers on the Rîmnicu Vîlcea road, then left at Bengeşti, and twelve kilometers on a smaller road. Right direction, wrong distance. It will be pitch-dark before I even reach the turning. And in my condition, I could hardly get on the bike in broad daylight with a stepladder. Still, there is no place for me to sleep at the wedding, as much as I would love to displace the groom, so I make my round of thanks. At the last, I clasp Miţicu's hand. The gold canine glints mischievously. It feels as if we are holding each other up with our right hands.

I fetch the bike. There are still a hundred people ambulatory enough to follow me out to the road. I have been with them for some two hours, but they act as if it has been two years. I wobble away, waving my thanks over a shoulder and nearly falling off the bicycle in the process. The fields beyond the road are already invisible. The road wavers in front of my eyes like a strand of seaweed, coiling under water.

There is a remarkable thing about this night, this seventeen-kilometer junket through the dark—I do not encounter a single sober person between the wedding feast and the hotel. This does not surprise me much. I have been seeing quite a number of drunks on the streets of the Romanian towns. They are still dressed in their work clothes, well shaven, respectable—just totally blitzed. And the sober people who pass them on the sidewalks wear expressions of sympathy and understanding.

A figure staggers out in front of me. I drift around him. I turn onto the smaller road. The white oaks on the right tiptoe into the road whenever I allow my attention to wander. I pass through dark hamlets. Peasant men on jangling, lightless bikes condense out of the blackness in front of me and glide past, mumbling songs in broken, bleary voices. In the roadside shadows, between the crafty oaks, I glimpse elderly couples making their way home on undulating paths, supporting each other by the arms in touching displays of marital solidarity. The very few automobiles—boxy, beaten-up Dacias (some of these also without lights)—drive gingerly by, emitting sounds of laughing and singing. For the first and last time in this country, I experience what perhaps many Romanians experience every weekend: a feeling of community in inebriation. It is a fine, cool night, trembling on the edge of rain, and for once, I feel as if I should be here.

•

Two days later, I arrived in Piteşti only to learn that my mail had been delayed. Outside the hotel, a dozen policemen and soldiers lounged and talked. A few of them fixed me with arrogant stares and adjusted their gun belts meaningfully. From this, I was supposed to infer that they didn't shoot me only because they were nice guys. Inside, the receptionist was a vision, with bleached hair, scarlet fingernails, glistening Mercurochrome lips, and wide bands of dark purple over her eyelids. She was talking to a squat woman with black curls and heavy, plastic-rimmed glasses, who moved aside as I approached.

"Yes," the receptionist said in French, "empty rooms still. One hundred thirty lei each night, private toilet, showers at the end of the hall. Breakfast included."

Not bad, actually. Under twelve bucks. Only 30 percent more than my budget for the entire day. "Fine." We traded papers and stamped things.

"Have you bicycled all the way from America, then?" the receptionist asked, laying a red-nailed finger alongside my U.S. passport. The woman with the black curls edged forward to steal a glance at the passport.

"No. From England."

The purple momentarily disappeared as the woman's eyes widened histrionically. "From England? On a bicycle?! Ohhh!" she exclaimed. "Did you hear that, Georgina?"

The usual conversation about bicycle touring followed. I ran through it mechanically, my mind on how long I might have to stay before my mail would appear, on whether I'd be able to buy any bread tomorrow. Georgina, the timid woman with the black curls, joined the conversation at some point, nodding her head and murmuring.

The first words I actually remember Georgina uttering were in English. She asked me if I liked Romania: a conventional question, but she put an unusual amount of urgency into it. Perhaps for this reason, I answered more superlatively than I usually did—"Oh *yes. Very* much." Her reaction was not what I had expected. She seemed taken aback, and hesitated, as if she was not sure she wanted to be talking to me. But then she went on, and we got onto the subject of letters, since I was waiting for some to arrive. "Yes," she said, "the mail is not reliable. In Romania you never know what will happen." Then she began to talk to me about England, and I started to tune her out. I assumed she had brought up England because it was sort of like America. I was brushing off my windbreaker and thinking about a shower. I was tired. I nodded my head to Georgina's words and hoped she would finish soon. A phrase finally broke through to me and brought my attention back.

"—father-daughter. Father-daughter in England."

Father what?

"You must understand. Father-daughter is in England. I hear nothing."

Her voice had grown quieter and more intense. She even had guided me a few feet away from the desk, away from the other woman.

"—and it is since 1974 now, and I don't understand it. He would not do that to me. He is father-daughter. And he loves her. So perhaps to me, but he cannot, he would not do this to her." She had me backed up against the wall.

"Why—? What—?" I said.

"I hear you speaking with Marianna and you say you are American. You say you were in England. Father-daughter is in England! So perhaps you will understand—"

Although she had literally cornered me, she still struck me as a timid woman. Her manner had the bitter edge of desperation; she seemed driven by a need that had swept over and obliterated her shyness.

"—but I just don't know. I wonder all the time what is wrong. There is nothing from him. I can't help to think—I send letters— I send so many letters. But I think . . ."

"Wait, wait," I broke in. "I'm sorry. I don't understand."

"It's father-daughter!" She nearly yelled it. "Here; I show you." She removed her hand from my forearm, where she had been gripping me, and scrabbled at the latch of her cheap maroon handbag. She was trembling. She stood awkwardly; her black hair had the same artificial sheen that the hair of the fat customs man had had: doll's hair. She rummaged in her bag, through lipstick and compact cases.

She held a picture out to me, a studio shot of a girl about twelve years old, in a white, ruffled frock. Her hair was jet black and curly, but longer than her mother's. "That is daughter," Georgina said. "And this"—she pulled another photo out from behind the first—"is father-daughter." It was an older photograph, perhaps from the 1960s, of a grinning man against a black background. He wore no uniform but had a close-cropped military haircut. He looked like the young F. Scott Fitzgerald: debonair and irresponsible. Georgina's eyes watched me searchingly. "You understand?"

"Yes. And, excuse me, your daughter's father lives in England? He's an Englishman?"

"Yes. And England, I know, is a free country. They don't stop people from doing what they want. If he wanted to—oh, but I *know* he wants to, he can't do this to me, to her, he would not—"

"Wait! I don't understand. What has father-daughter done?"

"I get nothing from him. Letters, oh yes, letters, fine. Nice letters, and he says—I know he cares so much. Until 1974. Then nothing. I hear nothing from him. This is his *daughter!*"—the word spat out, the photo shook before me—"He loves her. He would not do this to her, leave her alone without a word, without anything. He does not get my letters, I know. He would write, because in England you do what you want. But here"—and she gripped my arm again, pulled herself to within a few inches of my face— "here—oh, you can't understand. They don't send my letters out, I know it. They don't want I am writing to him. They take my letters, they throw them out of the way. He thinks I don't write to him. I never forget him, I write him so much!"

Sympathy was on my tongue. But she wasn't asking me for sympathy. It had been a long day for me, 110 kilometers of hills, and my mind was slow. I was tired and stupid. What did she want of me? Why couldn't I go up to my room?

"—and then I hear you are from America, when you talked with Marianna. So I know you will leave the country. You are driving through with bicycle, that is right? And then I think to me—my letters don't get through. But if I could get them out of the country . . . Then he would answer me! I know he would!"

I had a sinking feeling. "And you want me to—"

"You must understand. It is so hard to make you understand. If you can take the letter—I will write it, and you will take it. Wait until you are out of Romania. Oh, you don't understand . . ."

"Yes, I do, but—"

"No, you can't. Will you do this for me? Please. Please. I need your help." Her voice shook, became ragged. She was openly pleading.

"Well—I don't—I can't—"

The last thing I wanted was to get involved with anything that might anger the Romanian authorities.

But she was holding on to me. She was staring into my face. "Please. Please help me."

"Okay, okay. I'll help you." Cowardice, as usual, carried me along. The path of least resistance at the moment was to appease this intense, wild woman. Whatever it was that I was getting myself into was still a remote concern, but Georgina was right in front of me, and she alarmed me. "I'll take a letter out for you."

I thought of the down tube of my bicycle. I could remove the seat, place a rolled-up letter in the tube, and reattach the seat in two minutes. It seemed easy enough. But why agree to it at all? Would the authorities actually stop her personal mail over the years to an Englishman whom she had known—for how long?— perhaps for a couple of weeks a dozen years ago? If not, there was no point in my helping her, since the Englishman had no doubt decided to ignore her. And if so, then it would be risky for me to attempt to circumvent the police censorship, no matter how trifling the reason. For several years now, Romanian citizens had been barred by law from allowing foreigners to stay in their houses overnight. If lending a bed to an Englishman was grounds for a fine, did I know for certain that sending a letter to one wasn't grounds for imprisonment?

But the damn promise was out. The woman went on as if I had said nothing, but her words had taken a different tack: "—we cannot talk here. There are many men around this hotel, always. Men who say things, and talk to the police. It is very dangerous for us here. If they find out, it will be bad for me and my daughter."

"I've got to take my things up to my room, first," I said. "Then we can walk somewhere. Should I meet you down here again, in ten minutes?"

She took her hand away and looked toward the lobby café. There were, indeed, a few men sitting there staring at us. "Yes, yes," she said. "After ten minutes." The eyes of the men followed me as I went upstairs.

When I came back down, she was waiting where I had left her. She began to walk out, and I followed. I did not notice if the men in the café were watching; I kept my eyes straight ahead. Out on the street, we walked slowly, diffidently, among the crowd of pedestrians. The police, or soldiers, or whatever they were, were still grouped near the hotel entrance. I stayed slightly behind Georgina, and neither of us said anything.

She made for a small park near the hotel. It had a couple of dozen benches around the perimeter facing inward, gravel paths, and a statue of a Romanian hero rising from the middle. A minute passed in silence, and then she began: "I am so grateful to you that you do this for me. You are my only hope. I have waited so long for to meet someone who was leaving, who would take a letter, but I meet no one. It is difficult for us to talk to foreigners. They watch and they see. I don't want it to go badly for my daughter. They will make things worse if they know. And the hotel is so bad, so many people watching. Here it is better."

"When can you get the letter to me?" I asked. If what she said was true, it was not helping either of us to sit on the bench accomplishing nothing.

"Yes. Yes. I will write it tonight. I must put it in English."

"That's good. Then in case it's found, I can claim it's mine." Keeping my private correspondence in the down tube of the bicycle? How could I possibly look more suspicious? Perhaps it would be better to keep it with my other letters. If it was in English, I could read it beforehand to make sure there was nothing funny about it. "You'd better give it to me unsealed, so it will appear to be one of my own letters. The guards can't read much English." I hesitated, before the lie. "I won't read it, of course."

"Yes, I'll leave it open. In English. We will meet here, in this park, tomorrow. At 5:00 in the afternoon. We will just sit and I will give the letter to you."

"Five o'clock? But I may not still be here. I'm waiting for some important letters"—the irony of the situation did not escape me— "and if they arrive tomorrow morning, I'll be leaving. I have to. My visa is running out, and I have to reach the Bulgarian border in a few days."

She looked at me, once, then gazed out again, at the people strolling by, at the granite, implacable hero with arm and fist raised high. She answered in an indistinct voice: "In the morning, then."

"What time?"

"I will bring it to you without an envelope. Open, just a folded piece of paper. We don't have to say anything. I will just hand the letter to you. It should be quick. Oh, they can't find out! It will look worse if we sit for a while—"

"Which we're doing now—"

"—they might notice us, then. Even in the park there are people watching. And if they know what I have done, they will make it much worse for me. They watch my daughter. Yes, she! She has done nothing. But father-daughter is in England, so she is watched. And they can make it so much worse. You must understand!" She was talking faster and faster, her voice taking on an hysterical edge. "So you will help me. You must help me. You are my only hope. There is no one else. Oh, please. Please help me." Her face crumpled. She was crying. She brought a hand up and rubbed her glasses back and forth on her nose, as if the action would wipe away the tears—or perhaps because she was embarrassed and didn't know what else to do. I noticed, with her hand reaching up, her wide masculine face tilted downward to meet it halfway, how short her arms were. Georgina was built like a wrestler.

I didn't answer for a few seconds. I had already said it four times. But I said it again, wearily: "Yes. I'll help you." And I thought: Stupidstupidstupid.

Her face was averted and her hand, still on her glasses, hid her eyes from me. "I must go now" came from her in a strangled tone, and she started to rise.

"But what time should we meet tomorrow morning?"

She was on her feet, and she looked back at the bench—not at me, but at where she had been sitting. The tears were gone. And she replied, it seemed to me brusquely, with surprising force: "No. Not tomorrow morning. We will meet at five o'clock." Then she hurried away, waddling, the narrow soles of her shoes stumping awkwardly over the gravel. Within a few seconds, I had lost her in the darkness.

·

In November 1982, shortly after I had left Romania, I read in a newspaper in Greece that Ceauşescu had thumbed his nose once more at the Warsaw Pact by calling on both the United States *and* the U.S.S.R. to dismantle their nuclear arsenals. I met other travelers who had heard about this; favorable comments were made about the fairness and courage of Nicolae Ceauşescu. Because Romania's foreign policy is something of an irritant for the Soviet Union, Americans like it; our newspapers dwell on it.

But there are other aspects of Romania than its foreign policy. Thinking of my days actually spent in Romania, I remember the pictures of Ceauşescu everywhere, his name on the tops of buildings, articles by him and about him in the propaganda sheets, books of his in translation in little book carts in the streets of Piteşti. I could not escape the feeling, during that time, that I was looking at the face not only of a maverick but of a megalomaniac.

Nicolae Ceauşescu was the protégé of Gheorghe Gheorghiu-Dej, who became premier of Romania in 1952. Both Ceauşescu and Gheorghiu-Dej were proponents of a nationalist brand of Communism. Emphasizing Romanian folk culture and the Romanian language, they appealed to the deep resentment of the working class toward Soviet-style internationalist Communism. In this, they were simply returning to the prewar concerns—territorial integrity, a fierce ethnic consciousness, hatred of the Magyars—that had been disrupted by Moscow. From 1946 to 1952, Moscow had shown an incredible ignorance of the most deeply felt concerns of the Romanians: it had promoted "Danubian Unity," which meant cooperation with Hungary, and it had set up a Magyar Autonomous Region within Transylvania; it had tried to prove that the Moldavians and the Walachians were separate peoples (perhaps with an eye toward eventually annexing Moldavia); it had produced scholarly "evidence" that the ancient Dacians were actually Slavs and that modern Romanian was a Slavic language. No better way could possibly have been devised to outrage the Romanians, and Moscow paid dearly for its obtuseness—in May 1952, Gheorghiu-Dej, with massive popular support, purged the two Moscow-trained leaders of the Romanian Communist Party, Vasile Luca and Ana Pauker. From that moment on, the PCR was firmly in nationalist hands. Moscow never recovered a dominant voice in Romanian internal affairs.

The actions of the nationalists began to draw hopeful attention from the West. In 1958, in a closed meeting, Gheorghiu-Dej managed to extract from representatives of Khrushchev the promise to remove all Soviet troops from Romanian soil. A few weeks thereafter, that promise was fulfilled. (The details of that meeting have never been divulged, and as every other Bloc country except Bulgaria still has Soviet troops stationed on its soil, there is much envious speculation as to how the Romanians pulled it off.) With the Soviet troops gone, Gheorghiu-Dej began to act more boldly. In 1962, he stepped up relations with China and Yugoslavia. In the same year, Romania began to vote independently from the East Bloc in the United Nations. In 1963, the government closed down the Maxim Gorky Institute of Russian Studies in Bucharest and discontinued the obligatory study of Russian in both the lower schools and the universities; French was reinstated as the most common foreign language. Street names, cinema names, and school names were changed back from Russian to Romanian. In August, jamming of radio from the West was halted. By the end of 1963, Khrushchev had determined (it is thought) to rein in the disobedient Romanians, and he paid a threatening visit to Gheorghiu-Dej. But the deftness and luck of the Romanians held—Khrushchev was removed from office shortly thereafter; his clumsy handling of Eastern Europe was one of the reasons cited for his removal. The Romanian press hardly bothered to report Khrushchev's downfall. On April 26, 1964, at its annual congress, the Romanian Communist Party issued the statement that formalized its break with the economic policies of the Soviet Union. The West was paying close attention.

Gheorghiu-Dej died in 1965, and Ceauşescu, at the tender age of forty-six, replaced him as First Secretary. Ceauşescu continued the policies established by his predecessor, only with more nerve. He enlarged Romania's role in East–West diplomacy. He greatly increased trade with Western countries. He openly ridiculed the notion of a COMECON that did not allow for significant economic ties with capitalist nations. He attained Most Favored Nation trading status for Romania from the United States. He called for the dissolution of both NATO and the Warsaw Pact as a first step toward real détente. The Soviets were angry. And now the West was paying very close attention.

Unfortunately, Ceauşescu's popularity on nationalist issues encouraged him to promulgate a personality cult—a natural extension of his political growth under Stalin, his appeal to the emotions of his subjects, his claims to being the defender of the Romanian people against the Soviets (and the Magyars). Not satisfied with being both First Secretary and the president of the State Council, Ceauşescu created, in 1974, the office of President of the Republic and had himself installed in it, a maneuver that also made him commander of the armed forces. Now he could claim to represent Romania in a twofold capacity: ideological and political, at the head of both the country's argument and its army.

Who else did the country need? In the years after 1974, Ceauşescu ousted more and more old Party members, purges became more frequent, cabinet shake-ups became almost routine after economic or political crises. As more and more high posts were vacated, more and more relatives of Ceauşescu appeared to fill those posts. His wife, Elena, already on the Central Committee, became first deputy minister (the State Council's number-two slot). His son became the Youth Minister and a member of the Central Committee. His brother Ion became deputy minister of agriculture, his brother Ilie, a major general in the Romanian Army. His sister's husband is a full member of the Central Committee; his wife's brother is a Central Committee member and a cabinet minister. The family has acquired all the earmarks, including the arrogance, the confidence in continued power through succession, of a dynasty.

John Lukacs, writing in *The New Republic* in 1982, sketched the situation with the astringency that only a Hungarian could muster:

> The dictator of Rumania is Nicolae Ceauşescu, a former cobbler. . . . His private train has twelve cars. He had himself photographed with a jeweled scepter in hand; as well as standing over the carcasses of wild boars and bears which he shoots as they are driven before his august presence. He was also photographed dancing the Rumanian *hora* with Richard Nixon. The grinning, dark, and jowly faces of the Californian and Wallachian Presidents, both chief executives from the edges of civilization, oddly resembled each other.

With the cult of personality has come a more personalized, and therefore a more vindictive, rule. In 1977, the coal miners in southwest Romania initiated a strike (illegal) which closed down the mines of the Jiu valley. Ceauşescu traveled to the area, and after talking with the strikers, he promised them better working conditions. He also promised that there would be no reprisals taken against them for the strike. The miners halted their action. Ceauşescu immediately had hundreds of them arrested and sent the rest back to work with a 40 percent pay cut. The arrested miners were deported to their native villages, where very few of them would be able to find employment. If the strike had hurt production, the punishment of the miners hurt it more—per capita productivity in the mines plummeted; sabotage increased. Ceauşescu's response to the strike had been personal, kingly; not the response of a politician calculating quotas or determining the best way to quell unrest, but the response of a man whose feelings had been hurt, whose dignity had been compromised.

Ceauşescu has been clear about the value he places on internal security. (Some Romanian priests have estimated that fully one-quarter of the Romanian people have either been in prison at one time or have a close relative who has been in prison.) In the same year that Romania failed to support the U.S.S.R.'s invasion of

Afghanistan, Ceauşescu criticized Poland for its leniency toward "anti-socialist" elements—that is, trade unions. He declared that the Polish government should be firm and "resolutely rebuff" those agents of imperialism. In the previous year, 1979, Ceauşescu had already shown Poland how to rebuff such tendencies—he had crushed Romania's own fledgling free trade union movement, the SLOMR, so decisively that few people in the West have ever heard of it. His advice to Poland received little attention in the West; his criticism of the Afghanistan invasion received a great deal.

Naturally, internal security necessitates strict censorship. Ceauşescu on the arts:

> Artists and writers should not depict the backward mentality and contemptible dreams of certain people. . . . We do not need an art that denies realities, that misrepresents them and depicts them in black colors. . . . Such an art has a sickly nature and is therefore very harmful.

One writer whose works were deemed harmful was Paul Goma, who on his release from a Romanian prison in 1977 went into exile in Paris. In 1981, he wrote a book, *The Dogs of Death*, which dealt with political persecution in Romania during the 1950s. The book is said to have particularly angered Ceauşescu, whose response, again, was more emotional than well considered, especially when one remembers that no Romanian citizens had access to Goma's book: one of Romania's spies operating in France was ordered to liquidate Goma (along with another dissident writer, Virgil Tanase, who had published an article entitled "His Majesty Ceauşescu the First, King of the Communists").

The workings of the assassination plot read like pulp fiction. The spy, known only as Mr. Z, had spent eight years in France, secretly gathering economic and scientific information. According to his account, he decided soon after receiving his orders that he could not kill Goma and Tanase. But if he disobeyed, he would have to defect, and if he defected, he would be separated from his relatives, who might suffer persecution for his disobedience.

So Mr. Z defected secretly, informing the French police of the plot on the condition that they help him fake an assassination in order to give him time to get his family out of Romania. The French agreed. Goma, Tanase, and François Mitterand were brought into the plot.

One imagines that Mr. Z and his new associates had a certain amount of fun during the James Bondian antics that followed. At a cocktail party, Mr. Z poured poison from a fountain pen into Mr. Goma's glass, and Goma walked around with it for a few suspenseful moments until a disguised French agent "accidentally" knocked the glass out of his hand. Mr. Z's superiors took the unforeseeable failure of this attempt stoically. Then Mr. Z told Bucharest of his plan to kidnap and murder Tanase. Bucharest gave the go-ahead, and Tanase was subsequently grabbed on a Parisian street and hustled into a car. He disappeared for three months. President Mitterand acted up a storm at press conferences, voicing "grave concern" at the disappearance of Tanase and postponing a planned visit to Romania, while Mr. Z collected his reward for a successful assassination: a vacation for him and his family in the West. So while Tanase hid in a house in Brittany, Mr. Z packed up his family's bags and defected. Everything went smoothly until the Paris daily *Le Matin* broke the real story just a couple of hours before the last of Mr. Z's family, his mother, was to leave Romania. Her departure was barred immediately.

The publicity, of course, boosted the sales of Paul Goma's book. *The Dogs of Death* is a grim account of the experiment in brainwashing that was carried out by the Communists in Romania in the years 1949 to 1952. One thousand teenagers were rounded up on various charges of anti-revolutionary activity and put in a single prison. There, they were "reeducated"—through a calculated process of torture and demoralization that reminds one of the lunatic experiments of the Nazis. Torture in the Stalinist prisons was common, as the Romanian writer Virgil Ierunca points out in his postface to Goma's book. But the experiment described in *The Dogs of Death* was unusual in that it sought to organize the torture on a scientific basis:

It was discovered that torture can become an absolute weapon against which resistance is impossible, as long as two conditions are fulfilled: that the torture go on uninterrupted; and that the prisoners themselves apply it to each other. United by the evil they have both perpetrated and endured, the victim and the executioner thus become a single person. In fact, there is no longer a victim, ultimately no longer a witness. Undoubtedly, this is why the truth has taken so long to come out.

The experiment succeeded in breaking down all moral and physical resistance of the prisoners, and the "students" of the prison, as Ierunca calls them, were sent to other prisons to continue the process of reeducation. The experiment was discontinued in 1952 only when a prisoner died, in broad daylight, while under torture—an incident which caught the attention of the Western media. Still, as Ierunca has written, it took many years before the truth was revealed, before any of the participants in the experiments could bear to remember what they had done.

The prison in which the experiment was begun still stands. It is on the outskirts of Piteşti. And ever since word of that special prison began to leak out, "Piteşti" has been a catchword for the darkest nightmares of Romania's citizens.

•

On my way to the post office the next morning, I wondered what I would do if the missing letters had arrived. I could pack up and be gone by 9:30. But would I really leave Georgina?

She would be upset. Still, I had *told* her that we should meet in the morning, and she, inexplicably, had ignored me. If I left, it would be her own damn fault. I dribbled the problem across the smooth stones of Lenin Plaza. The worst of it was that I didn't think taking the woman's letters out would help her in the slightest. But whatever I told myself, I knew deep down that I wasn't going to leave. I had been trapped by my own spinelessness.

There was a woman selling lottery tickets by the door to the post office. She had no chair, and the bottoms of her legs were marbled with broken blood vessels, perhaps from years of standing, day after day. I bid her good morning, and she broke into an appealing, crack-toothed smile.

Inside, there were no letters. Feeling sorry for myself, I walked back down to get sympathy from the lottery woman. I complained to her in Italian, and she played her part beautifully. Although she didn't understand the actual words, she caught the mood from my tone of voice and wagged her balding head in consolation, clucking her tongue. As I left, I bought a lottery ticket from her. I couldn't figure out from the printing on the ticket what the prize might be. Permission to leave the country, I thought waggishly. Ho ho. I threw the ticket away as soon as I rounded a corner.

Now what? I thought. The plaza shone in the low sunlight like a vast slab of gray ice. It was a Wednesday morning—a workday. A few people cut long shadows through the brilliance, making patterns of swinging legs scissoring over the stone. A small child trailed its mother in a stumbling walk, threatening to fall. A man and a woman stood between me and the sun, silhouettes arguing in loud voices; his hand gripped her arm convulsively.

The logical thing to do was to look for food. Pitești was the largest of the towns I had visited, and it seemed plausible that there would be a greater variety of food here, something beyond green peppers, apples, and carrots. I entertained visions of finding grapes, perhaps even oranges. Who knew? Perhaps I would find milk for sale!

I spotted a supermarket off Lenin Plaza. Through the glass I could see full shelves. But inside, only two customers stood at the cash register. The rest of the store was empty. A bad sign. I had learned one rule of thumb in Romania: where there was no crowd, there was nothing worth buying.

But I had plenty of time on my hands, so I perused the shelves methodically. The aisle nearest the door was devoted exclusively to wine. The bottles were crammed onto the white aluminum shelves by the hundreds, with more set out on the floor. Some of the wine was Cotnari, a sweet white, in tall green bottles carrying labels slapped on haphazardly, with insufficient glue. Then a succession of wines with strange names: Murfatlar Pinot Noir, Dealu Mare Cabernet, Odobesti Galbena. But the bulk was a vast amount of the nameless, fizzy Romanian red wine, sold in squat bottles of one or two liters, shaped like water-cooler jugs, without labels, and priced so low that anybody could afford them. I knew from the hospitality I had received in the past few days that this was the ubiquitous table wine of Romania. It wasn't good and it wasn't strong, but it eventually did the trick.

The second aisle contained more wine. Bottles of *tsuica* were also there, and *rachia*. The third aisle was devoted to the harder liquors: domestic Scotch and vodka, an assortment of colored liqueurs and schnapps in smaller, dusty bottles.

The fourth aisle contained jars of fruit. Not jam or preserves—the fruit appeared to have been boiled whole or in quarters for a short time, then bottled in sugar water. I recognized pears and apples. Boiled apples? The pears just managed to look edible. The apples looked like embryos in formaldehyde. The cherries were sepia. The bottled fruit overflowed into the fifth aisle: more cherries, plums, and a few discolored peaches. In the sixth aisle, still more bottled fruit: pears again, and what looked like bruised or smashed apricots: brown pulpy blobs.

I moved to the back of the store, where two more aisles had been squeezed in. Tubes of mustard. Tubes of caviar. Pickled peppers. Tubes of horseradish. Pickled onions. More pickled peppers. Next aisle: a small stack of disk-shaped tins with the cartoon of a grinning pig stamped on each top—pork spread? Salt. Mixed vegetables, pickled. Chocolate bars. More pickled peppers. More pickled onions. That was it.

Except for the meat and cheese counter, which stood hard by the two cash registers. It was tiny, built to hold no more than two dozen pounds of food (I had seen larger ones in the *alimentari* of hamlets in southern Italy), and it was nearly empty. Only a string of the familiar pale pink sausages, looking like polyurethane foam tubes, lay coiled, a forlorn little pile, in one corner. Below the counter, in a freezer, were four or five plastic bags containing frozen vegetable pieces—peppers, carrots, potatoes, peas, and a few other kinds which I could not identify in their present state of mutilation. A woman stood behind the counter with a look of proprietorship on her face. I wondered what she possibly could think she was guarding. There were no cheeses, no fresh vegetables, no milk, no eggs. There was more than what the Hungarians had said there would be, but damn little, all the same. I was crushed. So much for the big-city supermarket. I could practically feel my salivary glands shutting down.

I found another supermarket a few blocks away. It was just the same, without the pink sausages. Seen through the windows from outside, they both looked so full, so promising; no doubt they could illustrate magazine articles on Romanian prosperity. But the fullness was almost an insult: did they think the towns-people could be so easily fooled? The tall SUPERMARKET signs on the flat metal awnings out front, the modern aluminum-fluorescent interiors, the shelves filled to overflowing: these were transparent veils thrown over the fact—there was nothing to buy. Like a magician assured of the stupidity of his audience, the government attempted illusions that hid nothing.

The only meat store I could find was closed. Through the window, I saw a few slabs of pork fat hanging from the ceiling, and more of the pink sausage. There was no notice about when the store would be open. Deva had had far more than this, and Deva was a smaller town. Of course, Deva was in southern Transylvania, a grazing area, while Piteşti lay in the industrial region of northern Walachia. Still, only three hundred kilometers of road separated Piteşti from Deva; didn't the damn country have any means of transport?

I wandered into a couple of fruit and vegetable stores. At this midmorning hour, only three or four people stood in line, but I could find no enthusiasm for buying. Only the potatoes looked healthy, and that was probably because potatoes hide their diseases exceptionally well. The women behind the rough-wood counters had the same look of wild guardianship that I had seen in the supermarket. They stood motionless, implacable; only their eyes moved, following my meek steps from one crate to another, like eyes in a portrait that stare at you no matter where you stand in a room. Even if my clothes hadn't been different, they would have known that I wasn't Romanian. Who but a foreigner would wander about looking for vegetables that weren't there? The natives got immediately into line and bought what was on the sloping shelf in front of them. I kept browsing, hoping for miracles.

The stares made me feel I owed the women something merely for having walked through their door, and I bought a few soft apples that were dimpled like golf balls, as brown in spots as old banana skins. I sauntered back out into the sunlight, asking myself if I would ever feel like eating them. It was now or never; I bit into one of the apples and tasted bruise.

A depression was settling on me, and I decided to head back toward the hotel. As I passed the cafeteria on the plaza, I saw knots of people standing out front. The workers inside were setting up fancy cakes in the long display windows. I stopped to admire, along with everyone else. Some of the cakes were enormous, weighing perhaps twenty pounds, and all of them were wonderfully complex—detailed replicas of houses, boats, children sitting in trees, even whole village scenes. They had been ingeniously put together with colored sugar frosting, chocolate squares, Life Savers, glazed grapes, and candied orange sections, licorice bits, and so on. There was a little factory with meringue smokestacks and ramps made out of sugar wafers. There was a tractor on doughnut wheels.

As each cake was set out, a sigh of satisfaction would exhale from the crowd and hang in the air like a happy mist. Children bumped their heads against the glass. The bakers waved to them from the display cases. The children were thrilled beyond words. I was reminded of my eighth birthday, when my mother baked me a cake in the shape of a steamship: the portholes were Life Savers and the smokestacks were Tootsie Rolls. Every other year, I had had an ordinary cake, with the privilege only of picking the flavor. But that one year, for some reason, my mother had devoted more energy to the task and had come up with a marvel: a cake that seemed to sail across the green-marbled Formica of our kitchen table. And I was enchanted—it is the only birthday before my adolescence that I can remember with any clarity.

Eventually, the line of cakes stretched more than fifty feet behind the long glass windows of the cafeteria. But there were no prices on the cakes. And for all the exclamations, all the excitement out on the street, no one seemed prepared to buy any of them. People stood with their hands in their pockets and smiled; they were admiring the cakes, not choosing them. Perhaps the cakes were not for sale.

I went inside the cafeteria and stood in line at the counter. The people ahead of me were buying pieces of a plain sheet cake that lay cut up on the counter's surface. In the midst of yards of empty counter space, only this and one other cake, a wretched little thing with green frosting, were for sale. I bought the same cake as the others had done, figuring they knew what they were doing. I also asked for a glass of water. The water wasn't bad, but the cake was unappetizing: tasteless and heavy, with an artificial smell. I felt as if I had been written into a bad movie. How could the irony be clearer? Outside, the people admiring cakes that they couldn't buy, pressing their faces to the glass like forlorn Dickensian street urchins; inside, the line waiting for the mealy sheet cake that was sold alongside the sludge they called coffee.

I left half my piece of sheet cake on the table and walked out. The display of cakes was a bravura performance, an advertisement for the skill of the Romanian bakers. But what kind of pride in Romania could the cakes arouse if the store could not afford to let them be eaten? Who, in the end, would eat the cakes, and who would only feed on their resentment? I left the plaza with a feeling of bewilderment and disgust.

.

A Hungarian, who lives in a land poor in natural resources, will tell a simple story about Romania. God was distributing all the riches of Central Europe among the nations there. For Hungary, he set aside a flat, dry plain; for Bulgaria, a bare, rocky mountain; for Yugoslavia, hot dry air and poor soil. But for Romania, he carved out a beautiful land of rich earth, powerful rivers, majestic mountains, fertile plains, vast resources of coal, oil, and iron. The people of the other nations cried out: "Why does Romania have such riches, while we are poor? Now Romania will be greater than all of us, and rule us after a short time." And the people pleaded for God to restore a balance. So God created the Romanians. And the other nations were satisfied.

Few people who are not Hungarian would seriously suggest that there is anything genetically deficient about the Romanians. But the story raises an important point. Given the fact that Romania is by far the best piece of real estate in Eastern Europe, why *is* the country so poor? Given that the goods for subsistence living are practically there for the taking, why do so many go hungry? What is being done wrong? Because something is clearly being done wrong. It is a bizarre experience to bicycle through field after field of freshly cut wheat stalks and then to arrive in a town in which there is no bread. Or to pass hundreds of sheep in the Transylvanian hills and then find no dairy products in the stores.

The richness of the area has been acknowledged for close to two thousand years. The Roman province of Dacia (which comprised Transylvania and Oltenia) became legendary for its prosperity, and was called, in the Roman writings, Dacia Felix. The colonists who were transported to the new province made much of the soil, of the gold, silver, and salt deposits. Much later, in the nineteenth century, the region became the most important granary of Europe, providing principally wheat and maize, but also barley, rye, and oats.

Romania suffered impoverishment during World War I, but it also doubled its population and more than doubled its size at the end of that war, when the Treaty of Trianon in 1920 awarded Romania, among other things, all of Transylvania and the eastern edge of the Hungarian plain—regions of vast natural wealth. So up until the Second World War, Romania remained a prosperous, if primitive, country.

But the last year of the war brought terrible destruction with it. And then the Russians took over, and went about depleting the country as best they could. Soviet-Romanian companies, the notorious "Sov-Roms," were set up; although ostensibly owned half by Romania and half by Russia, the Sov-Roms were really conduits for the transfer of raw material from the former country to the latter. Huge amounts of grain, coal, iron, and oil were carted out of Romania under terms that were only a hair's width short of being outright theft. No other Eastern European country suffered so much from Soviet economic imperialism. It was only after

Stalin's death in 1953 that the Sov-Roms were dissolved, as it gradually became clear to the Soviets that if they killed this albatross they would have to wear it.

Then, in the early sixties, with the economy in a shambles, Gheorghiu-Dej began the move away from Moscow. The country had always done well during the rare instances when it had been left alone, and under Gheorghiu-Dej's direction, the Romanian economy improved at a startling rate.

Yet it is important to specify *how* it improved. Both Gheorghiu-Dej and his successor, Ceauşescu, placed a premium on industrial expansion. Although they differed sharply from the Soviets on matters of relations between the two countries, they concurred with them in the belief that a country could be hauled, by sheer force of will and through the imposition of strict five-year plans, into the twentieth century in a relatively short period of time. The problems inevitably caused by such rapid development—dislocations of large populations, pollution, dysfunctional management, insufficient and inefficient distribution of newly interdependent goods—were viewed as minor inconveniences. By 1958, industrial output was four times what it had been in 1938, according to the official statistics. But the real commitment to producer goods over consumer goods came in 1958 and 1959, when the phrase "rapid and all-round industrialization" became the rallying cry for the following years. Every plan since 1960 has put emphasis on industrial growth at the expense of the production of consumer goods (such as food).

This unrelenting stress on industry, combined with the inefficiencies and losses in agricultural production that were inevitable after the rapid farm collectivization of 1961–62, has strikingly affected the content of the Romanian GNP. Before World War II, only 30 percent of the national income was produced by heavy industry. By the mid 1970s, that figure had risen to 65 percent. During the same period, food production fell from 32 percent of total economic activity to 13 percent. Farmlands were turned into oil fields or strip mines. Hundreds of thousands of hectares were converted to industrial crops: oil seed, sugar beets, hemp, flax, and cotton. At the same time, collectivization practically wiped out the subsistence element in agriculture among the peasant population. A country that had few roads and fewer trucks, that had been distinguished by the self-sufficiency not only of each region but of each village, suddenly found itself in need of a sophisticated transport system. Transylvania became the mining center, Walachia increasingly turned to heavy industry and oil, and agriculture was concentrated in Moldavia, where enormous fields were devoted now to a single crop, to wheat or maize, to peas, tomatoes, cabbage, or potatoes. For the first time in Romanian history, villagers were dependent on trucks and schedules, on bureaucratic organization, for their food.

I can remember a depressing sight. From time to time, as I pedaled along a road through the flat country, I would pass a dump truck—just the sort of truck used in America to haul gravel—parked at the edge of a field. A squadron of workers, sunburned women, would be lugging pails of vegetables from the fields up to the road, where they would deposit them at the feet of three or four men who stood at the back of the truck. The men would pick up the pails and, rising from a squat to a stretch, hands over their heads, would throw the vegetables, in a high wide arc, over the back of the truck and into the bed. It looked like an Olympic event: the Vegetable Heave. I would hear the thumps of the vegetables landing in the truck as I biked past, and I would remember the battered and smashed produce in the vegetable stores.

The loading of tomatoes was the most painful to watch. Cycling out of Polovragi, I came across a tomato truck which was nearly full. It seemed to me that the tomatoes were coming apart even as they were being thrown. I went on by; fifteen or twenty minutes later, the full truck caught up and passed me. A veritable river of tomato juice and crushed tomato skins was pouring out the back, through the narrow slit between the bed of the truck and the hinged rear panel. The stream was flowing so thickly that the truck left behind it on the road's surface a continuous band of tomato rubbish two feet wide. For the rest of the way to the next town, I had to be careful to avoid this wide, stinking stretch of tomato carcasses so that I would not foul my tires and brakes. The whole disgusting affair reminded me of the story reported in *Pravda* (not without a strange relish) about the coal car in Russia that had so many rust holes that it had arrived at its destination without a single piece of coal left in it.

It was in the late 1970s that widespread food shortages were first reported in Romania. There were rumors of public unrest, even of riots. Ceauşescu was worsening the situation by exporting a continually larger fraction of the country's food in order to get hard currency. The black market became the scene of desperate scrambling for products and services that had utterly disappeared from the open market. Lawrence Graham, an American researcher in Romania, reported that the most widely used medium of exchange on the black market in 1980 was not money but Kent Long cigarettes.

Bread rationing was instituted in October 1981; food hoarders faced six months to five years in prison. The economic targets announced that autumn were the lowest in twenty years. The IMF began to demand austerity measures in 1982. The demand had the usual result of punishing the victims: commodity prices were raised dramatically, and Romanian citizens were ordered to cut back on energy consumption. By this time, Romania, once the granary of Europe, owed $91 million to the United States for grain imports (which it could not pay), and President Reagan rejected a bid for another loan of $65 million in March.

I began by asking, "What is being done wrong?" To my mind, one answer can be discerned in the following notice, which I ran across in a January 1984 edition of the *Times*:

> Romanian farms in private hands will receive financial incentives this year in an effort to meet increasing food shortages, the Government announced yesterday.
>
> The incentives include tax relief, easy credit and fixed purchase prices. In return, small farms employing two or three hands must follow "new production objectives."
>
> Every farm will have to have a rigid quota of animals, consisting of one cow, two pigs, four sheep or two goats, at least 10 hens and 12 rabbits.

This is the action of a martinet. Instead of encouraging cooperation from the bottom up, Ceauşescu has consistently chosen to impose control from the top down. When productivity falters, his response has been to replace a minister and to establish yet another controlling council. While Hungary met production shortages in the late 1960s with decreased centralization, Ceauşescu has tried to combat inefficiency by outlawing it. The irony of the article quoted above is that Ceauşescu is attempting to encourage private enterprise even as he betrays the fact that he doesn't understand what it is. With his quotas, his strict control, he annuls the efficiency and flexibility that are the principal advantages of private ownership.

A second answer seems plain. A government cannot utterly sacrifice the well-being of its people for the sake of growth in international trade, because it thereby damages its work force and consequently its ability to produce the materials of trade. (For this reason, if for no other.) By 1981, reports of sabotage by the workers were widespread in Romania. The per capita productivity of the country is astonishingly low. Underfed, overworked, out of hope as they stand in the long lines, the Romanian people are demoralized, and it cannot be expected of a demoralized people that they be either honest or industrious.

I will give only two examples of the Romanian government's willingness, its determination, to boost its industry at the expense of its citizens' welfare.

In 1965, the Romanian government invited William Randolph Hearst, Jr., to Bucharest and informed him that it was interested in founding joint American-Romanian companies. Starting capital and end products would be shared by the two companies, while the production site and the labor would be provided entirely by Romania. Much was made of this proposal by Americans, who saw in it a break with the other Communist nations, a step toward capitalism and the West. But far more significant, it seems to me, is the ominous note struck by the promises that the Romanian government dangled, like carrots, before Hearst's nose: the labor would be cheap, and it was absolutely guaranteed that there would be no labor trouble. While Americans commented favorably on the reduction in Romania of Soviet economic influence, they passed over the fact that the Romanian people were being farmed out as Third World subjects to toil for American capitalism.

The second example: after the earthquake in 1977, emergency aid came flowing into Romania from countries around the world. The aid mostly took the form of bandages and drugs, for the treatment of the more than ten thousand people who had been injured. Ceauşescu asked, after some days, that the aid be suspended. He thanked the other countries for their concern but said that it would be better for them to wait until Romania had had a chance to specify its needs. The countries contributing the aid complied. After a few days, the Romanian Foreign Ministry announced that what the stricken country really needed in this time of crisis was not bandages but computers and other technical machinery. Russia responded by donating $22 million in emergency aid, mostly industrial parts. The other countries followed suit, but with varying degrees of suspicion. It looked like a maneuver no less self-serving, and only slightly less bare-faced, than Somoza's appropriation for his personal use of three-quarters of the international aid that poured into Managua after the 1972 earthquake. At a time when eighty thousand Romanians found themselves homeless, their government was tending its wounded factories—and stocking up material so that it could build more.

.

While out for an afternoon walk, I stuck my head into one of the vegetable stores again. Just for the hell of it. But I was lucky— a few crates of grapes had arrived only moments before. By the time I reached the counter, some forty people stood behind me. Everyone was buying huge amounts of the grapes, more than they or their families could eat. It occurred to me that each person was perhaps buying some to sell to friends—friends who had not been lucky enough to be at the store themselves. The shortage of food had already cultivated in me the urge to hoard, and I almost bought a couple of kilos myself, but resisted it. I took two handfuls and walked out, grinning. In five more minutes, the grapes in the store would be gone.

Then more luck. At the café with the cakes in the windows,

eggs were for sale. The bakers formed a protective phalanx around a tower of crates, and a woman lifted the eggs down from the top. A score of hands reached up from below with bills between their fingers. There was an unbelievable din. One of the bakers kept pushing people back, but the crowd would swell forward again, against the table, against the crates. I came up to the back of the mob and debated entering the melee. I could boil a few eggs and take them with me when I left Piteşti. But the crates were emptying quickly. It looked as if they would be gone before I could get to them. I came away.

I was learning slowly. Some of the products that I had thought nonexistent in Romania were, in fact, available—but only briefly! You had to be in the right place at the right time. I wondered, all of a sudden, about milk and cheese. Perhaps they, too, were periodically available.

I found a man who spoke French. "Yes," he replied; "people begin to line up at five in the morning, right outside that door." He pointed to where the mob was still cramming itself into the café. He held a dozen eggs under his arm, and his hat was askew. "The cheese and milk are brought in around 6:30."

I could guess the denouement. "And when does the store run out?" I asked.

"Usually by 7:00 or thereabouts. Maybe a little before."

Eek. I could think of better things to do at 5:00 a.m. "You actually get up that early to buy cheese?" I asked.

The man guffawed. "Me?! No, no. My wife does."

Of course. I could see it: a patient, motionless line of women, standing wrapped in their shawls in the purple light, while their cheese-loving husbands slept.

•

It was exactly five o'clock. The bench Georgina and I had agreed upon was occupied by an old woman with a big black dog. Just in case Georgina had taken a bench somewhere else, I walked slowly around the park, trying to appear nonchalant, then sat on an empty bench next to the one with the old lady and the dog. I had forgotten to bring a book. I studied the bench, the worn grass, the gravel. I looked at the stone hero. I looked at the clouds. After ten minutes of this, I couldn't help noticing that I was being watched.

The benches were set in a straight line along one side of the path, about twelve feet apart from each other. Between my bench and the next one to my left stood an oak tree. And fixedly staring at me, partly hidden by the tree, was a man sitting at the next bench. I first noticed him out of the corner of my eye, and I glanced in his direction to see if my impression was correct. I involuntarily glanced away again as I met his eyes. My time on the streets of Romanian towns had partly accustomed me to being stared at, but they had not trained me to stare back. I looked at the man again, intending to hold his gaze. But his deep, blank eyes stared into mine without the slightest response on his face, and after a couple of moments, against my will, I looked away again.

Partly to reassure myself, partly because I had nothing else to think about, I pondered the phenomenon of staring in Romania. I was a WASP. Staring, to me, was an affront. But it wasn't considered so by the Romanians. When they saw something out of the ordinary, they simply gawked. Yet the staring was not provoked just by my Western looks. I had often noticed Romanians watching each other. But "watching" is too active a word to describe it. The word implies too much the apparent backing of an intellect. The most unnerving thing about this is that the man who stares at you, on the street, in a bar, virtually everywhere, has no trace of curiosity on his face. He doesn't scrutinize you, he doesn't spy on you—he just *stares* at you. And the stare is unanswerable, because it carries no message. There is nothing you can do in the face of such a stare except to pick up a stick and charge at the man. But then he would probably run from you, fixing you with that same incurious eye over his shoulder as he ran.

Two feet walked into my line of sight, and stopped. I looked up and saw the man who had been staring at me. He was balding, in his mid-forties, with a swarthy face and close-set, deep-set eyes. He gestured to the bench and said, in Romanian, what must have been "May I sit there?" I took my right arm down from the back rest, picked up the pack, and slid to the left. The man sat down. There were empty benches all over the park, including the one he had vacated moments before. Out of the corner of my eye, I could see him, his face no more than eighteen inches from my own, twisted in his seat and staring directly at me.

I felt the beginnings of alarm and glanced at my watch: 5:25. Where was Georgina? I looked slowly around the park. All my movements were self-conscious now, and after two or three minutes, I made a show of stretching and stood up. I nodded foolishly to the man, who only stared back at me. I walked down the gravel path to the hero and pretended to read his inscription. In the twilight, a spotlight had come on at his feet, and the shadow of his nose spread up over his forehead in an inverted triangle; it was difficult to appear heroic in that lighting. He looked as if he had stepped, just at that instant, on a land mine.

I circled to the other side of the statue and slid my gaze carefully back to the bench. The man was gone. I walked around the park. I couldn't see him anywhere. I made another circuit, looking for Georgina, before sitting down again. But she was not in the park, either. What in the hell was going on? Perhaps Georgina had recognized the man watching me and had been scared away. Perhaps she had known he was an informer. She had been seen talking to a foreigner—she had been seen crying and pleading with me. Those were probably grounds enough for surveillance. I realized once again that I had no way of knowing the extent of the spying, or the arrests, or for what reasons they might be initiated. It was crazy of me to have committed myself to action in a situation that was so utterly mysterious to me.

Yet I could not bring myself to leave the park. Perhaps Georgina would arrive any minute and explain that the bus service in Piteşti was unpredictable. Or maybe she had had to work overtime unexpectedly. There were, in fact, several possible explanations for her non-appearance that were eminently reasonable.

I just didn't believe any of them.

Meanwhile, the man had reappeared. He was sitting on the first bench to my right. Of course, he was staring at me. I was beginning to feel glad that Georgina had not come, whatever the reason. Even if this man was just an idiot. If Georgina had given me a letter, I would have seen eyes under every bush between

Piteşti and the Bulgarian border. Now she was handing me, tied up with a ribbon, the opportunity to bug out. The letter wouldn't have helped her in any case.

After half an hour more, it seemed pointless to stay on, and I was cold. It was completely dark now. There weren't more than half a dozen people still scattered on the benches. The poor man on the bench next to me was probably getting cold, too.

I got up. I scrunched on the gravel past him, and felt his eyes following me. He was tireless. I had no letter; in no conceivable way was I guilty. I was tempted to turn to the man, bring my nose close to his, and scream as loud as I could. I wanted to see *something* in those eyes, fear or anger or menace. I wanted to convince myself that he was, after all, a human being. But my upbringing prevented me. The training from birth to be polite is harder to go against, I think at times, than the training not to murder. I passed by the man's bench with no more than an ironic nod in his direction. He stared back. In my life, I have been polite to the damnedest people, and it never has done me the slightest bit of good.

⋅

I stayed in Piteşti for another two days, but my letters never arrived. I walked to the park again at 5:00 p.m. on the day after my vigil there and sat and waited for half an hour, but saw neither Georgina nor any man keeping an eye on me. I returned to the hotel, completely at a loss.

Finally, I had to head for the border in order to avoid a visa violation. I stood once more at the edge of Lenin Plaza and regarded the post-office building. That year, basic food prices had gone up 35 percent, meat prices 64 percent. Postal rates, meanwhile, had risen *400* percent. The average Romanian now had to work thirty-two times as long as the average American to earn the postage for an airmail letter. Discouragement? I knew what Georgina would have said. But I had lost Georgina.

I circled for the final time around the knot of soldiers on the corner by my hotel. The last thing I can remember doing in Piteşti, while heading for the road to Giurgiu, is stopping and buying another lottery ticket from the old woman with the cracked teeth and no place to sit. I threw the ticket away as I left Lenin Plaza.

GIURGIU AT LAST—the border town into Bulgaria and my Romanian visa would run out tomorrow. I wheeled down the roughly paved streets and was happy.

The day had begun with pinching cold. I rode half the morning wearing sweatpants, three shirts, and a wool cap over my forehead; I had thick wool socks on my hands and I still could barely feel them. No doubt about it: the autumn was ending.

But the roads were kind, and I made good time. The plain stretched generously before me. South of Videle, I hit oil fields, and I bicycled for miles between pumping rigs, on asphalt slimy with a film of petroleum. Thick black goo oozed from the edges of the plunging pipes, and the dirt between the rigs glistened. When I lost my way and asked directions from a man, his face and hands were nearly as black as the dirt. The small rigs tilted gracefully around us like the wooden toys of birds that dip and drink water out of a bowl—but many of the rigs were motionless: the oil fields produced fewer barrels each year.

I arrived at Giurgiu just before three o'clock. The clinging, cold fog had been defeated by midmorning, and the afternoon was mild and still. The glow from the low sun delicately fired the colored leaves on the old beeches and sycamores in the town, until they seemed to burn slowly on the branches.

As Romanian towns went, Giurgiu was quite pleasant. The

center of the town lacked the usual complex of factories or strip mines, and the low stone houses set among trees seemed richer and happier for their accompaniment of rustling foliage, their illumination in a shifting patchwork of light and shade. The streets were paved and fairly clean. And the carpet of fallen leaves on the grass and sidewalks softened everything, from the sounds of footsteps and wheels to the sight of abandoned and collapsing farm machinery, pushed into careless piles at the edges of a farm cooperative's property. I even saw a beer garden, spread out between two white oaks, its aluminum tables and chairs scattered haphazardly; it was the only beer garden I had seen in Romania.

The tourist motel's prices were ridiculous. Fortunately, and to my surprise, the campground adjacent to the motel was still open. I waited behind a foreign couple who were berated at great length by the woman at the desk and eventually refused permission to camp, for reasons that I could not understand. I worried that I would have the same trouble ("I'm sorry, but Westerners must stay in our hideous and overpriced motel, right next door, you can't miss it"), but my passport was accepted, and I rented a tiny bungalow made of pasteboard and plywood. It had just enough room for me on one bed, my luggage on the other, and the bicycle in the narrow space between. To get out the door, I had to crawl to the foot of the bed and clamber over the bike's rear wheel. I changed into long pants and made a trip to the communal bathroom to wash my face.

I hadn't forgotten that pleasant beer garden, so I locked the bungalow and headed back up the street. The other drinkers in the garden seemed fairly sober. Many of them looked like clerks and civil servants stopping for a couple of beers on their way home. They wore sport jackets and rough-cut trousers, button-down shirts with an occasional tie. It seemed a friendly, mild, middle-class crowd, merely glad to be done with work. Today had been one of the working Saturdays.

As the garden filled up, the tables ran out. I saw a man looking for a place, with a brimming mug of beer in one hand and a bulky, seamed briefcase in the other, so I took my feet off the second chair and sat up. He came over with a grateful nod and collapsed backward into the chair—an eloquent pantomime of the fatigue of a man who has just finished his forty-eight hours.

He was around forty years old, appealing because he wore an expression of good-natured eagerness, a desire to like and to be liked, to help and to be able to count on help. He had fleshy cheeks and a wide, straight nose, unusually light brown hair that fitted around his head like a soft brush cap. His hazel eyes were close-set, but managed to look ingenuous all the same. It was an eminently sociable face.

Made happy by the wonderful weather, the two of us talked to each other a good deal while drinking our beer. He spoke only Romanian (which by now held for me the glimmerings of known words and familiar phrases), and I spoke a mixture of Italian and French, trying to puncture the barrier in whatever way I could. We had to repeat phrases over and over again, and we relied heavily on body language. Even after great effort, we understood each other only a quarter of the time. At intervals he would slap his thigh in excitement and exclaim, in the most engaging way, with a smile, "Oh, if only you could speak Romanian, the things you could tell me!"

After a while, I got up and bought us two more beers. He took the opportunity to reciprocate a few minutes after that. The beer made us more patient, and we plowed on. Here is some of the information that the hazel-eyed man and I managed to throw to each other, over the language wall:

His name was Petra.

My name was Brian.

He worked in an office in Giurgiu, doing a job that required a good deal of paperwork. He didn't like his boss. The money was okay.

I came from America. From Boston, which was in Massachusetts. A bit north of New York City. Naturally, it was a beautiful town, and quite old—at least by American standards.

He had been born in a village outside Giurgiu, Daiţa. He hadn't been back there in more than a decade. His father had been a cobbler and an alcoholic. The old house was gone, and his

mother lived with him in Giurgiu. He had never been outside
Romania. He had been to Bucharest, though, two or three times.

I wanted to make my living as a writer. There was no way to
count on that, though.

The food lines were something terrible. Didn't I think so?

I did.

He'd waited an hour to get some meat a few days ago. The
lines hadn't been like this a couple of years ago. It had been this
bad when he was a little boy, after the war. Some people blamed
the lines on Ceauşescu; the organization, they said, was stupid and
corrupt. He, I should remember, wasn't saying this; he didn't
know. Ceauşescu was no doubt a fine leader. But some people said
that he was messing things up.

I traveled by bicycle. No, really. The bicycle was locked in a
bungalow in the campground. I had brought the bicycle from
America. Actually, I preferred cycling in the mountains to cycling
on the plains, so I had enjoyed the Carpathians very much. No, I
hadn't seen any bears, but I *had* seen two vipers. Yes, the Carpathians were beautiful.

It was true, one could not buy a Bible in Romania. Well . . .
at least, it was difficult. Why did I ask?

There was this fat guy who almost popped my sleeping bag
looking for Bibles at the border.

Really! Well, people were allowed to keep their old family
Bibles. They were heirlooms, after all. His family had *two* Bibles.
And his dear mother still lit devotional candles every evening, in
her own room. He'd just bought her some, in fact. All the churches
were open on Sunday; sure, a lot of people went. But perhaps,
for some people, it wouldn't be very wise to attend. Him? Oh no,
he didn't go.

Bibles were available in all the bookstores in America. And
practically everywhere else in the Judeo-Christian world, for that
matter. It was only my good luck that I hadn't had one with me
when I went through customs at the Romanian border.

Was I a Christian?

No. But I liked the Bible. And I hadn't liked the fat guy at
all.

He had a daughter. She was fifteen. She was very intelligent and quite good-looking. She had learned French in school. She wanted to go to France in the summer sometime. He didn't know whether it was difficult to get permission. He hadn't really thought about it much. No, no one in his family had a passport. You had to wait a long time for those. Oh, was it necessary to have a passport to go to France? Well, he probably should have known that. Where was France, anyway?

France was a part of Europe. It was about 1,500 kilometers west of Giurgiu. His daughter would enjoy seeing France. There was good food there. There were also Bibles in the stores in France.

Come to think of it, since both his daughter and I spoke French, we could get her to be our translator. If I came home with him, we could talk more easily about things. We could have some dinner, too. Was there anything I had to do this evening, anywhere I had to be?

Nothing, nowhere.

.

During the walk to Petra's apartment, I thought about the ignorance of Romanians concerning the rest of the world. Here was an intelligent man—a government worker, I guessed—who could read and write. Yet he didn't know where France was. And of all the countries of Europe, France was Romania's closest friend, the only country with which Romania had any significant cultural exchange. Petra hadn't the faintest idea what documents he might need in order to travel to a foreign country; the very idea of travel abroad seemed so baroque to him that he had never stopped to wonder at his own ignorance of it, or of its prerequisites. This lapse, I felt, was connected to the Romanians' inability to read maps, their lack of knowledge about the village just fifteen kilometers down the road from their own. To Petra, France was not a place to which one could appeal or escape. France could not be a point of reference, because it wasn't even a spot on the map. It was a word, and one of the clearest lessons in Romania was that words meant nothing—they were the comet's tail of the revolution:

bright but insubstantial, forever pointing away from the direction in which the comet was going.

Petra lived in the huge complex of apartment blocks just south of the town center. From the beer garden, it was a fifteen-minute walk. We took several turns, and each one opened up a new vista of blocks receding over hundreds of yards. Walking in the middle of a slow, dense crowd of workers, I found my sense of direction disrupted, and I began to worry that I'd get lost when I tried to return to the campground.

The complex looked as if it could house something like fifteen thousand people. I found myself wondering where in the world these thousands of apartment dwellers had been living just twenty years before, when this monstrous park of concrete towers, and scores of others like it across Romania, had been just a construction project in a five-year plan. Giurgiu gave the impression of having tripled its population merely by throwing up these buildings and then filling them with people. It was a magic act—but with a sordid result.

Not the smallest concession had been made here to humanize the environment. The streets ran straight and severe between the buildings; the tiny plots of ground trapped between stretches of pavement were left with their dirt and dying grass; the gray concrete of the walls and balconies remained unpainted, so that it had become stained and streaked by the rust and dirt that was washed by the rains from the metal window frames and railings.

Not even words, labels, the cheapest of decorations, were used by the Romanians to soften this reality. In America, someone living in such a complex (we would call it a "residential park") would have an address like: Tower Green, 650 Lakeshore Drive, "Seven Oaks" Building, apartment 6A. But the addresses in Romania read like computer cards: Progress Street, number 10, block 5, stairwell C, floor 2, room 2. The envelopes for sale in the post offices in Romania were all preprinted with little boxes for these numbers, and other boxes for the sector, the province, the locality, and the postal code. You had to be careful not to write, say, the stairwell letter in the space reserved for block numbers. If you were writing to someone who happened still to live in a village, or if you were writing to friends back in the United States, then the post-office workers yelled at you for ignoring the printing on the envelope. At the project in Giurgiu, even the word "room" was rejected, perhaps as too polished. The apartments in Giurgiu were called, with unkind accuracy, "cells."

Petra and I reached the path to blocks 7 and 8, as large as junior-high schools and identical except for their numbers. We went to stairwell C of block 8. We ascended the low-ceilinged staircase to floor 3. Turning to the left down a narrow corridor, gloomily lit from the ceiling by 40-watt bulbs in square white flimsy plastic cases, we reached cell 5. Home.

Petra jangled and jiggled his key in the lock of the door, stooping to get a better view in the twilight. Finally, he had to ring the bell, laughing to me about the troublesome locks. He was embarrassed, but I could sympathize with him, since I had had frequent trouble with my hotel-room keys. The door was opened by an extraordinarily pretty girl. Petra had said she was fifteen, but she looked eighteen. She was blond, with a round, sensuous face and a woman's figure. I immediately wished that she were one-third as attractive; after months on my own, she was a reminder that I didn't need.

Petra stepped in and gave his daughter a hug and a kiss; he introduced me, but didn't tell me the girl's name—I never learned it. Then he hailed his mother, who stood in the background in a black shawl and black voluminous skirts. She came forward as I entered the tiny front hall and greeted me severely. I wasn't given her name, either. She had cataracts but was not yet blind. Petra pecked her on the cheek, fished the prayer candles out of his briefcase, and handed them to her. She pressed them to her stomach and quickly disappeared into a room beyond the kitchen. There was a furtiveness to the transaction, even here, in their own apartment.

The family was completed by three younger children, two of them nearly infants. The third was a small boy, about eight years old, with black hair and the complexion of a Gypsy. He had the plump, confident look that one sees so often on well-loved and pampered Italian boys. There didn't appear to be a wife.

The apartment for these six people was minuscule. Doors from the dining room led to a kitchenette and two small bedrooms. A bathroom was squeezed in next to the kitchenette. That was all. The total floor area couldn't have been more than five hundred square feet.

It immediately became apparent that Petra's daughter did not speak French as well as Petra had told me she did, with such fatherly pride. In fact, either she knew practically no French at all or she was too shy to utilize whatever words she did know. Once I had been seated at the dining-room table and the old woman had set about preparing dinner for us, Petra would speak to his daughter for a few seconds and then wait, his eyes shining hopefully, for her to relay the words to me in French. At this point, she would look embarrassed and not say anything. She would instead become busier at cleaning off the table. When she did finally speak, she would usually say, *"Ohhh . . . je ne sais pas."* Her embarrassed smiles were charming.

Her father did not seem disappointed in the slightest that his daughter, who could speak such excellent French, was failing as a translator. He suspected, I think, that the fault was mine, but he was unwilling to be disillusioned or in any way irritated with his guest. So, faced with an evening of more halting conversation, he brought to the table a liter-and-a-half bottle of red wine.

Presently, food began to appear. The daughter and her grandmother carried the broth, then the rice and small pieces of pork fat, then the cabbage and bean salad, from the tiny kitchen to the cramped dining room. Only Petra and I ate. That was the traditional arrangement. The grandmother retreated immediately to the kitchen, and the daughter either stood by the table and waited for her father's next wish or continued to tidy up the room. The tidying, I knew, was being done for my benefit. I had been a surprise. There probably would not be enough food for everyone tonight, and I did my best to eat sparingly.

The two smallest children had been put to bed. The young

dark boy was sitting to my left on a small sofa piled with quilts which apparently also served as his bed. He was watching *The Muppet Show* on the television set behind his father's head. The show was in English with subtitles; I hadn't heard much English for weeks. I soon became more interested in the television than in what Petra had to say, since I rarely understood him (he had begun to speak faster). So I attended to his words with half a mind, while my eyes more and more moved unstoppably to the television screen at his back. Miss Piggy had locked Kermit the Frog in a packing case because he wouldn't marry her. The Muppet Studio was being taken over by pirates. The little boy sat on his little sofa, entranced. The bottle of wine, I noticed suddenly, stood empty.

Petra, becoming more grandiloquent, ordered his daughter with a sweeping gesture of his arms to get another bottle of wine. She hesitated. The meal was over. Petra was getting drunk. He spoke in a louder voice, and the girl went. The old woman reappeared in the room for a moment and shot a poisonous glance at her son. She muttered something to him, but he stared her down. She retreated to one of the bedrooms and slammed the door.

A second bottle as large as the first appeared and was placed between us. More of the red wine went into my glass. I remember being glad that the wine was fairly weak. Conversation, by this point, was largely fruitless: neither Petra nor I had the presence of mind any longer to be able to interpret the other's speech, and the daughter's translating skills only worsened as Petra bullied her more and more.

But Petra was the kind of man who became loquacious and grand when he drank. He was, by now, talking to me practically nonstop, waving his glass in the air with the demeanor of a Viking chieftain proposing toasts of mead with the skull of his enemy in his hands. He seemed to become increasingly possessed with the desire to convey deep and noble emotions to me.

Petra grabbed his daughter, as she passed his chair on one of her trivial and incomprehensible errands, pulled her into his lap, gave her a mighty kiss, and said to me, beaming, "My daughter!

Isn't she beautiful?" His eyes were red. The girl looked at me just for a second, saying then, in the first complete French sentence I had heard from her, *"Mon père est un peu ivre; c'est pas bon."* She glanced away, humiliated, trying to smile at her father's coaxings. Petra's hand was on her breast.

I felt particularly sorry for the girl, who seemed acutely conscious of my presence. As an outsider, I was a new witness to her father's pleasures. In my own inebriated state, I simultaneously endeavored (a) to act and appear sober, so that she would not think she had two drunken louts on her hands, and (b) to act and appear drunk, so that I would not seem coldly to judge, to mock, or even to notice her father's condition. It was a measure of how much wine I had, in fact, consumed that I imagined for a while that I was succeeding at both objectives.

As the second bottle grew emptier, Petra began to abuse his daughter in earnest. He enjoyed making her pour the wine for him, since he knew she disliked his drinking. He would point to our two glasses and say roughly, "More wine!" If she hesitated, he would pound the table and scream it at her. She would flinch and fix him with pleading eyes; then she would pour. I tried to make myself invisible.

I had been waiting for an opportunity to escape for the past half hour, but Petra had made it difficult for me to take my leave casually by embarking on an extremely long and emotional harangue about what great friends we were. He kept grabbing me by the back of the neck, hauling me forward until my face was half a foot from his, fixing me with his red and excited eyes, still brimming with good nature, and declaiming the wonder and thrill of friendship. He was nearly overcome with the thought of it; he was rendered, now and then, for long seconds at a stretch, speechless by the thought of our friendship. At these times, he could only hold me by the neck and wag his head in joyful contemplation. I marveled at how likable he still was, in his present state. I also had had the opportunity to notice that he was both bigger and stronger than I had initially thought. I didn't envy his daughter trying to put him to bed.

I at last got my chance to leave when Petra let go of me and stood up to get a third bottle (he apparently no longer trusted his daughter with the task). I explained quickly that it was late and that I had to get an early start the next day, since the customs might take a long time. Only when I stood up did I realize how drunk I was. The room wavered. The boy was asleep, fully clothed, on his sofa. The television was turned off. I brutally suppressed a last, sweet desire to kiss Petra's daughter. I made my way carefully to the door. Petra grabbed the girl for support and came after me. She pulled his arm around her shoulders and guided him, with the experience of a halfway-house volunteer, into the front hall. Petra was past remonstrating with me for leaving. He had reached that stage of drunkenness in which he could accept everything, cheerfully aware as he was that he couldn't understand the reasons for anything. I thanked him for his hospitality, and thanked especially the girl, for waiting on us and for her patience. I gave her what I hoped would be an encouraging, a commiserating, and a compassionate smile. She smiled crookedly back, staggered under her father's weight as he lunged forward to shake my hand, and said, with a last pathetic attempt at explanation, *"Mon père aime beaucoup le vin."* She was on the verge of crying.

.

On my way out of the housing project, exactly what I had feared would happen happened. I got lost.

My being drunk didn't help. Now that they were empty of people, the streets seemed longer. It took me forever to get from one corner to another, and each corner merely showed me another street boxed in by buildings. I dimly recalled that the entrance to the complex had been deceptively small.

My plight struck me as emblematic of the situation for many people in Romania. I had a vivid image of myself wandering, drunk and poorly fed, through a maze of inhuman buildings, wanting only to get out, but unable to find the way. I imagined the Romanian Everyman, trapped behind the clifflike walls of his bureaucracy, finding no one to help him, seeing only the frighteningly long vistas, stumbling along without a passport, or even a good idea where France was.

I tried to concentrate on the matter at hand. The thought of a night spent on the cold sidewalk horrified me. So when I came across a clutch of late-night partyers, standing at the intersection of two streets with bottles of beer in their hands, I fell on them with great relief. They were even drunker than I was. But they knew their own territory, and they gave me directions. They also laughed at me, which I was willing to accept. I thanked them and headed off again. Ten minutes later, I was out of the project.

More of the alcohol had entered my blood by the time I reached the bungalow. I flopped down on my cot and watched the bike spin around for a while. Presently, I fell asleep, and dreamed. I was waiting for my Budapest friend in a cathedral. We had agreed to meet at one of the columns in the transept. A minister and his wife, both old and kindly, were walking up and down trying to decide where to hold the prayers and where the benediction. The minister was saying, over and over, "It's always prayers in the chancel and benediction in the nave. Let's try something different." I felt great tranquillity watching this pair, as they checked the lighting at various spots, angling the Bible in the sunlight and comparing the visibility for reading. It didn't even bother me that my friend hadn't shown up. The minister and his wife finally settled on a spot against the north wall of the nave for prayers, putting the great Bible up in the light as if they were hanging a picture; they both looked so pleased. Today, at least, there would be prayers in the nave. This pleased me, too—immensely.

Then I woke up. It was 3:30 and I desperately needed to go to the bathroom. The run outside to the toilet was bitterly cold.

THE MORNING WAS SO FOGGY that I couldn't see the Danube. The old steel bridge seemed to float in the mist. I stopped once or twice and peered over the handrail, hoping for a glimpse of the river, but the bridge pylons hung downward for a couple of dozen feet, then dissolved to ghostly outlines and disappeared. At my level the mist was thinner, but the ends of the bridge were invisible.

The Friendship Bridge, this was called; it connected Giurgiu, Romania, to Ruse, Bulgaria. Completed in 1954, made entirely of steel, it was the largest bridge in Europe and one of the very few spanning the vast lower reaches of the Danube. Romanian and Bulgarian engineers had worked together for two years in order to construct it. Perhaps it was from their temporary cooperation that the name "Friendship" had come. It was not the best word to describe the relationship between the two countries.

From the Romanian shore, there had been a sharp ascent, an arc. But the bridge was huge; when I reached the top of the curve, the pavement didn't descend again but swept away levelly and lost itself in the fog. I pedaled for a while in the stillness that fog imposes. Nearly thirty years of weather had rusted the spiderwork steel. The asphalt looked as if it had melted, started to run, and then solidified again; the dew made it treacherous. Steel latticework emerged out of the fog in front of me and was swallowed up again behind. I could just make out an oval of pale gray below the bridge on my left; the tops of two pines defined themselves—an island. How wide the Danube was here! On a clear day, the view would have been stupendous. As it was, I might as well have been crossing a train yard.

I had realized this morning that I had unintentionally been following the Danube for the past two months. I had picked it up at its source, in the mountainous Schwarzwald east of Freiburg, in late August. I'd kept with it through the pretty, diminutive Donautal ("Danube Valley") into Tuttlingen, where it had been still no wider than a stone's throw. I met it again at Donauwörth, and crossed it at Ingolstadt, north of Munich. In mid-September, I stood on the bluff at Passau, on the Austrian border, and watched the Danube mix with the Inn; the point of confluence of the two rivers rippled and glittered in the afternoon sun, and the Danube continued westward, visibly larger. I left the river a few days later to see the Czech border, but caught it again near Melk, a day's ride west of Vienna. By that point, the river was nearly a furlong wide. I saw it at its most austere in Vienna, in late September, where it flowed through an enormous artificial channel, dark gray between flat shores; I'd taken a trolley out from the city center especially to see it, and marveled (as I suppose everyone has) that Johann Strauss could have called it blue. Beyond Vienna, the Danube changed, from the German Donau to the Czech Dunaj. But I hadn't a visa to enter Czechoslovakia, and I didn't see the river again until I spent a night in Komárom, Hungary—on the Czech border. On my side of the river, the people called it Duna, in the delightfully soft Hungarian intonation; and the Duna here seemed just as soft—it flowed by pensively in the darkness. Then I followed it around the Danube Bend to Budapest, where it was at its most splendid—a silver blade between the Buda hills and the plain, moving with the confidence and power of the ocean tides. But beyond Budapest, I lost the river. My route took me to Romania, while the river flowed south into Yugoslavia. Near Belgrade, the Danube turned to the east, and after cutting through the highlands of the Banat, it became the border between Romania and Bulgaria. At times in Romania I was near it, and I caught now and then the Romanian word for the great river in conversation: Dunarea. At Tîrgu Jiu, I was less than a day's ride from Turnu Severin, the town by the "Iron Gates" gorge of the Danube, where one still could pick out the remains of the bridge built by the Emperor Trajan for his conquest of Dacia. After that, my roads kept me always north of the river, although we moved in the same direction. It was not until I left Piteşti and angled south toward the border that I approached the Danube again, and I raced it toward our crossing as one might race a train. I felt as if I would be seeing an old friend again.

The sighting of the Danube at Giurgiu would have been my last. Some sixty miles to the east of that point, the river would leave the border and turn north into Romania, delving to the edge of the Soviet Union, before curling east again and emptying, in a wide, marshy delta, into the Black Sea. I, meanwhile, would be headed south, cutting more or less straight through Bulgaria toward Greece. I had looked for the chance to see the Danube so near the end of its course, where it would be slow and swollen— where it would look like an inland sea. And now I was blinded by the fog.

After a time, a spindly tower condensed out of the mist in front of me: a concrete box set high on converging steel beams. Other towers identical to it stretched out, fading like Cheshire-cat skeletons, to east and west. Guards with rifles strapped to their backs peered out of windows. A pair of binoculars traced my movement on the bridge. It was not a friendly welcome for a traveler on the Friendship Bridge. A fatuous American, I waved to the man with the binoculars, and he, a soldierly Bulgarian, did not respond. I left the towers behind. I was in Bulgaria. The Danube, unseen, had become the Dunav, and I took with me its name.

BULGARIA

I FOLLOWED AN ARROW into the customs building. There were quite a few people standing at service windows in the main room inside. The signs were only in Bulgarian, and no one else in the room appeared to be a foreigner. I hadn't the slightest idea where to begin.

"Well . . . He looks lost, don't you think? I'll bet he wants to come here."

English. I turned in the direction of the voice and saw a hefty man with a pale, slack face and quizzical eyes. A younger man, to whom he had spoken, sat behind him. An ashtray on the counter was stuffed with butts; as I came up to the window, the pale man lit a new cigarette on the butt of an old one and stubbed the latter out.

"Let me guess," he said, while the smoke from his new cigarette curled around his light gray eyes. "You're entering Bulgaria, right?"

"Uh, yes . . . I haven't got a visa, though. I need to get one here," I said.

He cupped his chin with the hand holding the cigarette, and the veil of smoke in front of his eyes grew thicker. "You don't need a visa to enter Bulgaria," he said pensively. "So I suppose it's no surprise that you don't have one."

This information went against everything I had heard concerning Bulgaria. My yellow State Department sheet on entry requirements said flatly: "Visa required, standard 1 month, inquire Bulgarian embassy for details." In the past, tourists had been thrown off trains at the Bulgarian border when it was discovered that they didn't have the right papers. I said, "There are *no* tourist visas? How long has that been going on?"

The man laughed pleasantly. "Let me have your passport." He flipped through the pages, with the ash trembling on the end of the cigarette in his hand. "My, my, an American. It looks as if you've been traveling all over the place. All of this on the bicycle?" He gestured toward the plate-glass front of the building, where my bike was visible.

"Yes."

He nodded his head and chortled once; the ash fell off his cigarette, and he blew it onto the floor. "Well, everyone says here that Americans are crazy." He applied a stamp about as official-looking as the ones used in tiny branch libraries and slid the passport back to me. "Now you're all set."

The new mark showed only the date and place of entry. I couldn't believe that was sufficient, but I wasn't sure how I could politely question the man's competence. "I heard that tourists had to buy a special visa," I said. "When did that regulation end?"

"Oh, we still issue tourist visas. But you don't want one of those." He turned to catch the eye of the young man behind him; suddenly they both broke into laughter.

"Why don't I want one?" I asked.

"Hm?" he managed, still laughing.

"Do you have to pay for one?"

"No, no. They're free." He flicked some ash in the ashtray and rolled the butt between his fingers. He seemed to smoke partly for the fun of playing with the cigarette. "But if I give you a tourist visa, then I have to sell you hotel vouchers for the first two nights. I'm assuming that you don't want to do that. You don't look as if you travel expensively." He smiled, and his dark friend snorted into laughter again. I was beginning to enjoy these two.

"Wait a minute," I said. "If this stamp in my passport isn't a tourist visa, then what is it?"

"It's all right, don't worry about it. It's all you need."

"But what *is* it?"

"Oh, I don't know—what do you call it?—it's an entry permit . . . It's a visa, too; it's just not a special tourist visa."

"But what is the difference between a tourist visa and an entry permit?"

The pale man answered with exaggerated patience, "I've already told you. A tourist visa requires two days' accommodation vouchers. What I've given you doesn't need that." He smiled reasonably.

"But," I sputtered, "why would anybody get a tourist visa if they could get this instead?"

He shrugged his shoulders. "I really don't know. Stupidity, perhaps." His companion broke up again.

"Oh, wait—" The pale man suddenly seemed to remember something. "There's one other thing you'll need." He put down his cigarette and searched beneath the counter, his gray hair flopping over his forehead. The cigarette tilted off the ashtray and began to burn a spot in the linoleum. There were similar spots all over the countertop. He shrugged, stopped, and looked again. He spoke to the younger man, who helped him look. Finally the younger man exclaimed *"Da, da"* and pulled out a stack of white cards. I marveled at their lack of organization. It couldn't be *that* long since they had had a customer.

"This is your statistical card," the pale man said. "It's important. Keep it in your passport at all times. Whenever you stay at a hotel, make sure they stamp the card. When you leave the country, the customs man will check the dates on the card to make sure each night is accounted for."

"I have a question about that," I said.

The pale man rolled his eyes. "Oh . . . always questions."

"Since I'm traveling by bike, it's possible that sometimes I won't be able to reach a hotel. What if I end up camping out for a night or two? Will the missing dates really be that important?"

He fixed me with his watery eyes for a moment. "Well, you know, it depends on the other customs man. If he is in a good mood, the whole card could be blank and he'd just wink at you. But if he's not feeling well that day, then he could give you some trouble. Drag you off and beat you, that sort of thing—"

"What?"

"I'm only joking. No; for just one night, I don't think there would be a problem. Two nights: that's not so good. And be sure not to leave a whole week empty, right? But one day, no one will care, I think."

I tucked the card into my wallet.

"Is that all?"

"Sure, sure." The pale man waved his free hand; with the other he was searching for another cigarette among his many pockets. The dying butt on the counter sent up a last gasp of blue.

·

I entered Bulgaria on Halloween—very late in the season to be bicycling in an area that enjoys only 180 frost-free days a year. On the map, Bulgaria looks like a southern country; after all, it sits near the southeastern end of Europe. But Sofia, the capital city of Bulgaria, lies on the same latitude as Buffalo, New York. Only the Gulf Stream keeps the rest of Europe from getting snow eight months out of twelve, but the Gulf Stream does not exert much influence as far east as the Black Sea. And nearly all of Bulgaria is cut off from the tempering effects of the Mediterranean by the country's three mountain ranges: the Balkans, the Sredna Gora, and the Rhodopes. Bulgarian weather is a thing of extremes: blasting, dry summers followed by bitter winters. I needed to keep pressing south or I would, at some point, find myself cycling in a snowstorm; a loaded bike will slide on a thin layer of snow and go down like a horse shot in the head. But this worry was in the background. The customs men had given me a lift. It had been the first really positive human contact I had had for weeks.

My road ascended the flank of a line of hills, sweeping the raised outskirts of the city of Ruse in a westward-turning arc. The hills were lightly forested with stands of bare oak and beech, alternating with fields scarred with stalks of wheat and corn. Occasionally I spotted a small vineyard. Below the road, on my right, I could see the backs of stone houses and sloping private gardens. I passed, now and then, a homeowner in his ratty weekend clothes, picking through his garden with his nose to his kneecaps. Some of the back yards served as moderate-sized orchards, particularly of apples. I saw women high on ladders, with their torsos lost in the leaves. A few people waved to me as I passed, and smiled. Nobody stared. I was feeling better and better. I noticed a sign for a campground among the trees on the left, and turned in, on the off chance that the place was open. Before the gate to the campground, in a small clearing, stood a circular wooden shack—a bar—with glassless windows all around. A group of men sat on aluminum chairs under the bar's awning, drinking. I nosed around the gate and confirmed that it was locked. No one at the shack spoke a foreign language, so I mimed to them my concern, and they motioned back that the campground was closed. Yes, they were sure. No, it would not be opened up just for one foreign cyclist.

I remounted the bike, and the men said, *"Dobur put!"* They repeated it. At length I understood that they were saying *Bon voyage.*

I started out of the clearing. Straining up the incline toward the road, I put all my weight on the pedal. Just at that moment, the gear slipped and the pedal shot down; the chain snapping taut yanked the front sprocket brutally to a halt, and the pedal arm broke with a resounding snap. It took about five seconds for the import of what had happened to hit me: the bike was now useless. And I hadn't the means to repair it. Suddenly my trouble finding a place to sleep seemed trivial. I was stranded.

Dobur put indeed!

•

On any bicycle that is capable of going anywhere, the pedals are attached to pedal arms, or cranks, which in turn are attached to the front sprocket. The front sprocket is the toothed gear that lies between the rider's feet while he is riding the bike; as it rotates, it pulls the chain around with it by means of its teeth. The chain powers the back wheel, which spins and makes the bike go. This whole assembly is called the drive train, and if any part of it stops working, then the bike immediately becomes about as mobile as an Exercycle.

What had happened to my bike was that the crank (pedal arm) on the right side had broken away from the front sprocket. Both the cranks and the front sprocket were still firmly attached to the bicycle, since they both still gripped the axle that connected the two cranks, but they were no longer attached to *each other*. When I rotated the pedals, the front sprocket didn't move—so neither did the chain.

I had never heard of this happening before, even though I had traded many equipment horror stories with other bicyclists during the past seven and a half months. This, by the way, is something of a cyclist's game. Whenever two cyclists get together, either at a hostel or for a quick chat by the side of the road, a pattern of conversation establishes itself. First, the cyclists will talk about their routes, often delving into the side issue of explaining (defensively) why it is taking them so long to traverse them. Then they'll mention the longest day they've put in—and neither one of them will quite believe the figure on which the other insists. Third come the hospitality stories, which, believe it or not, are an oblique form of one-upmanship, since it is understood that the more hospitality you finagle, the better traveler you are. Finally, still seeking competition, one of the cyclists will ask the other, "Had any problems with your equipment?" and the dramatic accounts begin.

These are always told gleefully if the problem has been resolved, and with a mixture of relish and dismay if it hasn't been. The more exotic the problem, the more fun it is to talk about, and the greater the stature the victim gains thereby. The highest compliment one cyclist can bestow on another in this game is to declare that he has never heard of the other's problem before. This implies that the victim has been touring so long, so arduously, that he has discovered a novel form of equipment failure. He is a pioneer in disaster.

I can remember standing outside the youth hostel in Passau, West Germany, on a cliff high over the Danube, in the company of three other cyclists, examining the freewheel (the rear sprocket) on the bicycle of a fifth tourist. The freewheel, a thick piece made of steel, had split right through the middle; it looked as if a bolt of lightning had struck it. And what the four of us said, several times, enjoying the words, while the fifth looked on in gloomy satisfaction, was: "We have never heard of this happening before." Ever since mid-August I had been able to hold my own in these contests by describing the time that I had broken ten spokes in seven days, between Salzburg and Freiburg. That story always elicited respect—but never amazement. Everyone on tour with a heavy load breaks spokes; it's just unusual to break them that often. Now at last, after more than half a year of relatively little trouble, I had a catastrophe on my hands—and I could be sure that it was practically unique, because the crank-and-front-sprocket assembly was designed to last for the life of the bike. If I ever made it back to the West, I would be able to win plenty of contests.

Not that the thought gave me much consolation at the time. In fact, I was pretty upset—an unsporting attitude due, primarily, to anger at myself. For I had suspected that something was wrong with the front sprocket for months. As long ago as April, in England, I had felt a certain crappiness in the motion of the pedals, but I had not gotten around to isolating the problem until mid-July, when I was in Spoleto, Italy (a remarkable piece of procrastination, now that I thought about it). There, while working on another part of the bike, I had noticed that the right pedal and the front sprocket moved slightly with respect to one another. The Italians who were with me at the time confirmed that bikes were not supposed to do that. But the bicycle still worked, new crank assemblies were expensive, and I was cheap. I opted to keep riding and stop worrying. I only hoped that if it ever *did* break, it broke in a Western country. I knew that between Vienna and Athens there were no bicycle shops capable of servicing a ten-speed Japanese bicycle—in fact, there were practically no bicycle shops of any kind.

And now, examining my disabled bike in Bulgaria with anguish, I could hardly believe my earlier nonchalance. How could I have been so stupid as to ignore a looming disaster? Moreover,

I had compounded the stupidity. There is a special tool for removing cotterless cranks—that is, cranks that are not attached to the bike by means of cotter pins. Logically enough, the tool is called a "cotterless crank remover"; it weighs perhaps seven ounces and costs about six dollars. For some reason that, just outside Ruse, I could no longer fathom, I had neglected to buy this tool, even though my bike had cotterless cranks. Therefore, I could not take the first step toward repairing the problem, which would have been to remove the right crank. And the Soviet Sputnik bicycles, the only touring and racing cycles I had seen in the East Bloc, all had cottered cranks. I was not likely to find a cotterless crank remover anywhere in Bulgaria. It was therefore not at all likely that I would be able to get the bike fixed. I had to face the facts: I had fucked up.

I recognized one source of consolation as soon as I got off my rear end: it was downhill all the way to Ruse. I swung onto the bike and coasted. About halfway down the ridge, an idea occurred to me. Perhaps I could weld the sprocket and crank together! It would not be necessary to remove the crank in order to do so. A clumsy job, perhaps, but not impossible (?). And I could easily find a welder at any machine shop, even with no knowledge of the language. Welding was not a normal procedure in bicycle work, by any means—but it wasn't normal to be in Bulgaria, either. A small hope, at least. I would see what I could accomplish the next morning.

I followed the signs from the ridge road toward the center of town. I began to pass through tree-lined and crepuscular suburban streets. The square stone houses with their red-tiled roofs and low-walled balconies looked comfortable. The sidewalks on the main streets were crowded with people. I heard laughter. Feet moved quickly over the pavement. A large number of children, high-voiced and sure of themselves, flitted around their parents. After my time in Romania, these people seemed boundlessly energetic, full of life and cheerfulness.

Inside the city, I pushed my bicycle like a scooter down the streets. The stone houses gave way suddenly to larger buildings of two and three stories, and the trees retreated into ornamentality.

The streets widened, and I hit cobblestones. I stopped a couple of times and asked after a hotel. (The Bulgarian word for "hotel" is "*hotel*," pronounced with a German *ch* at the beginning; alas, I didn't know the word for "cheap.") Everyone pointed in the same direction. It worried me a little that although I didn't specify which hotel I wanted, all the people I asked were clearly directing me toward the same one.

I rolled past a floodlit park lanced by a tall memorial column, made a left-hand turn, and found myself at the hotel. It was called the Dunav: six stories high, latticed with aluminum supports for its tiny balconies. I recognized the restaurant and disco bar through the windows of a block that swung out from the tower like a two-story parking garage.

"Do you need some help?" a deep voice asked me in accented German. On the sidewalk stood a slender man in his late twenties. He wore dark glasses, although the light had been failing for the past half hour. His neat black hair had a modish cut, curving smoothly down to his earlobes—the blow-dried, smarmy sort of cut now affected in the United States by New Right junior senators. His mustache, sprinkled with a few dozen gray hairs, looked no better: its full, clipped shape weighed down on his mouth like a disguise. His hands were in his pockets. He wore a slick gray winter jacket, polyester black pants, and black shoes with a reflective plastic finish. He was not alone but stood in a loose group with four or five others. Some of them looked as slick as he did; others were dressed like street toughs, American-style.

"Do you need some help?" he asked again.

"Well, actually, my bicycle is broken," I said warily.

"Broken?!" he replied in a raised voice. "How is it broken?" His tone implied that he suspected me of trying to put one over on him.

I reached down and spun the pedals. My first audience. "It happened just a few minutes ago," I said. "I need to find a place where I can get it fixed tomorrow."

His response was immediate: "I can fix that. No problem!" He gave me a gesture of reassurance—his right hand waving down worries. It was a con man's gesture.

"You? How could you fix it?"

He shrugged. "No problem. It would take five, ten minutes. Listen, I used to do that kind of stuff."

"What kind of stuff?"

He paused. "I don't know the word in German." He pulled a hand out of his pocket and mimed making a weld; he imitated the sound with his lips.

"Ahh . . . *Schmeissung*," I said.

"*Ja, ja. Schmeissung*." He returned his hand to its pocket. I had noticed a heavy gold ring on his fourth finger.

I wondered if he possibly could have been a welder. He didn't look the type. The type he *did* look like was not East European at all but a certain kind of American, the type who ran a succession of crafty little businesses from the age of thirteen on, who talked a good line, who had a finger in more pies than you even knew existed; exactly the sort whom you couldn't trust, whom you could hardly imagine anyone, no matter how gullible, trusting. That type flourished in our airy American soil, nurtured by our particular national brand of gullibility. This was Bulgaria, and it occurred to me to feel sorry for anyone in this country who had the genes of a self-made man, even a sleazy one. I wasn't aware of the particulars of economic organization in Bulgaria, but I imagined it was pretty tough to be a fifteen-year-old in Ruse with plans of buying firewood wholesale and peddling it retail from a bicycle-drawn cart at a 200 percent profit. Chances were good that you'd do poorly in your studies and would get slapped into a technical school, where they would train you to be a welder. I could picture this guy with his gold ring and blow-dried hair chafing on the job, holding the spit of fire to a monstrous seal and cooking up one moneymaking scheme after another. Most of the brummagem little schemes I could think of were not possible in Bulgaria. They required a free market. Yet the man had claimed that he *used* to be a welder. He had gotten out of the job somehow. And his shades, his ring, his well-cut fancy pants suggested that he was doing pretty well: he was better turned out than most of the people on the street. So into what line had his entrepreneurial spirit led

him? I had a fair idea, and that meant I didn't want to have much
to do with him.

"Look," he said. "We can meet early tomorrow morning. I'll
take you to the place where I can fix your bike, my old workplace.
I'll knock on your door in the morning. Just give me your room
number."

"I haven't checked in yet," I expostulated. "How could I know
my room number?"

"Check in right now. I'll wait. Just come back out and tell me
what the room number is."

One of his cohorts took a step in our direction. They were
anxious to be off. "Stilyan," he said, coaxingly. Stilyan gave him
the reassuring gesture.

"No," I said. "Don't wait. I won't come out again. You can ask
at the desk for me."

He knew perfectly well that this meant I didn't trust him. "All
right," he grunted, "we'll do it that way. What is your name?" He
quickly added, "I've got to know who to ask for."

What could it matter? I thought. "Brian Hall."

"My name is Stilyan," he said. We shook hands. I could feel
the big gold ring, like a wart. "I've got to go; I've got some business
to take care of." He turned away, and the pack hurried off.
Business? Hmpf. I sincerely hoped that Stilyan would not bother
to come for me in the morning.

                                    •

When they took my passport at the desk inside, I asked, just
for fun, if there were any other hotels in town. Yes, there was the
Prima, they said, a *wunderschön* hotel just a couple of blocks—oh
. . . *other* hotels? No, those were the only two . . . But why did I
need another, these two were so nice! They had the deluxe
restaurants, the disco bars, the nightclubs . . . Everything a tourist
might desire.

Both the Dunav and the Prima were administered by Balkanturist, the state travel agency, whose mission was to make each
Westerner's stay in Bulgaria as expensive as possible. The Dunav
was comfortable enough, but it had exactly the international high-

rise hotel interior that I tried to avoid. Once I was inside the swinging glass doors, I could have been anywhere in Europe, in any of ten thousand large, expensive hotels. The lobby was carpeted in green, and a number of leather chairs and hassocks were scattered across the floor like fat calves grazing on the sward. A couple of square end tables with wood-grained plastic finishes held magazines of the *Beautiful Bulgaria* variety in German and English. Potted something-or-other trees with small dark-green leaves flanked the elevators, the granite stairs, and the yellowish glass doors at the entrance. The promise of the Dunav's exterior had been appropriately fulfilled within.

Up in my room, I stood at the large window for a while and contemplated the night over Ruse. The streets were nearly deserted. A few figures, bundled against the cold, hurried through the park. The moon was full, but my window faced west; all I could see was the opalescence of the tree branches, the wan light on the paving stones.

From three floors below, the sound of the disco bar came up to me, vibrating through my feet: a muffled *oomp-oomp* POW, *oomp-oomp* POW. They had started early. "Everything a tourist might desire"—except quiet. And a little taste. These six-story piles of carpeting and fiberboard ceilings offered all the comforts, and all the vulgarities, of home.

I drew the curtains.

•

After a little while, I came back downstairs to the restaurant; it was packed. This late at night, it served more as a bar than a restaurant. The air swirled with cigarette smoke. As always in Eastern Europe, the lighting was dim—not for the sake of atmosphere, but for the sake of electricity. Maybe they'd have more wattage for the lights if they didn't use so much on the rock and Gypsy bands that drowned out conversation in every restaurant. Tonight there was a common combo: electric keyboard, two electric guitars, a mike for the singer. But the players were on break, so we were blessed, for the moment, with the quieter strains of canned Gypsy music.

After some searching, I commandeered a chair at a table for

two. The other chair had disappeared. A waitress fought her way to me after several minutes, looking as ill-tempered as she had every right to look. I ordered a beer.

Virtually all the customers in the restaurant were Bulgarian. This was no surprise. I had heard that during the summer, Bulgarian tourists could hardly get into the Balkanturist hotels, since their function was to bring in hard currency. But the tourist season ended every September, and the hotels not only began to fill with Bulgarian travelers, who could now take their holidays with a little more self-respect, but they also became the favorite hangout of the locals. After all, the hotels were the fanciest acts in town, and they could add to their glitter the mystique of being Westernized.

This was an interesting switch. In the West, expensive hotels are the farthest you can get from the natives. Here, except in summer, and after supper was over, the townspeople flocked to them. The rooms and corridors of the Dunav lacked all local color; the restaurant, without a shred of Bulgarian decor, overflowed with it. Here was the smell of Bulgarian tobacco. Here was the food: sour soups and sour cream; beef-and-onion lozenges oozing oil; cabbage, black pepper, and paprika. Here were Bulgarian faces: oval, almost Mediterranean, not the wide-boned Slavic faces of the Russians or the Poles. Here was the language—incomprehensible to me but beautiful, a Russian-sounding mix of *v*'s and *bl*'s and *zh*'s, articulated with a frequent blowing out of the lips. And most curious of all, here were the gestures: a close speaking distance, frequent use of the arms, and head gestures, as in Albania, the reverse of the rest of Europe: a nod for no and a shake for yes.

I ordered a beer and mused on the brighter side of things. It was a delicious pleasure to sit in a crowded room, surrounded by Bulgarians, and not be stared at. I fit in better here than I had in Romania. My beard was not a rarity, and my facial type, though not exactly Bulgarian, was closer to southern Slavic than it was to the swarthy Latinate faces of Romania. For the two weeks I had been in Romania, I had felt as though I were on a stage; here, it seemed, I could retreat into anonymity.

Things could be worse. I finished the beer and left money on
the table, catching the waitress's eye and pointing back to the table
as I threaded my way out. As I pushed through the door into the
anteroom, I nearly ran into someone who was pulling it open from
the other side. Cold air still clung to his clothes—I saw shades, a
slick gray winter jacket, polyester black pants.

"There you are!" Stilyan said. "I've been looking for you." He
held the door to the restaurant open for me.

"Uh . . . no, thank you—I've just had a b—"

"Aannhh, come on! I'll buy you a drink." He had hold of my
arm. "Come on. It's cold outside; you've got nothing else to do."

He was right. I had hoped he would forget all about me, but
if he insisted on being a pest, then it would help me to know more
about him. We went in.

"Why were you looking for me?" I asked.

He shrugged. His hands moved incessantly: fingering his
shades, picking his nails, tapping a cigarette pack against the
tablecloth. "We didn't settle anything about tomorrow," he said.

My heart sank; so he was really going to try to go through
with this. I couldn't think of anything to say, so I sat there, brushing
my fingertips worriedly over the tablecloth. "Well . . ." I finally
came out with, "it's not that important, is it?"

"Of course it's important!" When he spoke earnestly, Stilyan's
eyes seemed to retreat into the flesh around them. "Look: you are
stuck here with a broken bike and you don't speak a word of
Bulgarian—"

"*Blagodarya,*" I interjected. I had been practicing. "*Dobur put!*"

"—you don't speak five words of Bulgarian, and you've hardly
got a bike that's seen every day around here. You don't know how
to get around town, and you can't talk to anyone about how you
want it done or how much it might cost—"

"Well—"

"—so how are you going to get it fixed? If you take the bike
into some little shit shop, you'll be dealing with a man who doesn't
know what he's working with. He'll probably do something wrong.
I'll get the bike fixed for you. We speak the same language *and* I
know what I'm doing."

He was saying, in effect, that I needed him. And unfortunately, I wasn't so sure that I didn't. It was true that I didn't know my way around town. And a question I had put to the woman at the Dunav desk about bicycle repair brought the blankest response.

"We must meet early tomorrow," Stilyan was saying. "I've got some business to take care of in the morning, so we should go down to my old workplace before that. Say about 7:30?"

"Uh . . . okay," I said, "7:30."

We drank, and a lull followed. Stilyan couldn't keep still. Tapping his fingers, flitting his glance continually about the room, turning first one way and then the other in his chair as if he were trying to find a comfortable position, he reminded me of a person at a party who is intent on meeting people, on making many contacts. The question resurfaced in my mind: What does the opportunist do in a Communist country? I decided it wouldn't hurt to probe a little; partly, I was simply curious to discover if my suspicions were correct.

"Where did you learn such good German?" I asked. "That doesn't seem to be a common achievement in this country."

Stilyan shrugged and made a belittling gesture. But I could see that he was flattered. "Oh . . . Talking to all the German tourists, you know. Thousands of them come through here in the summer."

"But what do you talk with the Germans about? Tourists aren't very interesting—"

Suddenly Stilyan laughed.

"What is it?"

It had surprised him, too. This was the first time I had seen him unguarded. This laugh, more than anything else, reconciled me to going out with him the next morning. "No, they are not interesting," he said. "Not interesting at all. But they are lucrative, you understand?" His smile made his mustache smaller, and he consequently looked more trustworthy; he ought to try smiling more, I thought. "Everybody who comes here wants leva, and nobody wants to get it at their hotel. And why should they? My rates are better." He laughed again, this time self-consciously.

"Here, let me show you." He reached into his jacket pocket

and pulled out a fat wad of bills. Several hundred leva. Now I understood why he kept his hands in his pockets on the street and why he hadn't taken the jacket off in the hot restaurant. Stilyan said, "You are a German tourist. You don't like the exchange rate at your hotel. So you come meet me." He mimed ducking into an alley. "Now I take the marks and I count out the money." He counted out fifty leva in fives and ones directly under my nose, then handed the amount to me.

"How much have you got?" he asked.

"Fifty leva."

Stilyan turned his hand palm up. He was holding ten leva.

"Let me see that again," I said.

He counted the money out again. I watched carefully. He handed me the money. I was certain this time that he had given me all of it. He turned his hand: ten leva were in his palm.

"What if the person counts it?" I asked.

He shrugged. "So I made a mistake. What's he going to do? Go tell the police? They'll put him in jail for two weeks for trading on the black market. So he says, 'Hey, this is not enough,' and I give him the rest. Here, watch."

Stilyan handed me forty-five leva. "Okay, you're the tourist again. You count your money and you notice that it's not fifty, the way it should be. So you get angry and you say—"

"Hey, what's the big idea? This is five leva short!" I said, trying to sound like an indignant middle-ager from Hanover.

"Very good. And I—"

"Thank you."

"—and I say, 'Oooh, I am so sorry!' " Stilyan feigned contrition. "But I must make sure you are not lying," he said, and took the forty-five leva back. He counted through it quickly. "Oh yes, you are right, silly me, it's only forty-five. I do this all day, you know, so it's no surprise I make a mistake sometimes." He handed the money back to me. I counted it again, and it was still forty-five. While I was counting, Stilyan pressed an additional five-note into my hands, acting now as if he were in a hurry. He also feigned irritation at having been caught cheating. "I walk quickly away now, angry because I have not been able to cheat you. You feel good, because you have always been told how the black-market traders in Bulgaria are not honest, but you knew you were too smart for them and you have proven it." Stilyan smiled with remembered malice. "You put the money in your wallet and walk off whistling a tune."

"But—" I said, confused.

Stilyan misunderstood. "Exactly! But! Later you count it. Or better, perhaps you never count it; perhaps you never notice and you let the next trader cheat you the same way."

I counted the money. Forty leva. I couldn't help laughing. "How did you do it?"

He showed his palm; ten leva were nested there again. "While you were counting; when I gave you the five leva. The money you'd already counted was already out of your mind. The Germans always think they are smarter. But they are stupid." He downed the rest of his beer and wiped his mouth. "That one is a harder trick to pull. You were more suspicious than most. Usually I don't even give back all forty-five leva; I watch how they count the money I give them the first time. Many people count money by flipping up the edges of the bills; when they are in a hurry, it is very easy to fool them by giving them folded bills—they count one note twice. However, you count your money by sliding the bills across, from one hand to another, so you would notice a folded bill. But when you slide them like that, you don't have a good grip on them, and it is easy to take one back, especially if I thrust the extra bill into your hands quickly. Actually, most people don't count the bills a second time at all. I can usually tell if they will by how wary they are. It's always easy to fool them, because they are nervous. They want to get away as quickly as possible. And I make them more nervous by looking around all the time; I act as if the police are going to discover us any second."

"And what about the police?" I asked. "Don't you have to worry about them? Have you ever been caught?"

Stilyan grimaced and flashed me the reassuring gesture. Or perhaps he was signing for me to speak more softly. His own voice

Page 108

became faint: "Oh, the police . . . I just—they're no problem . . .
I just give them a little . . ." and he rubbed the fingers and thumb
of his right hand together.

He seemed embarrassed to admit it. I think he would have
preferred me to believe that his was a dangerous job, constantly
threatening imprisonment. Buying his way out of uncertainty
perhaps struck him as an ignominious means of securing his
livelihood. But I had asked, and he had not lied. Assuming that
his embarrassment was real (and I could think of no reason why
he would feign it), I could see that he was being remarkably honest
with me.

"And what do you do with the hard currency once you get
it?" I asked. "Where does it go?"

He shrugged. I had reinstated him as the authority figure,
and the shrug, I was learning, was part of his repertory of swaggers.
"Everyone here wants hard currency. If the hotel rate is half a
leva to the mark, I offer the tourists two leva for three marks; then
I sell marks to Bulgarians one-for-one. Everyone is happy. The
tourist gets a better rate, the Bulgarians get hold of some hard
currency, and I make a good living."

"And why do the Bulgarians want hard currency so much?"
I asked.

Stilyan looked surprised by the question. "Well, they need
hard currency for the Corecom stores, right?"

The name was new to me. "Corecom?"

"The hard-currency stores. Everybody wants blue jeans and
stereos. There are even these little stereos now that you can carry
around on your belt. Everyone wants one of those. How are they
going to get Western things without dollars or marks?"

This fit what I had been told. In Bulgaria, many of the most
sought-after Western goods, such as blue jeans, could be bought
only in special shops. All the customers, including Bulgarians, had
to pay in hard currency at those shops. The shops were nominally
for tourists, whence the currency rule, and originally the only
Bulgarians who bought things there were the ones who could
prove they had gotten the hard currency "legally"—namely, the
Party members, who usually had their hands in several tills. But

now, any Bulgarian could get his cherished Sony Walkman, provided he had the bucks—a fairer system, perhaps, but it made corruption more widespread. The Corecom policy directly encouraged large segments of the population to become involved in the black currency market.

It was time to go. I started to leave my own money for the beer, assuming that Stilyan's offer in the anteroom had been only a way to get me through the door. But he insisted now on paying. Strange behavior for a con man.

Outside the front door of the hotel, someone caught up with me from behind and said my name. I turned and recognized one of Stilyan's friends. He asked me a few simple questions, in broken German. It was bitterly cold now, and I wondered what he really wanted. Finally, he held out a hand that he had previously been keeping under an armpit, rubbed the fingers and thumb together, and said, with an embarrassed twitch of his lips, "Change money?"

•

I woke.

Gray-blue came through the window and suffused the room. I sat up, confused. It was cold. The curtains were open. Through the window I could see the top of a monument, a figure with arms outstretched, in a benedictory gesture, and far away, the tops of pine and oak trees, silhouettes against a violet sky. I was in Ruse, I recalled. I had to get up to meet someone. I noticed my bicycle leaning against the window. The bike is broken, I thought. Shit. I was stranded in Bulgaria. I was supposed to be helped this morning by a man who might cheat me. Shit shit.

I got out of bed and felt the radiator: lukewarm. For twenty-one leva, I didn't understand why I couldn't have heat. I fiddled with a knob on the side, but nothing happened.

Because of the importance of traveling light, I did not have adequate winter clothing—I had intended, long, long ago when I decided on this route, on that sweltering July day in Ravenna, to reach the Mediterranean by November 1. So I had no sweater, no down vest—just shirts of varying degrees of inadequacy and a windbreaker. For my hands, I used wool socks. I could buy warmer clothes, but where would I store them? I was overloaded as it was.

When I was on the bike I was all right; the exertion kept me warm. But I didn't relish the thought of wandering around Ruse looking for repairs on this wintry day.

Stilyan showed up half an hour late, wearing his shades and the gray jacket; he had added a pair of black gloves with tufts of brown fur sticking out at the wrists, and ankle-length black boots with zippers on the sides and pointed toes. Show-off.

We left the hotel and headed west, across Lenin Square. Morning mist was still dispersing in the air up to a hundred feet or so, and the gauziness was giving way to a shimmer of wetness in the light. We skirted the Freedom Monument, sixty feet high, and I recognized in a bas-relief on the base a scene from the battle for the Shipka Pass, one of the climactic events of the Russo-Turkish War. Stilyan paused to let me look at it, but he kept his distance. Perhaps it was not cool (the sixties word repeatedly came to me in connection with Stilyan) to be in the company of a tourist. We continued into the gelid shade of the maples and pines. Stilyan was greeted by three sets of people in the park.

We crossed a street and went north past the House of the Soviets. Stilyan met a friend on the corner. We turned onto Petkov Street: west again. At the end of Petkov Street, Stilyan met another friend. We veered left and passed the wide mouth of Georgi Dimitrov Street, adorned with shops and boxed-in trees. (Georgi Dimitrov: trained in Moscow, hero of the Reichstag fire trial; head of the Fatherland Front and then leader of Bulgaria from 1944 to 1949; currently resident in a Leninesque mausoleum on public display in Sofia; executioner in 1947 of Nikola Petkov, head of the Agrarian Party, proponent of free elections, former partner of Dimitrov's in the Fatherland Front and son of Dimitr Petkov, after whom Petkov Street was named.)

We headed up Deveti Street, crossing paths with a group of workers in blue cloth who hailed Stilyan and, at the end of the street, a man sitting outside his run-down vegetable store who drew him into a joke. Now we stood at 9th September Square, as the white-and-black plaque on the post office told me. I asked Stilyan why 9th September, and he said, "It's our national holiday; the Popular Uprising was on the ninth and tenth of September, against the Nazis, in 1944; the Russian Army came in at the same time. Fatherland Front was established, Dimitrov came home. All that stuff."

"Stilyan!" someone called, and there was another delay. Then we crossed 19th February Street. I couldn't help asking. Stilyan shrugged. "Pro-Russian day. 1887. Ten officers who favored the Russians were caught; they were plotting against Stambulov—a dictator—who didn't like the Russians. Or something like that. They were shot." In a Communist country, I reflected, a third of the street names were of people who had been executed, the second third were of the people who had executed the first third, and the last third were the dates on which the second third had executed the first third. "At the time, the officers were in a bad light. It seemed like treason. They were plotting to overthrow their own government. But that's different now, of course. There's a monument outside town for them—because we're friends with Russia now."

I searched his face for traces of irony. But Stilyan was not, I thought, an ironic person; he had simply been stating a fact—the Bulgarian government was on good terms with Moscow. Actually, I was a little surprised that he even knew some of the details, but on reflection I realized that he must have had all that drummed into him during his first few years of public schooling.

From 19th February Street, we passed into a lane which headed downhill. We were approaching the port. A woman was out beating a rug against her iron fence, the brown dust spurting up and then settling around her feet; she greeted Stilyan by name.

We came to another road with a low stone wall and a view. This was the boulevard that skirted the shelf on which Ruse sat, 150 feet above the river. I ran across the road and jumped up on the wall. At last, I saw the Danube.

I wasn't quite prepared for what I saw. For the immensity. I have no eye for distances, but the river was more or less a mile wide where I stood. One and a half million gallons of water were passing me every second. The gray-green stretched away and hazed into the blue of the sky; there was only a thin black line of Romania, barely discernible, to separate the two colors. The

Danube here was its own world, a vast acreage of one color, unreflective of the sky and unrelated to its shores. I thought of the pleasant little stream I had started with in Donaueschingen; the Danube had changed more than I had.

Several cargo ships at anchor were dwarfed by the green, and a number of fishing vessels glided among them; the port of Ruse sprawled below me to the left. Two ships were in dry dock. Even from the bluff, I could discern the white-blue glare and the falling away of heavy, almost molten sparks along the red-streaked sides, iron cliff faces, of a ship: welding.

Of course. Why hadn't I thought of it? In a busy port town, where else to go for a welding job than the shipyards? They might not do the best work there, but they certainly did the biggest. None of the piddling equipment I had seen on the painted board outside a machine shop near the Dunav for my bike: the knee-high canister, the desktop compressor, the pencil-thin nozzle. No —I would get my repairs from a bazooka-sized tool that could melt the crank, the drive chain, the whole bike in a matter of seconds. When I thought of my delicate, beautiful bike—as beautiful in its way as the rigging of a sailing ship—in the hands of a brute shipwelder, I cringed inwardly. If the man made a mistake, it was sure to be an impressive one. I might have considered the Danube a friend in one of my lonely moods, but the bike was the real friend. It, not the river, was the thing that stayed with me. Faces disappeared; the river *had* changed; the bike carried me on.

Stilyan was not interested in the view. He wanted to get on, so I jumped down. We started down a flight of stone steps, in the direction of the port. I carried the bike on my shoulder. "You seem to know a lot of people in town," I said to the back of his head.

Stilyan shrugged. "I have to," he replied, not turning. "Business. I can't advertise in the paper. If people need me, they have to know me. Believe me, nobody wants to deal with a stranger— only the tourists are stupid enough to do that."

"Do the tourists get thrown in jail sometimes, for a week or two?" I asked. This is what I had heard.

"Sure, it happens. Not often."

"And do the black marketeers work with the police sometimes? Do they turn in tourists for a reward?" I had heard this also.

Stilyan was silent for half a flight. Then: "No, I haven't heard anything about that. That's not good."

The stairs bottomed out in an old yard littered with cans and broken glass. A truck carrying gas canisters rattled by. We followed it, and crossed a narrow-gauge railroad track with rotting ties, entered through a gate in a high chain-link fence.

Here, Stilyan seemed to be friends with all the workers. We ran a gauntlet of greeting, between low warehouses roofed with tar paper and corrugated iron. A dark swamp smell hung in the air. It had remained cold; I cracked one or two puddles of ice as we walked. A couple of workers were hurriedly arranging barrels, pressing their bare hands to their sides between the intervals of effort.

Stilyan struggled with, and finally kicked open, a crooked door at the end of a ramshackle wooden building. A delicious wave of heat enveloped us. At the far end of a narrow room sat a man tending an iron stove who turned, stared, and yelled "Stilyan!" happily. He struggled to his feet and the two embraced.

The man was old and thin, almost emaciated, without many teeth. While he and Stilyan indulged in a bit of hail-fellow-well-met talk, slapping each other on the shoulder, Stilyan laughing and the old man wheezing, I moved immediately to the stove and tried to rub some feeling back into my hands. If the weather didn't warm up a little, I wouldn't be able to cycle through Bulgaria even if they *did* fix the bike.

From the conversation I inferred that the old man's name was Peyo. I noticed now that one of his hands was badly scarred, and he seemed to have a limp; little wonder, perhaps, that he also had a drinker's nose. A third man entered, a heavy figure in a leather apron, with a large cigar billowing smoke from between his lips. He, too, shouted delightedly, "Stilyan!" wrenched the cigar out of his mouth, and gave Stilyan a bear hug, which Stilyan, I could see, wanted to avoid.

This, I learned, was Vladimir, the welder. Vladimir was beefy and bluff; probably a gourmand, almost certainly a flirt. He looked like the sort of man who went through life consuming: liquor, food, women, friends, time. When Stilyan gave him my name, he lumbered forward and crushed my outstretched hand. Then he sat next to me on the bench, held his hands over the stove, and enveloped us both in a cloud of cigar smoke.

Peyo limped over to shut the door. Vladimir was demanding information about me from Stilyan in a huge voice, and Stilyan, with a grimace and a calming gesture, was trying to comply. The word *"Amerikanski"* floated to me, and I glimpsed out of the corner of my eye Stilyan's hands spinning like bicycle pedals.

We were in the workers' break room, Stilyan informed me. The room had two windows, both mostly obscured by tar paper that had been tacked around their frames to cut down on the heat loss. Hanging from the low ceiling were dozens of oily rags and dirty shirts, draped over aluminum wires apparently strung up for the purpose. The construction of the building—the posts, the cross beams, the planking—was so makeshift it looked like something thrown together in an afternoon; or worse, over a period of years, using odds and ends that had been dug now and then out of the scrap heap of the port. With the freezing air making its way in through countless holes, with cold drafts crawling up legs and down necks, it would be a dispiriting place to spend the winter.

Vladimir opened his locker. I saw a color photograph of a naked woman taped to the inside of his door; he had outlined her nipples in red pen. He drew out a pair of heavy welder's gloves and threw them on the table. My repair! I thought. I was wrong.

From behind where the gloves had been, Vladimir lifted out an enormous bottle of wine; he fished around some more and came up with two glasses. He winked at me. Then he groped among his boots at the bottom of the locker, spilling some of them out onto the concrete floor, and finally produced a mug. He hefted the bottle onto the table and arranged the glasses in front of us, putting the rather larger mug in front of himself. Peyo retrieved a glass out of his own locker and scurried to the table with an expectant, grateful air. Vladimir poured. The liquid was yellow-pink, with a curling bit of violet struck from it, occasionally, by the light.

"Vladimir makes this wine himself." Stilyan had a sparkle in his eye. "It is very good stuff. We used to drink it all winter long when I worked here. It warms you. Here, you'll see . . ." He raised his glass.

I drank, and could feel the blood come into my face. The wine was oily, like sherry, and burning. Perhaps Vladimir fortified it with *slivova*. Peyo was already showing the effects. He got up animatedly and added some wood to the stove fire. I noticed that the firewood, thrown into a pile around the iron legs of the stove, was a conglomeration of smashed furniture. Peyo was feeding in a chair leg as I watched; he followed it with a scrolled armrest. I wondered if it was easier, if it involved less red tape, to replace office chairs and tables lost to "depreciation" each spring (or simply to do without them) than it was to get the winter rations of firewood for the port workers raised.

Vladimir downed another mugful, then slapped his hands on the table and rose. He leaned over me, crushed my hand again, and said "*Amerikanski!*" Then he tapped his temple and broke into peals of laughter. He picked up his welding gloves and made for the door, the leather apron swirling around the edges of his paunch.

"It's time to fix your bike!" Stilyan was excited. This was his big moment, the moment in which he would prove himself. "Let's go, let's go!" When I looked at Stilyan's face, my last doubts about his motives, doubts that had lingered despite his kindnesses, drained out of me. He was not after my money. He was after my gratitude, perhaps even more after my respect. He was a man with connections, and he was proud of it. And like most of us, he flaunted the thing he prized before strangers. He was going to show me that he had the resources to fix a bike in a country that had never seen its like before, and that he had the influence to interrupt the work of Bulgaria's largest river port in order to get it done.

"It will be as good as new in just a couple of minutes," he said to me, as he ushered me out the door. I grabbed my bike from where it was leaning, dispirited, against the torn tar paper, and the two of us trotted after Vladimir's hurrying bulk. The sky was a brilliant blue. The cinder-gray of the yards had the clean look of filtered ash. Our breaths shone fleetingly in the air.

We stopped beneath a three-sided shed, its fourth side open to the Danube and the sharp river winds. Vladimir signed to an assistant, a thin young sycophant who took my bicycle. It was hoisted sideways and balanced on a block. A flint was struck and the thread of fire shot out, a cold blue that burned and hissed in the air. I turned away.

Stilyan had been right. It took no time at all. I stood with my back to the shed, looking out across the water, the cluttered piers and garbage scows, while the strange blue-white light flashed my outline on the ground in front of me. Three, four times, it flashed, like a peculiar, passionless heat lightning, sputtering. I didn't watch, both because I was afraid to see the attempt fail and because someone, somewhere, had told me when I was a child that it was dangerous to look at the flare of a welder's torch.

Then it was over. The sputtering ceased and I turned around.

It had not worked. Vladimir had stopped with an oath, and I saw him now striking the bike with an elongated adze, sending fragments of tortured metal in all directions. The weld splintered like ice, and the pedal jarred loose once again from the sprocket; now both pedal and sprocket had ugly, shriveled scars where the weld had been attempted. Vladimir drew the blue needle back into its sheath and lifted his goggles. Stilyan went to his side with a questioning look; in addition to my own dismay, I felt sorry for him. The assistant hoisted the bike off the block and I took it in my hands. I inspected it, alarmed: the damage was minimal. But the bike was still broken.

"What happened?" I asked, as we came away from the welding shed. Vladimir, behind us, went on to other business; the young assistant struggled again at the block.

"It didn't work," Stilyan answered, deep in thought.

"I know it didn't work; what I meant was, why didn't it work?"

"Vladimir says it is not the right metal. It just melts. The weld is no good. You saw the way it shattered."

When I had prepared for a bicycle tour, it hadn't occurred to me that I would need to know anything about welding. It chagrins me now to think that someone may read this account and say, "But of course—who could have expected such a weld to work?" I knew that the cranks were not made of iron or steel—my handbook told me that an aluminum alloy was used, for lightness: duralumin. But what that implied I didn't know, and I was a little ashamed about not knowing. This was my bike, my means of transportation, my life-style—I had gone some 10,000 miles without using a drop of gasoline. I fixed my flats and replaced my spokes, I rebuilt my own wheels when they needed it. I had begun to feel as if I could handle any mechanical problem that came along. And now the bike suddenly seemed not to belong to me; it had slipped out of my control.

·

It was the expression on Stilyan's face as we walked up from the port—determined, uninspired—that stayed with me while I waited for him outside the Dunav Hotel and watched the afternoon crowd. I sat on a cold stone wall in front of the hotel restaurant and kicked my heels impatiently. A German translation of Ibsen, which I had bought in Salzburg because it was cheap and would give me practice, sat next to me, closed, while my eyes ran back and forth, over the park, the streets, the busy sidewalks.

Stilyan was very late; I had just gone into the hotel for the third time to ring him up. Where in the hell was he? It was possible that he was trustworthy only when he was within earshot. I had known people before like that, and Stilyan would have fit well into their company—he had the same ambiguity, the same slipperiness, combined with an overt, ingenuous concern for the good opinion of other people. The real fear of these characters was indignity: the humiliation of seeing themselves in the eyes of others. Stilyan would be safe from my disappointment as long as he stayed away.

I had come up from the docks just in time to catch the tail end of the hotel breakfast. (This was the recurrent comedy at the Balkanturist hotels: when checking in, I would ask, "Is breakfast obligatory?" and the receptionist would answer with all suavity, "No, breakfast is *included*.")

Afterward, I went out in search of a better deal. At the Orbita office, a man confirmed for me that none of the Orbita student accommodations were available out of the summer season (despite what every last Orbita publication claimed). However, we got into a long conversation about bicycling, and eventually he admitted to me that other hotels did exist in Ruse, a fact which, despite all my mistrust of Balkanturist, I had begun to doubt. He rang up a hotel that was within four blocks of the Dunav and made sure they had a spare room; they had plenty. Then he told them to expect an American cyclist—he gave them my name and carefully described what I looked like. In this way, I presumed, the hotel would not accidently allow a different American cyclist to have a room there.

I emptied my room at the Dunav just before the noon checkout deadline and carried the bicycle with all its packs down the four flights to the lobby, where I told the woman at the desk that I was changing hotels. I felt a twinge of panic—this was the same woman who had checked me in, the woman who had insisted to me that the Dunav and Prima were the only hotels in town. I wondered if her embarrassment at being caught in a lie would make her unpleasant. But she merely smiled, handed me my passport, and wished me on my way. I even asked her for directions to the cheaper hotel, but she would not go that far. Perhaps she genuinely didn't know.

The other hotel was built around a central atrium, ratty and faded. I thought, How much more interesting, more attractive, is this seedy old building than the soulless Balkanturist hotel. The price of a room was a third of what I had paid at the Dunav. The man at the desk spoke only Bulgarian, but since he had been expecting me, we accomplished the registering, the stamping, and the signing with a minimum of exasperation. A pretty young woman with dark hair in a bowl cut sat behind the man and watched me with curious, diffident eyes. I found my room on the third floor, at the end of a high-ceilinged hall.

When I descended later, the young woman with the bowl-cut hair was cleaning the stairway carpet in the atrium. She wore a white maid's uniform and had a waiflike face. I was overcome suddenly with a feeling of tenderness for her. I wanted to make her day more pleasant, this slender, girlish woman who had to clean the spiraling red rug with its frayed edges and permanent discolorations. But all I could think of to do was to smile. She smiled back. On my way to the Dunav, I reflected on how curiously easy it was, sometimes, to feel better; that the smile of a woman on a stairway could linger with me and dispel the discouragement of a morning of failures.

But I had been heading toward the biggest failure of all. Stilyan had abandoned me, and I thought over the last few minutes of our time together that morning, looking for a clue in them to his present lapse.

As we walked up from the port, I had kept my mouth shut, while Stilyan pondered. I was afraid he would infer doubt about his competence from any suggestion I might offer for the afternoon. Once we had regained the level of the city, Stilyan led me down tiny streets to a wood-fronted shop with old tire tubes hanging on a nail over the door. An old man was working on the upended bike of an eight-year-old. Stilyan did not hesitate to interrupt, going into the shop, grabbing the man's arm, and drawing him unceremoniously out to the street. The old man didn't seem to mind (of course, he recognized Stilyan), and the kid—accustomed, like all kids, to shabby treatment from adults— ventured out in their wake. Stilyan led the two of them to my bike and twirled the pedals. The boy was fascinated, both with the exotic ten-speed bike and with its spectacular state of disrepair. But the old man chewed on his fingers for a few moments and nodded his head (in Bulgaria, I reminded myself, this meant "no"). Stilyan argued with him. He nodded his head more vigorously; Stilyan sounded as if he suspected the old man of holding out on him. The man pointed, and the two of them blocked out maps with their hands. I stood by and felt superfluous.

"Yeah"—Stilyan grimaced at me, as the old man disappeared again into the shop—"I didn't think he'd be able to do anything. But he gave me some good news."

"Yes?"

"He says there's a mechanic at one of the stadia in town who works with sport bikes. He'll be able to help us."

I wasn't sure of this at all: the Russian racing bikes were not equipped with the kinds of cranks that my bike had. But at least it was something to hope for.

We were back on 9th September Square. "Listen," Stilyan told me, putting his hand on my arm, "I can't go there with you now. There are some people I have to meet. For business. I'm late already."

"Whatever's convenient for you," I said.

"We'll go this afternoon. I'll meet you outside the Dunav at one o'clock, all right?"

"Stilyan, I really appreciate this." The hand waved me down. "No—this is extremely kind of you, to give me all this help—"

"I have to go now." He shrugged and stepped off the curb, plugged his hands in his pockets, and walked away across the square. The back of his carefully coiffed head receded into the light crowd. I saw him trot across another street, still with that studied demeanor of nonchalance, looking quickly in both directions, and then my sight was blocked by the shrubs in the square. He was gone.

Now this: the most puzzling part of the whole affair. Past three o'clock and Stilyan was nowhere to be found. Had he intended to leave me for good? The only two explanations were that he had forgotten or that he had gotten into some trouble—and neither of these seemed likely. Stilyan had stepped out of the picture as enigmatically as he had come into it. The last thing I had expected was a replay of Piteşti.

Damnitall! There was nothing for it—I would have to try to find the mechanic on my own.

When in doubt, I thought, ask the Dunav. The desk was good about everything except providing hotel information. I went inside, and the receptionist and I spread out a map and looked for stadia. There were three, all outside town. The woman didn't know which one might be the place to look for a bike mechanic, but only one of the three stadia was close enough to reach on foot anyway, before darkness fell. So I headed for it.

I hadn't much hope. If this one didn't work out, I would trudge out to the others on the following day. But deep down, I didn't expect anyone to be at any of them. They were all open-air stadia, and the sports season was over. There was no reason to expect a soul. I was going to them only because I had nothing else to do.

Well. It had been a long tumble down from the afternoon of the day before, when I had biked into the country in such an elated mood: the room troubles, the broken bike, the thwarted hopes of repair, the disappearance of Stilyan—each had taken me down a notch, until I had virtually resigned myself, without consciously acknowledging it, to leaving the country, ignominiously, on a train. I tried to tell myself, walking east toward the stadium, that I didn't care that much. But I did care—I had lost the freedom that the bike gave me, and would be captive now to train schedules and routes; I would have to depend on other people to take me south.

And now that I had hit the bottom of my spirits, everything started to go right again.

The stadium crawled into sight. As I approached the chain-link fence, I heard whirring and the sound of voices. I climbed a few feet up the wire and peered over the inner wall. What I saw made my heart jump: cyclists on ten-speed, lightweight bicycles. There were four of them on the concrete track, going through silent periods of intense effort, pumping faster and faster, then relaxing and talking to each other judgmentally. They were testing different bikes for a race. So much for the sports season being over.

I entered the track area, and the cyclists regarded me curiously, but continued to make their circuits—pushing hard, then slowing and discussing, dismounting sometimes to fiddle with a derailleur or a brake set. I could tell what they were doing from a distance— I knew the parts they were looking at, I knew what they were going to do to adjust them. Even though the Russian model of bike was different from mine, I felt as if I had come home.

A run-down shed stood at the far edge of the track, and I went over to it and peered in. There were tires on racks, boxes of inner tubes, thousands of nuts and bolts on wooden shelves, spokes, derailleurs on benches, pliers, screwdrivers, wrenches dropped or thrown everywhere. There was no one inside. I tried another door, to an attached shed on my right, and saw a score of Sputnik bicycles. None of them had cotterless cranks, like my bike.

"Dobur vecher!"

I turned around, and a fat man, short and balding, gave me a quizzical look. Black grease streaked his white shirt. He had to be the mechanic.

Of course, we had no common language, but we didn't really need one. I just showed him the bike, spinning the pedal for him, and he grunted. The cyclists started to drift in from the track, and soon all four of them stood in a circle around me. The mechanic invited them to examine the damage, and each one spun the pedals delicately, like a musician tapping over the keys of a piano to see if it is in tune. There were whistles of admiration, and although it was in Bulgarian, I could tell that they were saying, "We've never seen that before." It was my last audience, and my most appreciative: these guys knew what a feat it was to break a front sprocket.

Suddenly I understood a word, and my heart leapt. The mechanic had gone into his shack muttering "Campagnolo." I heard him rummaging: the metallic sound of bolts and wrenches being scattered by a searching hand drifted through the door. I could only hope that in that incredible mess he would find what he was looking for before Christmas. The cyclists crouched around my bike and twanged the spokes. The mechanic returned, at length, with a cylindrical, four-inch tool, and suddenly I knew that everything was going to be all right. He was holding a Campagnolo cotterless crank remover.

•

The repair was makeshift, but it worked. My cranks could not be replaced, because the Russian crank and axle sizes were different. But with the crank remover, they could at least be taken off my bike, and once they were off, a repair was not a hard thing to improvise.

The mechanic, Andrei, saw the wrinkled patches of metal where the welding had done its damage. He grabbed my coat, holding the crank-and-sprocket assembly under my nose, and said, *"Ne! Ne! Ne pffffffffft!"* He mimed welding. *"Ne pffffffffft!* Duralumin! *Ne, ne!"*

So various things were tried. The sizes of replacements were confirmed to be unsuitable, and a resetting of the pressure lock between the crank and the sprocket didn't work. Then two of the cyclists rode away with my crank on a moped to see if they could find a replacement elsewhere. After some minutes, during which Andrei and I tried and utterly failed to keep a conversation going in sign language, they returned with no results. Finally, Andrei drilled a hole in the crank arm and bolted it to the sprocket. It was the only solution we could see. It was potentially weak, since most bolted cranks use four bolts and there was no room along my crank for more than one. But weak was infinitely better than dead. Andrei gave me a replacement bolt, and advised me to dismount and walk the bike up the steepest grades, to keep from putting too much strain on the crank. Since that was what I did, anyway, I agreed cheerfully.

I took the bicycle out for a spin around the track, pulling hard two or three times on the pedal to test the bolt. The bike spurted forward; the bolt held. I tore around the track like a lunatic and whooped in delight. A couple of the cyclists jumped on their Sputniks and came onto the track with me. We raced each other for a minute or so, and they destroyed me. I loved it. My world was in my hands again. I would get the hell out of town and camp tomorrow night in the middle of nowhere, with no one's permission. Even now, all I have to do is picture that small stadium in my mind—the saddle-roofed shack, the concrete track, the sight of my feet turning the pedals, and a new black bolt spinning, like a twirling insect, with the crank—and I can summon again that feeling of delight.

Andrei refused the twenty leva I tried to give him. He also refused the ten. With an embarrassed grin, he motioned five, but I forced the ten on him. He looked at his friends, the cyclists, and laughed, the black-streaked belly vibrating like a tympanum. Then he reared back his head and held his hand, a glass, up to his mouth. He cocked it, and said the third word that I had understood from him in more than an hour of trying to communicate: "Vodka." A great shout of laughter went into the air.

THE NAME OF THE VILLAGE, five miles off the main road to Veliko Tarnovo, has long since escaped me, but its image is still clear in my mind: a casual jumbling of white stone houses on a mossy and muddy slope. None of the buildings reached two stories, and the plaster of most of them gaped at the corners, showing ill-fitted boulders. Frets of carved wood below the eaves and around the windows, decorated fitfully with painted flowers and curving lines, gave the houses a frail, Japanese look. It was a style I would grow to recognize as characteristic of Bulgaria: a predominant white and a stained-wood brown, in elegant, rectilinear patterns that looked, to an American's eyes, like meditations by Frank Lloyd Wright.

The cobblestone streets, shifting and collapsing on the soft hillside, formed the usual grid of right angles and straight lines. Mud had worked its way up through the widening gaps among the stones, and the going was treacherous. Spattered mud formed a dirty fringe along the bottom of every wall. Ruts in the lanes were a foot deep. An automobile would immediately have foundered, sinking in to its axles. My bicycle fared little better, and the mud clogged its chain and gears.

It was late afternoon.

At the lower end of the square—a treeless, empty rectangle of unwanted land—I found the village store. Battered and humble, it stood on squat wooden posts, about four feet off the ground, and looked like a peasant woman holding her skirts up while standing in a muddy road. A sad line of denuded poplars peered over its roof from the field behind.

I clambered onto the wooden porch and greeted the three villagers lounging there. They nodded silently back and fixed me with curious eyes. Two older men and a teenager—field-workers. They were tipped back in rotting cane chairs, smoking hand-rolled cigarettes. Their waistcoats were as dirty as the village square sloping up to the east. Mud caked their boots, and clots of the stuff, drying at the edges to a light brown powder, littered the wooden planks.

The oldest man removed the cigarette from his mouth with one dark-lined hand and offered me the other, wordlessly. Surprised, I shook it. His hand felt like a turtle shell. He gestured incredulously at my bicycle, at my short pants, at the sun which was floating down like a balloon. Our breaths were beginning to leave wisps in the air.

"*Studeno?*" he asked in a gravelly voice.

Student? I thought. Was he asking if I was a student? I motioned that I didn't understand.

The man tipped forward in his chair. He held himself tightly and shivered. "Brrrr," he said. "*Studeno!* Brrrr . . ." He replaced the cigarette in his mouth, and tipped back against the wall. The other men smiled at his performance.

So this was going to be my most frequent topic of conversation. "*Ne,*" I said, and mimed pedaling. "*Ne studeno!*" This was embarrassing—I couldn't put even a simple negation grammatically. How on earth could I tell them that I wasn't cold as long as I was cycling? "*Ne studeno; dobur.*" "No cold; good." Oh brother.

But the three men appeared satisfied. They repeated, shaking their heads: "*Dobur, dobur.*" I declined a smoke.

I entered the store. I wanted to buy some bread, and fortunately, someone had taught me the word for it. Now this, I thought, I should be able to handle.

There were two women in line, but the woman behind the counter, a hairy, hefty peasant with a black kerchief around her slick black hair, turned immediately to me. The customers waved me forward as if it were their greatest pleasure to yield their places to a foreigner.

"*Chlap!*" I said.

The hefty woman's expectant eyes remained expectant. She didn't budge. Apparently what I had said was not a word.

"*Chlap!*" I repeated. I formed a fat loaf in the air with my hands.

A disconcerted glaze crept over the woman's eyes. She turned to the others for help.

"*Gghlap!*" I tried. "*Gghlap?*" The word sounded like something a wide-mouthed frog would say. "*Hlapp?*" The women looked at each other. They nodded their heads to me—this meant they were confused.

"*Chlop? Chlyopp?*" I was getting nowhere. "*Chlob? Chlyob?*"

I had to get it right soon, or the women would simply stop paying attention.

"*Hlyapp! Hlyapp, hlyopp, hlyupp!*"

My only hope was pantomime, so I repeatedly held an invisible loaf over the counter. I squeezed it. It was a fresh, invisible loaf. I tore off a piece and ate it. It was good. "Mmmm . . . *Ghlop!*" I said, between mouthfuls. But although it was good, it apparently was not *ghlop*.

The teenager appeared in the doorway.

"*Hlob?*" I was trying. "*Hlob? Yllobb?*" I couldn't keep this up much longer; it was too hard on my self-esteem.

Fortunately for us all, the teenager had a younger, more agile mind than the women did; after studying my motions for a few seconds, he put his large, dusty head on one side and pondered. Then his eyes cleared and he shot a hand out as if to grab the word. "*Hlyab!*" he said triumphantly. That was all. He turned and swaggered back out, leaving the smoke from his cigarette to linger, gloatingly, behind him.

"*Hlyab! Hlyab!*" exclaimed the women, and reproached me with why-in-the-hell-didn't-you-say-so stares. A round beige loaf was retrieved from the back room.

"*Chlyab?*" I asked, holding the bread out.

"*Ne, ne—hlyab.*"

I could not reproduce the quick, rasping sound of the opening consonants. For the future, I decided I'd better save a piece of the old loaf and simply present it at the store counter when I wanted a new one. The procedure reminded me of saving a dollop of yoghurt in order to start a new batch. "Yes, the same, please— only larger."

As I mounted the bike and started off, the three chairs smacked down against the porch planking; I saw the men, just before I turned west at the end of the square, stand up and move to the front porch in order to keep their eyes on me. They smiled and waved.

The voice of the teenager followed me out of the village: *"Hlyab! Hlyab! Hlyab!"* He sounded victorious.

.

The road sidled west, through the line of bare poplars, crossed a leaf-choked stream, and turned south. The jarring rumble of the cobblestones gave way to a thumping across the planks of the rotting bridge, then to a humming over cracked and dirt-slick pavement. Shallow drainage ditches edged the bare fields; lines of poplar and oak fringed the ditches. Otherwise, it was a flat, fleshless landscape, marked only by the dry stumps of harvested maize and the low spidery remains of potato leaves. The sun had just set and the air was turning blue.

I pulled off the road to let a dilapidated school bus pass me, going north. The bus bounced and jangled over the ruts in the pavement like an old peddler's cart, making the noise of loose pots, and the driver, hugging the bucking wheel to his chest, stared blankly out at me with goggle eyes. I waved, and I glimpsed him just beginning to respond as the bus swept him out of my sight.

After a couple of kilometers, the soil began to look drier. I could camp anywhere here. Near the horizon, on my left, a line of shivering lights came into view. Distances were deceptive in the dusk, and I took the lights to be bonfires separated by great distances. I thought of the signal fires used in classical times to transmit news of victory or defeat. It was an appalling idea, that people were tending those fires on this great expanse of land, far away from their homes. What on earth were they doing it for?

The fires lifted up a gauzy curtain of smoke that muted the blue in the air to a sullen violet.

The temperature had already dropped, with the setting of the sun, close to forty. The night was going to be freezing.

It occurred to me that I might be more comfortable if I camped among the fires. Whoever was over there would not begrudge a traveler some warmth on a winter night, even though camping was illegal. I would not be able to talk with them, but at least I would have good light for reading. Or failing even that, I could divert myself by staring into the flames. An empty evening lay in front of me, and any kind of entertainment would be welcome.

I rode parallel to the distant necklace of light for some time. Then I came to a hard-packed dirt track, lying in the shelter of a line of oak trees at the edge of a stubble field. I dismounted and started down the rough surface. The road disappeared behind me. I walked for some time, while shadowy oaks slid one by one to the rear.

I gradually realized that I had misjudged the size of the fires. Squinting, I could see them more clearly, and my spirits sank. The fires were actually quite small. I could pick out individual tongues of flame, what I had thought were whole branches burning, moving fitfully in the gentle breeze. The fires burned only a few yards apart from each other. That explained their purpose—the villagers were burning off the old grass. This seemed like an odd time to be doing it. Perhaps, at least, the burners would have some *slivova* for the cold.

My path began, subtly, to slant downhill. The trees on my right dwindled, shrank to bushes, then to stands of tall grass, and finally dispersed to nothing. Darkness had fallen.

I was close enough now to see that no one was tending the fires. The villagers had gone home. They had no doubt taken their *slivova* with them.

Well, I had wanted to get away from people. The night before in Ruse, with my bike newly fixed, my first thought had been that I could escape to the countryside. I had looked forward to camping in some isolated spot. And now here I was, trudging between an empty road and a line of deserted fires. I wasn't sure anymore that this was what I wanted. Suddenly a bed didn't seem so bad.

An auburn light had awakened, playfully, on the front of my jacket. Now the nearest fire came to meet me. Several more hovered close behind it. I left the path, and soon I found myself in the midst of them, flutter-brilliant circles a meter or two across. The rest of the world receded into blackness, and I stood under a dome whose apex I could almost touch, in a scattering of creeping fires. The air here was warmer. I laid the bike down and wandered.

The bottom of the field lay another hundred yards to the east and was marked by a line of tall white willows. These were the only trees to be seen. As far as I could tell, the villagers had begun their burning here in the late afternoon. The gentle east wind had blown the fires uphill through the flattened stubble; they had progressed like a troop of reluctant infantrymen prodded from the rear. They had left behind them parallel lines of black ash and still continued to inch, murmuring, westward.

It was easy to see why the villagers had felt safe in leaving them: under the mild, steady breeze, there was little danger they would burn anything they were not intended to burn. Still, the practice disturbed me. I remembered how much of Corsica had been ravaged by fire. There, I had cycled through entire valleys, across large tracts, where nothing but black, branchless trunks had stood, where cinders had lined the road like broken bits of pavement and only fireweed had grown. A few of the fires in Corsica had been caused by lightning; some had been set delib- erately, by warring families; and some had begun as selective burnings which the peasants, confident of their technique, had abandoned. I, the city boy, had been shocked. I had assumed the peasants knew what they were doing.

The fires crept always westward, at an inch a second. The thin stalks along the ground caught quickly, focused to bright threads, then yielded to ash, all in an instant. Whenever a fire encountered a thicker tangle, it would dart forward, expanding, like a child throwing out her arms. Then it would return as suddenly to its normal size and creep industriously on. I had intended to cook and eat by one of the fires, but I had not realized how quickly they advanced. In the time it would take me merely to set up my stove, one of these fires would have moved several feet. And I couldn't build my own wood fire—the fields had been picked clean of dead wood by the village women, gathering for their stoves.

I carried my things upwind and raised the tent on a small plot of hay bounded by the dirt path and a strip of ash. This inflammable boundary would protect me in case the wind changed direction during the night. I did not want to be immolated in my tent by an innocuous little fire ripping its way back east.

I cooked and ate in my own darkness. The temperature continued to fall rapidly. The night was going to be even colder than I had feared. And I noticed, after I had cleaned my pan and utensils—a dreadful job, holding the light in my mouth and struggling with numb fingers in the icy water—that the fires, one by one, were going out.

There was something inexpressibly sad in the winking out of each light. They died like sick old men, flickering down to a desperate, fighting blue and then giving themselves up, suddenly, to smoke and silence. My source of both cheer and comfort was deserting me.

I left the tent and walked from fire to fire, trying to keep the fleeting warmth company. I would stand close to a fire when the yellow exuberance was upon it and would abandon it for another as soon as the death throes came. I was trying, in a worried, illogical way, to store up heat within me for the long night, since I could tell that my sleeping bag would not be up to this profound cold. A futile effort—but at least the periphery of the fires made tolerable places to stand while I counted the minutes until the time for sleep. It was too cold to sit still, too cold to read. And I didn't want to crawl into the sleeping bag yet: I would be too long on my back as it was. I had nothing else to do but chase the fires.

I walked farther and farther to find fires that now seemed always to ail and succumb shortly after I reached them. The field was huge—and no matter how far I walked, I could always see a fire or two, lonely doomed beacons, far ahead. Eventually I had to turn back. The chance was too great, if I went on, that I would lose my way.

In the starlight, I picked out the dim, pale, vertical lines of willows far off in the darkness. I walked toward them.

I had been waiting all this time for the moon to rise, and finally, just as I reached the tent, I caught my first sight of her— a dusky red irregularity, partly obscured by the lines of smog that hugged the horizon. She pulled herself, slowly, grimacing, like a gravid woman mounting stairs, up through the thicker air toward clarity: from red, to orange, to fleeting lemon, to sharp, crystalline, ruthless white. She was two days past full. The stars fled before their mistress; the sky turned toward the moon and became her mirror. The last of the fires, near the horizon, had died out as she rose, as if they, like the stars, were yielding, willingly, to a different kind of light: a cold and penetrating scrutiny. And in the way of one who has been alone for some time, I turned to the moon as she climbed the sky and spoke to her, out loud. "You're late," I murmured. "Where have you been?" But the moon was not personable like the fires. I would get nowhere by talking to her.

I started to tidy my camp, keeping my hands in heavy wool socks. My nostril hairs had begun to prick with each inhalation. I collapsed my mess kit and put away the stove. Bending to pick up the new loaf of bread, I felt a rock—the crust had frozen.

Hlyab. Studeno.

For once, I had all the Bulgarian words I needed.

DUSK WAS DARKENING the whitewashed plaster walls of the courtyard to slate. I looked around me, at a loss, at first, as to where to go. The place seemed deserted.

The monastery was arranged in the usual Bulgarian Orthodox pattern, with the church in the middle of a courtyard whose sides were bounded partly by high stone walls and partly by the monks' dormitory, the lay quarters, and the storerooms. These last three were housed in a single long building, all the doors and galleries of which faced inward. The arrangement served a defensive purpose, since the outside of the building presented a blank face to the world, broken only rarely by small windows, often barred. These precautions had been necessary in the embattled times of the Turkish occupation. The most protected part of the monastery, of course, was the church in the middle, which had contained the icons—and, sometimes, the revolutionaries.

The Troyanski Monastery was situated on the west flank of a small, forested ravine. The stones of the sloped yard, sinking over the centuries, had become so irregular that even to go on foot was difficult. New debris littered the sunken debris—the east wall was being rebuilt. The dormitory building, up the slope to my right, accounted for most of the north and west walls. It stood three stories high, with wooden galleries running the length of its right-angled face on each story. Rough wooden staircases connected the galleries at intervals, and the supports of the banisters were as thick as piano legs. I looked forward to sleeping inside. I imagined a clean stone room with a straw pallet and an oil lamp on a wooden writing desk.

The church, squatting halfway up the slope, was three-domed and small. It resembled three steamer trunks lashed together and set out on an ancient stone pier. Here was a portrait of the Levant: domes, inward-looking, on windowless boxes; a slope of stones descending to a dry ravine. The central dome was the tallest of the three, reaching a height of perhaps forty feet. It surmounted a squat cylinder, which rose from the rounded shoulders of the roof like a thick bellicose neck, punctuated by windows in the shapes of Norman arches. The muffled sound of singing came through the high windows, so I moved toward it, dragging the bicycle over the stones behind me.

Tonight would be my first contact with monks of any kind. Somehow I had managed to travel in France and Italy without encountering any, but to do the same in Bulgaria was nearly impossible, since the monasteries were the country's premier tourist attractions. Not only had they been spared, in general, the depredations of centuries of Turkish domination, but they had been regarded by Bulgarians, throughout those centuries, as symbols of future independence and as repositories of the national culture. The Bulgarians had lavished their art and architectural skills on the monasteries accordingly. Especially from 1820 to 1870, after the opening, at last, of a number of Bulgarian-language schools had contributed to a nationalist consciousness, renovation projects were undertaken to give back to national monuments both their opulence and their distinctly Bulgarian character.

I unfolded a page from *Let's Go*. The text assured me, as *Nagel's* had done, that a bed could be had here for just a few leva. I also learned that the slopes around the monastery offered excellent hiking. The passage ended with an anecdote about what to do if the guest rooms were full. Across the road from the gate of the monastery, it seemed, there stood an old barn, and one could sleep—illegally—in the loft. "If anyone asks you what you're doing in the hay," *Let's Go* concluded, "just say (or pantomime) that the monk dressed in black with the beard said you could sleep there."

A tinkling bell rang three times, and the singing abruptly ended. After a moment, four monks appeared on the porch—imposing black figures with hair down to their shoulders and chests. They saw me and looked away. I spoke to one, but he walked away while I was in mid-sentence. The second turned impassive eyes on me, shrugged his shoulders, and disappeared into the darkness. A third followed him before I could get his attention. The fourth monk didn't understand me, either, but at least he looked me straight in the eye. He went back inside and fetched a fifth monk, who approached me cautiously and said, *"Guten Abend, mein junger Freund."*

"Good evening," I returned, relieved.

He was shorter than the others, perhaps forty years old, with bulging eyes and a little red nose. He took my arm and led me off the porch. "Listen, my friend," he said, "you cannot stay here. That is what you wanted, was it not?"

Somehow, now that we had come to it, I was not surprised. "But I heard that there were rooms here for guests. I am perfectly willing to pay."

We stopped. A light went on in the dormitory. "Oh, I am sure you are willing to pay," he answered. "But we are not allowed to give you a room. The rooms here are only for Bulgarian tourists."

I tried polite bewilderment. "But in this guidebook"—I felt like an ass, showing him the few torn pages—"it says that anybody can stay. It was written for American students."

"Until two years ago, anyone *could* stay, even Western tourists. But we always had trouble with the Westerners—they wanted luxury. This is a monastery, not a deluxe hotel; they were not expecting small, bare rooms. They wanted heating and hot water. We don't have such things here."

"But I don't want such things," I expostulated. "I don't need hot water or heating, or whatever. I usually camp out. A room will be warmer than the outside even if it's unheated—"

The monk put up his hand to stop me and smiled. "Of course, of course—but I can do nothing. Two years ago, one of our visitors, an important West German citizen, complained terribly afterward. 'Auuugh, no hot water, no towels, no private toilet! Auugh! Auugh!' He wrote letters. It was very unpleasant. And so the police said, 'That is enough; no more Westerners. Only Bulgarians.' It is a rule from the police. It is out of our hands. Besides, you won't have to sleep outside. There is a wonderful new hotel in the town. *Luxus*."

"Balkanturist?"

"Yes. It is very new. It was built just a couple of years ago."

Aha! So that was really why Westerners were barred now from the monastery quarters. Balkanturist was right next door, welcoming us with open jaws. So much for the important-West-German-citizen crap.

"I can't go down to the town," I said, and pointed smugly to the bike. "It's pitch-dark now, and the ride is dangerous on a bicycle. I have no decent light."

The monk had not noticed the bike. His face fell. "Oh, you came up on that thing. Hmmmm." He fingered a heavy silver cross. "Well, it's not very far, you know. Only five or six kilometers."

"It's twelve," I riposted.

"Couldn't you just be careful?"

"Nope," I declared flatly. "Much too dangerous. I always stop before dark."

"Hmm," he said again, and sunk into silence. He apparently was unaccustomed to meeting with resistance. Finally he roused himself and took my arm again. "Here. Come with me. Take that thing with you." He gestured toward the bike. "But you have to promise not to tell anybody I did this for you, all right?"

"Of course," I said. I would get no mark on the statistical card, but I would have a room and some light. Good enough!

But—I should have known. The monk walked through the monastery gate and struck out across the street. We climbed a wooden fence on the far shoulder and descended a dirt lane. Out of the darkness, on the left, a ramshackle structure of logs and wooden slats materialized. A barn. The monk looked cautiously around and then hauled open the barn door. Inside, it was pitch-black.

"There is hay in the loft," the monk said. "You can sleep there. It will not be so cold. But don't let anyone see you go in or come out. It is strictly forbidden to sleep here." He looked at me; his eyes asked, Well, what would you have me do?

"You can buy dinner in the grill next door. It is not very good, I'm afraid. There used to be a deluxe tourist restaurant there—wonderful. All the tourists loved it, but it burned down last year. Now there is only this," and he waved to the bright noisy windows above us. It sounded like a vulgar, lively place. I was glad the other had burned down. "I must go now. Have a good night's sleep!"

I fished out my armlight and shined it into the barn's black interior. The loft and the hay were there. But the barn had no lights. The loft doorway had no door. It would be as cold within the barn as without. I wondered vaguely if there were any rats and clapped my hands, but I heard no scurrying. Aah, to be thankful for small blessings.

The logic that had brought me here had a certain charm. I was a Western tourist. I ostensibly demanded luxury. Therefore, the monastery was not suitable for me, since it did not offer hot water or a private toilet. Therefore, I had to sleep in the barn, where I could not even have a bed or any toilet at all. The arrangement didn't help the Bulgarian economy, either. Whereas the police demanded that I fork over twenty-one leva for a bed in town, I was willing to shell out four or five leva for a bed at the monastery. With me sleeping in the barn, no one got any hard currency out of me at all.

I threw my bag up onto the loft and concealed the rest of my things behind bales on the floor. So I was going to sleep in the barn, after all, as the guidebook had suggested I do if the monastery was full. And if someone asked what I was doing in the hay, I could truthfully say that the monk in black with the beard had given me permission. But thanks to the book, no one would believe me now; thousands of students read *Let's Go* each season, and they had been crying wolf in the barn for years.

In spite of myself, I laughed.

•

Outside the door to the grill I ran into the monk again. He paused before moving on. "Listen," he said. "I have some business to take care of right now, but I'll be done in about an hour. Why don't we meet again in the restaurant and talk a little bit, have some beer?"

I hesitated, surprised. This man was not only a monk but a black-stoled monk who cut not the corners of his beard, neither rounded the corners of his hair. The idea of him meeting anyone— especially me—in a restaurant for a chat and a cold one struck me as incongruous. "Uh, sure," I said.

He patted me on the back and swept out of sight.

By the time he returned to the grill, I had eaten two complete dinners of oily shish kebab, french fries, and cabbage, and was nursing my second bottle of beer over the Ibsen. Needless to say, I felt much better. When the monk appeared at my table, I offered him some of the bread, cheese, and apples that I had brought up from the barn for my dessert. He pulled out a terrifying knife, grabbed an apple, and sat down, carving it.

"Thank you," he said. "My name, by the way, is Yordan."

"Mine is Brian." We shook hands.

The men at the half dozen other tables greeted Yordan. Dirty and boisterous, squeezed between cracked shoes and worn blue caps, they had been shy with me and had confined their curiosity to eyeing me when they thought I wasn't looking. They now spoke to Yordan familiarly, if a little uneasily. Perhaps they, too, saw incongruity in a monk who sucked down brews at the local grill. Or perhaps his mere presence—like that of a priest at the poker game—awakened in them restraint, and therefore resentment.

"Shall I get you a beer?" I asked, starting to rise.

"Oh yes. Please," he said, and patted his stomach. "I am just breaking fast. Wednesday is a fasting day for us, you know."

I brought back from the counter Yordan's beer and a carafe

of wine for myself. Sleep would come easier to me if I got a little blitzed. Yordan had clapped on the table an enormous loaf of his own and another wedge of cheese. He attacked it all hungrily. I handed him his beer. "Fanks," he said, with his mouth full of bread, and took a swig.

In the better light, Yordan was truly impressive. His long hair and beard shone like jet-black anthracite. On his head he wore a tall cylindrical miter, also black, with a black fall behind. The silver cross hanging from his neck was about the size of a sword handle, and a similarly weighty silver ring encircled a finger of his right hand. The black stole was so large that the folds and curves of it looked as if they could conceal anything up to the size of a coatrack—a raft of scrolls, perhaps, or a scimitar.

"We don't see many cyclists up here, you know," Yordan said.

I felt like the bear in the bar in the old joke: "With these accommodations, I'm not surprised." But I said, "Oh, really?"

We talked about me for a while: the traveler's duty. But eventually the conversation turned to the Troyanski Monastery.

"The monastery is not very old as they go," Yordan was saying. "1600s. The church itself was built in the 1830s, by Constantin, and Zograf painted the frescoes a decade later." These names meant nothing to me. "You probably couldn't see the frescoes very well in the dark. You should take a good look tomorrow. They are famous. Like the ones at Rila, they are themselves Gospel. They illustrate important events from the Holy Book—even people who cannot read or who do not understand the liturgy, the people who stand out on the porch during the service or who are confused by the singing, they can look at the frescoes and learn."

"How difficult is it for the average Bulgarian to understand the liturgy?"

"Oh, an educated Bulgarian would have no trouble at all. This liturgical language of the Slav Orthodox Churches, it is called Old Church Slavonic. But it is also called Old Bulgarian. Bulgarian is the original language of the Slav Churches, also of all Slav literatures. You probably didn't know that; the Russians may think they are the only Slav culture, but when Turnovo rivaled Byzantium in the thirteenth century, when the religious texts of Bulgaria were among the best in the Christian world, the Russians still lived in a swamp." This was a feeling I had encountered already. Despite their much-vaunted friendship with the Russians, the Bulgarians seemed to resent the idea among foreigners that their country was little more than a province of Mother Russia. In the Bulgarians' eyes, I gathered, she was a stepmother at best.

Bulgaria had, indeed, proven itself fertile religious ground—even volatile. Yordan would not mention it, I assumed, but Bulgaria had not only been an important early propagator of the Slav Orthodox faith and its liturgy; it had also been the source of the greatest, the most widespread, and the most long-lasting heresy of the Balkan peninsula: Bogomilism.

The heresy began soon after the Bulgarian Orthodox Church was established. Beginning circa 940, the Bogomils had grown rapidly into as exotic a sect as any popular historian might wish for. They had named themselves after the Priest Bogomil—the word means "love of God"—and they propounded a strange and ascetic form of Manichaeism, according to which the earth and all material things had been created by Satan. From this central tenet, the Bogomils inferred refutation of practically every significant aspect of the Orthodox Church and its dogma. They scorned the priesthood and church buildings, the Eucharist and the sacrament of baptism. They hated crosses and Holy Tables and iconostases. They denied the incarnation of Christ. Most of the early Bogomils were peasants, and like peasants everywhere, they had led a miserable existence; they advocated rebellion among the serfs. In fact, they preached against manual labor of any kind. They were ascetics, and taught that men, to keep their souls from peril, must not eat meat or imbibe alcohol. The Bogomils did not think much of sex, either, which makes the heresy's longevity even more remarkable. Antiestablishment, anti-intellectual, puritan in the highest degree: Bogomilism was the Great Awakening of Bulgaria. Six hundred years before Martin Luther, the Bogomils founded the world's first Protestant Evangelical sect. The only reason they did not nail their theses to the church door at Preslav was that they believed paper and nails to be creations of the Devil.

Bogomilism spread as only the evangelical religions can—like a brushfire. Within 150 years, it had penetrated to all parts of the Byzantine Empire, picking up not a few adherents among the Byzantine aristocracy as it did so. By 1170, Bogomilism was expanding westward into Serbia and Bosnia, and began to influence the religious life of countries as far away as Italy and France. Council after council was convened to denounce Bogomilism, but it continued to grow like an ambiguous hothouse flower. The heresy did not die until the fifteenth century, when the Turks began their semimillennial domination of the Balkans and a good number of the heretics found the rigor they had been looking for in Islam.

But Europe was not to forget the Bogomils, and particularly not where they had come from. The word "Bulgar," in medieval Europe, came to mean, simply, "Heretic." "Bulgar" was a slur that people of the fourteenth century threw at Cathars, at Manichees, and, eventually, at heretics who espoused theories that had nothing to do with dualism. A remnant of this libelous use of Bulgaria's good name survives in the European languages today. In "lay slander," according to Partridge, heretics were also called sodomites. Bulgars were called heretics, and vice versa. The words were conflated. "Bulgar" entered old French as *bogre* and developed into the middle French *bougre*. From that, alas, we have derived the English word "bugger." So "buggery," etymologically, means "the condition of being Bulgarian."

Yordan was still talking: "Many of the monasteries played an active role in the movement for liberation from the Turks. Archimandrite Macarii was the abbot of Troyan during the Liberation, and he became a fervent patriot. He inspired many people in the neighboring towns—Novo Selo, Klisura, Sevlievo, Gabrovo—to join the revolutionary movement. The area around Troyan was the last to be defeated by the Turks in 1876—"

Another point: over four hundred monuments in Bulgaria honor the Russians who died in 1877–78, when the Turks were pushed back nearly to Constantinople by the armies of the Tsar, and the legends on their pedestals celebrate Bulgarian-Russian friendship in words no less grandiose than predictable. But the Bulgarians themselves never mentioned the Russo-Turkish War to me; when they referred to the Liberation, they cited 1876—the year of the April Uprising, when the Bulgarians carried out an ill-coordinated and doomed rebellion, without the help of a single Russian. They were crushed brutally by the Turks. Perhaps because it was a failure, or perhaps for political reasons, monuments to April 1876 were few and far between in Bulgaria.

"Troyan is also one of the most visited monasteries in Bulgaria. Which, in fact, is not entirely good. At least, *I* don't think so. Sometimes when we are doing a service, a tourist will come right into the nave with his camera and his guidebook. Ours is not a big church; we cannot ignore someone photographing the icons while we are reading. And then every time we cross the yard, everyone wants to take our picture. Foreigners talk about our vestments as if they were stage costumes. We are men of God, yet we are treated like curiosities!"

"How many tourists come?" I asked.

"In the summer, we get 3,000 tourists each day."

Three thousand! I found that hard to believe. But Yordan insisted on it. No wonder, then, that the other monks had done their best to ignore me. I felt abashed. Perhaps no tourists came this late in the year, but the monks were still reeling from three months in which they had been perpetually on public display. This was a bitter irony for the devout. They joined the monastery to embrace seclusion, and here they encountered hordes that could be matched nowhere else. I was the unexpected and unwelcome rearguard of an army that had only lately decamped and headed for its winter quarters.

"And how many monks are there in Troyan?"

"Only nine. We are not as many as we used to be. We do not live in religious times. Practically none of the Bulgarian youth go to church, and many of their parents . . ." Yordan gestured significantly to the workers around us.

"How does the monastery support itself?" I asked. "Where does the money come from?"

"Well, we own land, you know. There is a cooperative farm which belongs to the monastery—it uses land that has belonged to the monastery for three centuries. Our income derives from that."

"The farm is owned directly by the monastery?"

"Well . . . yes, and no. That is, it *is* ours. The government oversees its operation and buys up its produce. We, the monks, are paid by the government. But that should go without saying—everyone is."

"And how would you describe relations in Bulgaria between the Church and the government?"

An immediate reply: "Very good."

A pause. I waited.

"The Church in Bulgaria has always been identified with freedom, with the people's struggle for self-fulfillment and self-expression. The Church was a progressive force during the Liberation; the government recognizes that."

"But the government disestablished the Church in 1944." I had, alas, very few facts to work with, but now and then I could make an intelligent comment.

Yordan continued, unruffled: "Oh yes, yes. I agree that relations did not begin so well. Under Stalin, there were many problems. The government is the first to admit that. Stefan was dismissed in 1948, when he opposed the disestablishment, and other abuses. The Church had no patriarch for five years. But self-government was returned to the Church in 1951, and Kyril became the new Patriarch in '53. Now the situation is much improved."

Yordan's smile was blank and sincere. This seemed to be as far as I would get. Of course, it was possible that he was telling me, essentially, the truth. I doubted, however, that the relationship was as bland as he stated it. I did not trust blandness in Eastern Europe. When I spoke to people about their culture, or their neighbors, they responded with a depth of feeling that thrilled me, even when I found it inexplicable. The blandness surfaced only in political conversation. It seemed a great deal was left unsaid; emotions were stored behind the smiles that blossomed at the ends of sentences and waited for me to switch the subject.

"And this Kyril—he is still the Patriarch?"

"No; Kyril died in 1973." And suddenly Yordan's eyes took on the gleam of a great idea. In his enthusiasm he grabbed my leg, under the table, and gave it a squeeze. "Of course! I don't know why I didn't think of it before—you are very lucky to have come here today, Brian."

"Oh really?"

"Tomorrow morning there is a special service in our church. It's the sixty-eighth birthday of Kyril's successor, our present Patriarch and head of the entire Bulgarian Church, Maksim. He is coming to Troyan to celebrate it! Maksim was born in Oreshak, a village a few kilometers down the road"—where I had bought some cheese—"and he was a novice and a monk here at Troyanski Monastery. Since you are interested in Church matters, you should come."

"Sure," I said blithely. "What time does the service begin?"

"Six o'clock."

Gulp.

"But you don't have to come at the beginning. It will last until 9:00. Come around 7:30 or so." Yordan grabbed my leg again. "And we can meet after the service, all right? Perhaps you would like to stay in the area tomorrow. And although I cannot give you a room in the monastery, I can let you use my private bathroom. It is a very good bathroom"—the idea of ranking bathrooms was new to me—"and I am sure you would like to do some cleaning up. You could take a bath in my room."

"Ye-es. Perhaps." A hot bath would be very welcome, but the conversation had taken a disconcerting turn. Yordan's hand remained on my leg, beneath the table.

"Well, we will see." Yordan removed his hand. "Let's meet after the service. Say, at 9:30; right outside the church." He dropped his loaf and wedge of cheese into the satchel. "I have to go now. It's late." He stood up.

"Yordan—"

"Yes?"

"Just out of curiosity, how many beds for guests are there in the monastery?"

"Oh . . . about two hundred."

"And how many would you estimate are empty tonight? Just a rough guess."

Yordan smiled, with a touch of rue in his wet brown pop-eyes. "About two hundred. Did you really want to know?"

"Just gathering material," I said aggrievedly.

Later, in the barn, I made a bed in the loft and carefully arranged things so that, once in my sleeping bag, I could pull an enormous quantity of hay down on top of me. Inside this cocoon, I began to warm up. Perhaps I would get a decent night's sleep, after all.

•

At 7:00 in the morning, the mist was as much within the barn as without. I jumped down from the loft, chased by broken strands of hay. Dressing appropriately for the service was out of the question—most of my clothes were hardly decent enough even for the road. I had no choice in the matter: the church would not be heated, and I would have to stand motionless for close to two hours. I put on everything I had.

The cobblestones in the courtyard glistened. I could make out tire tracks curving like palm-tree trunks through the frost. I crossed the yard silently, and the singing drifted to me like the mist. I passed through the porch and went in at the door.

At first, I saw only teardrops of flames. Then my sight enlarged and took in other things. A small cruciform room. Float lights before the iconostasis. Bearded men in black on the raised choir. A congregation of half a dozen women and a couple of men, all elderly. Painting, fresco, mural, portrait, on every inch of wall and ceiling: all of it dark purple, nearly invisible, in the feeble light.

Two faces turned my way and regarded me for a moment, then renewed, incuriously, their contemplation of the floor. Following the Orthodox tradition, I bought a candle and lit it, pressed it into the bowl of sand. Then I retreated to one of the bays along the west wall and sunk back into the semicircle of wood. The others ignored me, for which I was grateful. I lost myself in the music.

•

Seven men performed the service. I recognized Yordan and the other monks from the night before. I was also able immediately to pick out the Patriarch Maksim, who could not have looked more the part if he had been cast by Cecil B. deMille. He was dressed like the lesser monks, but whereas all the others had jet-black hair, Maksim's hair was a pure, marvelous white. His beard reached nearly to his waist. He was a slender man with a slight stoop, and he sang in a strong voice that ran easily from note to note.

The music was a delight. It advanced like a snake, writhing over the dark intervals with its eyes fixed always on some point beyond the horizon. Its aim could not be of this world; one could sense that without understanding a word of the text. Most of the time, the music was a recitative: the singer used only two or three notes, wandering between the tones in a dazed sleepy ecstasy, like a pilgrim moving among the relics of a shrine. Time, then, would stop and wait for the line. Or the singer would rouse himself, take up the line, and rush along the filament of a single note, building up momentum toward the climactic moment when the pitch would suddenly shift, dropping down a fourth perhaps, or stepping up once and then again, following an old, plaintive mode, and he would enunciate an important word on the new note like a shard of cut glass. What a shame that I could not understand that word!

An undercurrent to the music was the talking of the monks. The tradition of the Church required the celebrants to carry forward the singing continually, but it did not require that they always attend to it. Sometimes the spoken words nearly drowned out the liturgy. The monks appeared to be talking over the logistics of the service, for they accompanied their words by pointing and then changing their positions; or they argued over who should be next to hold the censer; or they reminded one of their number to head for the sanctuary. There was something appealing in all this: perhaps, with Maksim added to the Matins, their routine was broken and they were forced to improvise. Now and then I decided the monks were just chatting. They would lean on their elbows over the railing of their station and talk casually. When this happened, I could not help feeling annoyed, as I would at people who talked during a concert. At the same time, the irony of the situation tickled me. I wanted the monks to show more respect for their own performance; in this desire, I betrayed the fact that the service was less a religious occasion for me than an aesthetic one.

For the loud talking compromised only the drama, not the liturgy. The reading flowed on, unruffled; God would not fail to hear His praise merely because of ambient noise.

The recitatives were prayers and scripture readings. Now and then a hymn would come, suddenly at the end of a prayer, and it was thrilling to hear the one chanting voice joined all at once by the others, to hear the singing mount above the plane of the recitative and begin to grope heavenward. The hymns were brief, like voluptuous swellings along a branch. I had thought that the recitatives were at least partly improvised: they showed so little form, and the liturgy on which they were based was so huge, I found it hard to believe that the notes were memorized. And perhaps, in a strict sense, they were not. Yet every time one singer joined another, in a hymn or a prayer response, the two or three of them moved together in flawless unison. They were singing from texts that displayed no musical notes, and this was the most thrilling part of all: the music seemed so spontaneous, so free, yet the singers, by moving identically, without ever looking at each other, proved themselves to be utterly in control of it. It sounded like genuine inspiration taking all the singers at once. Here, I could imagine, was reflected in music one of the paradoxes of Christian theology: the freedom that came from submission of will to the Christ. Here was the sound of a communion of souls.

Yordan was singing now, in front of the Deacon's Door. He held a cross before him, stiff-armed, while the voluminous sleeves of his black stole hung to his knees. Then he raised the cross aloft, two or three times, as he sang on a higher note, wavering now in a tone of supplication. The women to my left fell to their knees at the first elevation of the cross and kissed the floor, rose back to their knees to cross themselves, and bent down again to kiss the floor, repeatedly. The two men remained standing.

A military man came into the nave from the west door and stood next to me, startling me. He was a young man with an officious little mustache and pudgy cheeks. He rocked on his heels and looked around. He was making a show of curiosity, as if he had never before seen the celebration of this strange cult. After fidgeting for a few moments, he began to wander slowly around the west end of the nave. He held his hands behind his back and kept a cheerfully arrogant expression on his face, watching the peasants as they crossed themselves. After a time, he nonchalantly wandered out, with his hands still behind his back, leaving the door ajar.

The paranomarion flew open and a procession emerged. Yordan led with the primiker, the processional taper, and a monk followed, swinging the censer. Maksim came next, swaying now as he sang, so that his black robes billowed out to right and left. Two monks took up the rear, holding the banner. The old women renewed their crossing and bowing.

The military man appeared again, with an old peasant woman, the monastery's factotum. They carried a light wooden table between them. I knew just enough about the Orthodox service to know that this was out of the ordinary. While a prayer continued from the Holy Door, two monks came forward and helped guide the table, arguing with each other about where it should go. Then the four of them put it before the ambon, under the central dome. The military man and the woman walked back out. Then the woman returned with a white linen cloth and spread it over the table.

The woman left again, then entered the nave with a large plate of cookies in her hands. Another hymn rose, while Maksim— Cookies? I looked again. Yes, it was a plate of cookies. She deposited it in the center of the table. She went out. The hymn flowed on. She returned with a plate of little chocolate bars. More hymn. Little cakes followed, then more cookies, and small loaves of buttery bread. As the plates began to collect on the linen cloth, the monks who were not singing, without leaving their stations in the apses, told the woman which way to arrange the food. They pointed and spoke, while she extrapolated trajectories from their fingers and shifted the plates around accordingly. A space was reserved in the middle of the table, and at last, the old woman brought in the centerpiece—a hemispherical mound of pure white with a single candle rising from it. The candle was the same tan slip of wax as all the others, but the others were offertory candles. This one was a birthday candle. After the centerpiece had been laid, the old woman retreated and took up a position next to me in the corner. She smelled of sheep.

For the next forty minutes, the monks slowly advanced on the birthday food. They uttered recitatives, they melted into hymns and exquisitely melodic responses, they changed their positions with the same bewildering frequency as before. But all the while they gradually drew nearer to the table. They outwardly ignored it, they never looked at it; yet it drew them in inexorably. Eventually they were close enough to it to form a circle, and from that moment on they did not retreat or break the circle. They sang on and on, slowly tightening the ring, sometimes moving around the table in a graceful, measured step. There was something predatory about their movement. As gentle as they appeared, as excruciatingly patient, they reminded me of wolves circling in for the kill.

Finally, the monks were at the table. I had a vision of Maksim singing a wish in a slow, sober recitative and then blowing out the candle. But instead, he picked up the plate of cookies and raised it over his head. He sang a prayer, probably of dedication. The women to my left recommenced crossing themselves. When the great cross had been held aloft, the women's obeisance had made a powerful impression on me. It was strange now to see the same action performed for a plate of what looked like sugared pecan puffs.

Maksim lowered the plate, and the circle of monks rotated; now one of the monks, occupying Maksim's former position, raised a bowl of chocolate squares. Another prayer of dedication was sung, and then again the circle rotated. It was the most impressive birthday party I had ever seen. I remembered again the cake shaped like a steamship that my mother had made for me on my eighth birthday. That had been nothing like this. What I had missed by not being Patriarch of the Bulgarian Orthodox Church!

Like all birthday celebrations, this one ended too early. The last plate of food was lowered to the table, and a last prayer was sung. The bell rang. The monks relaxed and broke their circle. I expected them now, at last, to throw themselves on the food. After three hours of singing they must have been ravenous. But decorum prevailed, and they carried the table out of the nave, through the vestibule, and onto the porch. There the food was shared among all of us, clergy and congregation alike. The old factotum cut the cakes and arranged the cookies and chocolate squares on napkins for each of us. The white mound turned out to be made of a bleached grain, delicately sweetened. The pecan cookies were delicious. The pudgy-faced military man ate his portion quickly, rather like a pig. He was the only one to take seconds. I was still very hungry and wanted to do the same, but no one offered me more, so I sadly watched the food—the best sweets I had had in months—being whisked out of sight.

Now I noticed other military men. The courtyard held a dozen soldiers. A couple of them led Maksim off the porch, behind the church, to a line of black Mercedeses. Maksim gave his brothers a round of farewell hugs and climbed into the largest of the cars, a new Mercedes limousine. He drew the curtains on the windows. The soldiers ran to the other cars, and within seconds the line was gliding past me, reflecting the church and the pines in their shiny black hoods and doors. In the arrogant, capable way of expensive cars, they crossed the rough courtyard quietly and easily and slipped through the front gate.

.

Yordan had disappeared, and I waited for him outside the church. I had yet to decide what to do about his offer, but as it turned out, no decision was necessary. There followed one of those inexplicable lapses that had been plaguing me in Eastern Europe: Yordan did not show up. I spent some time examining the frescoes on the outside of the church and wandered around the galleries for a while admiring the wood trim. But waiting and admiring come hard on a fine sunny day when it is late in the year and you know you should be heading south. Finally, after nearly two hours, I gave up. I returned to the barn and fetched my things out of the hay, waving goodbye to some of the men who had been in the grill the night before, who now were working on the tumbledown monastery wall.

A bus drove up to the monastery just as I mounted the bicycle. And as I looked around a last time, coasting down the road toward Oreshak, I saw Yordan getting off the bus. His back was to me.

He was carrying two large paper sacks in his arms, and he was hurrying, perhaps to meet me. But I was already on my way—my spirit was turned toward going—and I did not call to him. A few seconds later, the monastery had slipped from sight. The Bulgarians were not very punctual, I knew, but Yordan had made me wait too long. I wanted to get over the Troyanski pass before nightfall, and I resented the loss of time. Perhaps, if I went quickly, I would reach a hotel and a hot bath in the Stryama valley.

All the way to Oreshak, I wondered what Yordan had been carrying in those paper sacks.

•

Much later, when I read the memoirs of Georgi Markov, a Bulgarian dissident, I came across his description of an altercation that took place in an unidentified year in Sofia:

> We all know about the incident that occurred inside the Alexander Nevski Cathedral during last year's Easter service. The initiative was taken by a newly promoted Party or militia chief who had been alarmed at the rising number of young people attending church. According to other rumours, though, the idea of the attack on the Easter service had come from the Soviet Embassy, from whose windows the mass gathering of believers looked like an open anti-Soviet demonstration. Under the auspices of the security service a shock detachment of Komsomol activists, mainly students, had been formed and instructed in hooligan behaviour. On entering the cathedral, shouting, laughing, jeering, pushing and offending members of the congregation, they had aimed at disrupting the service itself. The climax of their outrage had been to pelt the officiating priests with eggs and other missiles so as to provoke the churchgoers. In any event, their objective was achieved. The Patriarch had to call in the militia, who were already deployed, in readiness in the adjoining streets. Needless to say, the militiamen seized this opportunity and rushed in, arresting numerous people and bundling them into police vans. An hour later the Komsomol hooligans went peacefully home, while completely innocent young people were subjected to strong pressure to ensure that they would not dare attend another Easter service. . . .

There can be no doubt that this action boomeranged, and later it was admitted in Party circles that it had been an example of the militia's consummate stupidity. The very next day people started to flock *en masse* to all the churches in Sofia.

Reading this, I thought of Yordan's assurances to me that the Church and the government of Bulgaria were on excellent terms. I had not quite believed Yordan; still, the picture that Markov painted was so utterly different it took my breath away. I thought again of the tiny congregation that I had seen, and of Maksim climbing into the Mercedes and gliding, with his escort, out of sight. The Patriarch in Markov's story was Kyril, who died in 1973. If he had been looked on so poorly by the government, what kind of man had been allowed to replace him?

Curious, I telephoned a Bulgarian exile who was a friend of a friend and asked him about the Patriarchs. He worked for Radio Free Europe, so I figured I would have to take what he told me with a grain of salt. Kyril, he said, had been all right. A cautious man, but a religious one. Maksim, however, had been a member of the Holy Synod in the Soviet Union. He had been "trained" by the Soviets. This Bulgarian exile had insisted to me, his voice ragged with indignation, that Maksim was a colonel in the KGB.

Could it be true? What a fascinating thought! I wondered now what might have been going on in Maksim's mind on the day that I had seen him: November 4, 1982. I checked the dates of the investigation into the shooting of the Pope and confirmed that Mehmet Ali Agca had begun to talk about the attempted assassination in May 1982. By September, the Bulgarian government had grown alarmed at the allegations made against its operatives, and on September 8, seven weeks before I landed at Ruse with a broken bicycle, the Bulgarian news agency printed this:

Agca's testimony changes so often and is so controversial that we would not be surprised if one fine day, on someone's suggestion and for some promise, he even "confesses" that the Bulgarians ordered him to kill the Pope.

Which, of course, is exactly what happened a short time later. Maksim, as the head of an autocephalous Orthodox Church, was the "Pope" of Bulgaria. If he was, indeed, an officer in the KGB, it was conceivable that his organization had tried to kill his brother in Christ, Karol Wojtyla. And on November 4, he celebrated his sixty-eighth birthday peacefully, with six monks, eight old peasants, and one young stranger in attendance. He was presiding over a dying Church; its lifeblood was being sucked out by his superiors. Had he thought, while riding away from the monastery in his limousine, drawing the curtains over the bulletproof glass, of a great basilica, of a key-shaped colonnade jammed with people and echoing to the sound of shots?

I WOKE, WITH BRIGHT LIGHT on my face, to an important day. November 7, 1982: the sixty-fifth anniversary of the Great October Socialist Revolution.

(Perhaps the name confuses you, too. It seems that the Russian Tsars, faithful to their title, had never abandoned the calendar of Julius Caesar, even though, by 1917, more than three centuries had passed since Pope Gregory had given his name to a new, improved model and the discrepancy between the two calendars had grown to thirteen days. So after the Western world went to sleep on the night of November 6, with Kerensky still in power in Petrograd, Petrograd itself woke on the morning of October 25 to find the Bolsheviks occupying most of the buildings and Kerensky in flight to the front. 1917 gave us the ten days that shook the world, but the world couldn't even agree on the dates.)

So today the sixty-fifth celebration of the Bolshevik takeover in Russia would be held. I had been seeing the number 65 for days, plastered on walls and jury-rigged in steel or neon on the tops of the tallest buildings. This had struck me as a little comic, since sixty-five years ago Bulgaria had been a kingdom under Ferdinand and about as close to a socialist revolution as England had been. When Russia pulled out of the Great War and exhorted all sides to make a socialist peace, not only did Bulgaria keep fighting but it kept fighting on the side of the Central Powers, at war with Russia, on which side it had been since 1915. I was curious—would November 7 ring hollow, here in a country that had celebrated it for the first time only after Russia had done so twenty-seven times?

I ate breakfast on a deal table out on the gallery of the Bansko hostel in cold, brilliant sunshine. New snow flashed like cut glass from the high mountain slopes, but it didn't appear to reach below five thousand feet. When I paid for my bed, I mimed to the woman that I needed a stamp for my statistical card, but she looked blank. I had missed too many days—I urgently needed her stamp. We rummaged in the top drawer of her business desk and came up with an old mailing stamp that had nothing to do with Bansko or with her establishment. I purposely applied too little ink, then struck the stamp three or four times, to make it look as if a hotel clerk had tried successively to make a good print. The effect was pleasingly illegible, and I wrote the proper dates above and below it.

I heard the loudspeakers as I came out of the narrow gate into the alley. Bansko was a museum town and about as picturesque as a tourist might wish. The streets wound around the old houses with a pleasing randomness, forking, doubling back, and dead-ending in courtyards encircled by rough stone walls with terra-cotta or cut-stone tops. Glare-white mountain peaks stared with the blankness of cats over every wall, gazed into the gardens hidden behind the studded doors.

I turned into a square paved with bluish flagstones, where new brick benches and brick-encircled trees attested to recent tourist development. The loudspeakers were perched at the tops of four metal towers, set at each corner of the square. The volume was too high and the sound quality was bad. The square was empty, except for a man at the far corner who was fixing the last mooring on a loudspeaker stand. I sat on a bench and listened for a few minutes to the ragged voice, while the man bent over the cable and twisted a wrench. Then he got up and sauntered away, without looking back. The voice exhorted the flagstones and the brick benches. Now and then I would glimpse someone, a couple of blocks away, headed somewhere else. Perhaps I was too early for the official celebration.

Heading out of town, I passed several other loudspeakers, but I didn't see a soul. Hemmed in by walls, the streets were square stone gutters, swept clean by the last rain. Finally, at the edge of town, just where the road opened up and arrowed north toward Razlog, I came to a crowd. People were setting up stands, and there were a few banners leaning against cattle trucks. The hyphens on the banners stood out sharply, and I no longer needed to transliterate the words to know what they said: BULGARIAN-SOVIET. There was a loudspeaker here as well, but there were no walls or stones to amplify it, and the people milling around, adding wood to wood, talked above it. At the edge of the crowd, older men stood in knots and smoked cheroots. A lot of the little Soviet-made cars were congregated here with each trunk opened wide to display a live pig inside; some of them had two. The farmers were taking the opportunity of the socialist holiday to sell their pigs. How convenient that this most important of Soviet days should fall near pig-killing time—the first winter's frost. The men ignored me, chafing their hands in the cold and talking—I supposed—about pork prices. The pigs, peering over license plates and rear lights, followed my movement with intelligent eyes.

Past Bansko, the going was easy. Joyous, in fact—a long, gradual climb through a treeless landscape, under a high blue sky. I cleared the Predel pass at 10:00 a.m., with Mount Vikhren rising on my left like a gathering tidal wave flecked at the curl with white foam. I took in the clean chill air and looked miles into Yugoslavia, then began the long descent into the Struma valley, heaving a sigh of relief. No more snow worries. The valley into which I was dropping sloped gently south, for ninety miles, over the Greek border and straight into the Mediterranean. The headwind that greeted me at Simitli, the town at the bottom of the pass road, had come directly from Amphipolis.

There was no sign of a celebration in Simitli: still streets and shut-up houses, a farmer guiding an ox-drawn plow. Then a village, scattered across the slope, also with nothing going on. At a second hamlet, at last, I found a celebration in full swing. *Kebabche* stands lined the road, and a small, dense crowd plugged the village's only side street. But there were no loudspeakers or banners, not even neglected ones. The affair seemed to be entirely apolitical, expressing nothing more than the thrill of a holiday, much like our Fourth of July. I stopped to buy some *kebabches* (oily plugs of spiced ground beef), and a crowd of children glued itself to my bicycle. On sale in the booths were shoes and handbags, nuts, tobacco, hard candy, and large jugs of red wine. The people made a tremendous noise, and I listened to the laughing cadence of the conversation. At some undefined point between the Predel and this village, I had crossed into "Pirin" Macedonia—Bulgaria's share of that ancient, disputed land. Now I wondered if I was hearing Macedonian. People had died in the struggle to preserve Macedonian, for the right to pronounce their vowels in a slightly different way, to resort to an unusual back formation to represent the definite article. They had won the language battle, but they had lost the ethnic war. They did speak Macedonian, but the Bulgarian government claimed there were no real Macedonians.

At Delchevo, on a dry pan of land a dozen kilometers from the Greek border, I turned east on the road to Melnik. The road reverted to sand and clay, while the hills around me grew steeper, acquired points and cliffs. Around a sharp bend, past an ugly green vegetable stand with plywood nailed over its windows, I came upon Melnik, suddenly, on my right. The town was squeezed into a narrow ravine by sinuous cliffs of barely lithified sand. Two wide paths of stone and sand wandered up through the town on either side of a dry streambed and dissolved almost immediately into twisting tracks. The concrete Balkanturist hotel glowered down from the right slope onto the small houses below, like the manor of a medieval town.

While I was standing by the streambed uncertainly, a villager came up to me, took one look at my bicycle and my beard, and pointed to the fancy hotel, wiping it figuratively off the slope with his hand.

"*Nix chotel. Nix.*" He pointed to me and rubbed his fingers. Too expensive, he meant. "*Turisticheski. Turisticheski Spalnya. Ist besser. Billig.*" He gestured up the left bank of the stream.

I could hardly believe it. He was directing me to a hostel. In

Melnik, at last, I had found a villager who was not proud of his *luxus* tourist hotel.

Nor did Melnikans seem very proud of November 7. As at Simitli, there were no signs of a celebration. The town was silent, swept by sand. I started up the left bank, passing between houses jumbled against each other like crystals of salt thrown into a fold of cloth. Melnik's architecture was uncharacteristic of Bulgaria: the Greek merchants who had lived and prospered here had clearly been an influence. With pyramidal roofs and mullioned windows, whitewashed walls and, frequently, overhanging second stories, the buildings struck a balance between Bulgarian delicacy and Greek matter-of-factness that somehow failed to be attractive.

The *turisticheski* was a white stone building, squatting on the crown of a promontory, with a view over the village. Flanking it on the right was a row of concrete pit toilets. All the doors and windows of the hostel had been thrown open to air it out, but there was no one inside. I called and waited. After half an hour, a young woman arrived to close the windows. She looked a little displeased to have found a guest, but she took three leva, anyway, and gave me the key to the back door.

That night, as I lay in bed in the empty dorm room, I thought about November 7. Had that been all? Loudspeakers on an empty square, a pig market at the edge of town, *kebabche* stands and shoe stalls by the side of the road. The political spirit had been so lacking, a different kind of spirit had managed to grow in its place—people had been out to enjoy themselves, to make some pleasing use of an official holiday. The villagers had succeeded in making the Soviet day their own.

•

Bulgaria rose to prominence in the ninth century by fighting the Byzantine Empire. The first great Bulgarian chieftain, Khan Krum, annihilated the Byzantine Army at a pass in the Balkans in A.D. 811 and killed the Emperor Nicephorus I. Krum was a pagan who worshipped the sun, and he cut off the Christian Emperor's head, hollowed out his skull, lined the skull with silver, and drank his favorite wine from it for the next three years, during which he continued to terrorize the only civilization that he knew. In 814, Krum died suddenly, while laying siege to Constantinople. His death may have saved the city.

But the glorious pagan days were short-lived; Bulgaria's very success demanded that it conform to the prevailing winds of change in order to further its ambitions. So in the year 870, Boris I, only the third Bulgarian ruler after Krum, converted his subjects forcibly to Christianity. After having wavered for several years on the matter, Boris I chose the Eastern Church over Rome for the faith of his country, primarily because the Latins had refused to grant him a patriarchate. The pagan Slavs south of the Danube became Orthodox Christians practically overnight, and Boris's decision, based on expedience and ambition, established a connection that would direct Bulgaria's religious and political affairs for the following eleven centuries.

Under Boris's successor, Simeon, Bulgaria reached the first peak of its power, growing to an empire that stretched from the Adriatic to the Black Sea, from the Danube to Gallipoli and far into Macedonia. Simeon declared himself "Emperor of all the Bulgars and Greeks," and the fact that his Church was Orthodox did not reconcile him with the Byzantine Empire. In fact, it prompted him repeatedly to lead campaigns against Constantinople, with the aim of gaining the Byzantine crown for himself.

After his death, however, Bulgaria weakened and lost Serbia in 933. Then Byzantium, not having forgotten Simeon the Pest, attacked and regained eastern Bulgaria in 972, in the process capturing Boris II, who was carted off to prison in Constantinople. In western Bulgaria, an area still independent from Constantinople, a Macedonian named Samuel assumed leadership in 980, called himself Tsar, and built a new, if smaller, Bulgarian Empire. It was during Samuel's reign that Melnik appeared for the first time in the historical record: as a fortified village of eastern Macedonia, hidden among the steep foothills of Pirin, a few kilometers east of the Struma. Melnik was essentially a fortress, and several other such strongholds probably existed along the Struma valley at that time, in order to guard this flat and easy access from the Aegean into the heart of western Bulgaria. But it is unlikely that any of them were as naturally protected as was Melnik, which had been built into the back of a narrow valley and resembled a mussel, with its houses peering suspiciously out through the crack of its mouth. The population of the village was predominantly Slav, with perhaps an admixture of Greek blood— a legacy of the ancient Macedonians, Christians as early as the fourth century, who had been displaced by the pagan Slavs at the end of the sixth.

While Tsar Samuel labored to rebuild Bulgaria, a series of power struggles in Constantinople culminated in the emergence of a new emperor: Basil II, who turned to the Bulgarian Problem with the determination to remove this thorn once and for all from the side of his empire. The war dragged on for nearly two decades, but the Bulgarians finally suffered an overwhelming defeat at Belasitsa, just a few kilometers from Melnik, in 1014. Basil II then committed an act of cruelty that shocked even that cruel age: he blinded his 15,000 prisoners. One man out of every hundred was left with one eye. The 150 one-eyed men led the 14,850 blind men back to Samuel. As the story goes (Constantine Manasses included it in his *Chronicle*), Samuel's heart broke at the sight of his men, and he fainted. Whether or not the story is true, it is a fact that Samuel died within two days.

Melnik remained subject to the Byzantine Empire until 1204, when the Latins, diverting from the Fourth Crusade, barbarically sacked Constantinople and set up a Latin emperor. In the chaos that followed, a feudal lord by the colorful name of Despot Slav took over Melnik and made it his capital, only to be defeated a few years later by the Bulgarian Tsar Ivan Asen II. In 1246, Melnik became subject to the Nicaeans, who clung to power until 1330, when they lost Macedonia to the Serbs. Stability came to the region only when the Ottomans appeared on the western side of the Bosporus and proceeded to overrun everybody. By 1371, Melnik was in Turkish hands.

The influx of refugees over the years had made Melnik at least as much a Greek town as a Bulgarian one, and now a great number of Turks settled in the little valley. There were probably a few Serbs there as well, and it is possible that Sephardic Jews arrived, too, fresh from the Spanish expulsion. In the middle of chaos, Melnik was growing. People were attracted by the town's secure position in a precipitous cul-de-sac. By the sixteenth century, Melnik had become the chief town of the district, and its sweet red wines became famous as far away as Vienna. In its heyday, the town numbered something like 20,000 people, fully half the size of Sofia.

The First Balkan War originated in the impossible situation that had arisen concerning Macedonia. Bulgaria, Serbia, and Greece each considered Macedonia theirs, since all three had held it at one time or another. (Many of the Macedonians themselves wanted autonomy, but no one paid serious attention to that—the region had not been autonomous since antiquity.) Ridden by internal weaknesses and corruption, Turkey was not the power it had been, and in 1912, Bulgaria, Serbia, and Greece allied against the ailing empire and drove Nazim Pasha's armies back nearly to Constantinople. But too many victors spoil the spoils, and there was violent disagreement over who had promised which parts of Macedonia to whom, and when. Negotiations broke down by the end of the year, and Bulgaria made the grave mistake of attacking Serbia and Greece by surprise, in 1913, precipitating the Second Balkan War. Austro-Hungary did not come to Bulgaria's aid, as King Ferdinand had rather foolishly hoped, and Bulgaria quickly lost both the war and a good deal of its territory. The Turks recaptured land west to Adrianople, and in the Macedonian settlement that followed, Bulgaria received approximately one-tenth of the disputed area.

What had been a bad time for Bulgaria had been a disastrous time for Melnik. The entire Turkish population of the town had evacuated during the First Balkan War, and at some point shortly thereafter, Melnik was burned to the ground. By 1914, only a handful of buildings were standing in the narrow valley. Melnik had boasted seventy churches in 1800; in 1914, only three remained.

Melnik did not recover from its burning. Its missing people never came back, and those who had survived the armies and the fire began to leave. By 1920, the recorded population was 721; by 1963, that number had fallen to 368. The town continued to grow tobacco and to produce a rather well-known wine; otherwise, it had slight contact with the outside world.

It did have something to offer, however: the attraction of a landscape that was unique in Bulgaria.

As usual, the painters came first. They would set up their easels at the mouth of the ravine and try to catch the evening light as it slashed past them and emblazoned with rose the pale faces of the sinuous sand walls jutting up from the town. Or they would walk among the hills at the head of the ravine, taking care not to step off the sheer cliffs that fell away from the far sides of gentle grassy slopes, searching for a good viewpoint along the twisting sheep paths. Or they would sit directly beneath one of the sandstone walls, where the bits of soft rock from above pattered down around them even as they worked, and sketch the hybrid houses, the riverbed paths, and the arid, scrubby face of the far slope in shadow. A sketch of the sand walls alone could be rewarding— some of them lifted razor edges, like the backs of basilisk lizards, into the sky, while others curved inward as they fell, forming concave scallops, and landed in loose piles of their own droppings. Towering columns of soft rock narrowed to spikes at the top and then widened out suddenly to support boulders the size of Buicks, balanced four hundred feet above the ground.

The painters helped bring the tourists. Bulgarians in Sofia saw the oils and the sketches and asked, "Where is this, somewhere in Somali?" Still more fancied they saw a resemblance to Egypt, and in a short time people were referring to the wind-carved mounds as the "pyramids of Melnik." Bulgarians from outside Macedonia gradually realized that a trick of geology and climate had produced a landscape in their southwest worthy of Hieronymus Bosch.

Eye-opening landscapes were nothing until mass tourism was invented to appreciate them. Centuries earlier, perhaps, people stopped and drew in their breath when they first came upon the foot of Melnik's valley—but to base a local economy on the beauty of its surroundings was an idea that had to wait for the internal combustion engine. The Turks, Greeks, Bulgarians, Serbs, and Jews of 1600 lived in Melnik because its market thrived, and its market thrived because those breathtaking walls of sand kept out thieves and hostile armies. Melnik's market in 1980 was virtually nonexistent—but more people passed through the town in two weeks in summer than had lived in the bustling market city of the seventeenth century. The walls repulsed no one—but they attracted tourists like Niagara Falls.

I first read of Melnik in my hotel room in Pazardzhik, when a paragraph in *Nagel's* caught my eye: "*Melnik* (368 inhabitants in 1963) will no doubt soon be a museum town visited only by tourists. In the magnificent setting of its hills of sand, carved by wind and rain into fantastic shapes, the town already attracts large numbers of visitors." In an overpopulated world, where cities and towns spread beyond their boundaries inexorably, like shock waves rippling out from an epicenter, the knack for depopulation appealed to me. I had encountered it before, in central Corsica, and I had loved it: the abandoned farm buildings, the empty vistas of newly encroaching maquis, broken by collapsing stone walls, the barely discernible terraces on the hillsides sighing back into slopes. Few have found it hard to see in tourism a certain vulturism, and the irony of Melnik's situation was too self-evident not to be delightful. Robust tourist statistics and an enervated village—the tourist as vampire. Because even while they put Melnik back on the map, the tourists probably helped to ossify it. The picturesqueness of museum towns tends to solidify into a lifeless gloss. Visitors from all over the world came to look around for an hour or so, bought lunch, perhaps, at a tavern in the village, and then moved on. They left money that went only to build tourist services, that thickened the polish on the town. Melnik, to the tourists, was a ghost town with a fine view. And the tourists, to the Melnikans, were phantoms, perhaps, gliding through with noise and cameras and vanishing as soon as the sun dropped behind the southern wall.

Melnik was on my way to Greece, and I decided to visit it.

The pages I had with me came from a 1968 edition of *Nagel's*—I wondered if Melnik had already died.

·

I stayed in Melnik for several days. I had had to hurry to get there, but the mountains were behind me and the danger of snow was largely past. I was ready to relax a little, in this dry southwest corner of the country, to acquaint myself with a locality—to try to meet and talk to some people. I had not really conversed with anyone, I realized, since that night with Yordan, in the bar-and-grill across from the Troyanski Monastery.

The traveler develops a talent for establishing a routine quickly, and for feeling, almost immediately, as if he has followed it for a long time. Otherwise, the homesickness becomes unbearable. I pegged down my routine in Melnik within a few hours of arriving there. It intensified my feeling of having stopped in a safe harbor, where weather and time no longer threatened me.

For three leva a night, I could not expect heat from the hostel, and I did not get it. By dawn, the empty room would be frigid. I slept by the window with the shutters open, so that the first shifts to lighter blue would waken me, and I dressed myself in the half-light with stiff fingers. Only one place in the village was open so early—a small café on the edge of the dry streambed that split the town neatly in two. I would run down the rough stone path, through the back yard of one house, across the dead garden of another, past Konstantin's, across the dry bed of a diminutive tributary, down a few crude stairs, past the white portico of the combination town hall–school, and into a depression below path level, where the door was a green wooden rectangle with the word KAFÉ stenciled above it in Cyrillic. Magda, the middle-aged proprietess, would have the dark, low room well heated by 7:00. From then until the sun cleared the southern rim of the valley, I would sit and write. There was rarely anyone to talk to. Men came in for five minutes at a stretch and drank their coffee standing up. Women appeared now and then, but they clustered around the counter, around Magda, and it would not have been proper, in any case, for me to converse for long with the women, even if they did speak something other than Bulgarian or Macedonian—which they didn't.

Magda's coffee was dreadful, but she also sold decent hot cider and an assortment of candies that she displayed on her counter in the same dark cardboard boxes in which she received them from some incompetent candy factory in the north. No Bulgarian specialties here—just cheap, sweet chewiness, produced by the ton. I eventually tried them all.

Fortunately, Magda didn't mind if I ate other people's food in her café, so at eight o'clock I would brave the freezing, dingy air and arrive at the door of the bread depot, thirty yards upstream, just as it opened. The depot was run by an elderly couple, who kept yoghurt and butter in crates at the back of the room, away from their inadequate stove by the counter. Every morning the woman would say the same thing to me, laughing and bobbing her head, *"Ehhy . . . ehhy . . . e studeno?"* and I would say, *"Da! Studeno!"* and we would chuckle pointlessly while the woman brought a loaf, a jar of yoghurt, and a lump of butter to the counter. The old man never moved—he leaned against the counter and let the stove toast his backside, nodded to me politely, and equably regarded his wife at work. I would return the empty yoghurt jar from the day before, which I had tried, and failed, to clean properly in the icy water at the hostel, and the woman would regard its streaks bemusedly as she placed it below the counter, too polite and perhaps too understanding to say the Bulgarian equivalent of "Whaddya mean, returning the jar in this condition?"

The bread, at 8:00, was very warm—a pale, damp, doughy football of heat—and I would put it under my shirt and make an end run with it back to the café. Against my skin, in that sunless morning valley, the heat of the bread was luxurious. The bread would steam on the table in the café like a boiled sponge. With melted butter, and that marvelous *bacillus Bulgaricus* yoghurt, it made a satisfying breakfast.

At 10:00, a plate of sunlight two centimeters thick would insert itself between the top of the southern rim and the top of the café windows. It would seem to hesitate, as if teetering over an edge, then tilt and slide gracefully into the valley. I would put my work away. By the time I went out Magda's door, the air was already warmed by the glare from the whitewashed walls, and the vegetable traceries of frost drew in their branches and disappeared from the rocks and tough matted grasses. I noted, with malicious satisfaction, that the Balkanturist hotel, on the south slope, would not receive the sun on its flat head until well past noon.

I bought food from two stores that stood at the mouth of the valley—the only two in town except for the boarded-up, poison-green vegetable stand on the other side of the road. Both stores were tiny, both run by heavy, middle-aged women. The woman on the left offered the white salty cheese that I had been eating for weeks now, but none of the yellow cheese—*kashkaval*—which I liked better. Sometimes she would be selling greasy little sausages. Jugs of the heavy Melnik wine lined her floorboards. The woman on the right sold rice from the Maritsa valley, pasta, and fruits and vegetables, meaning apples, onions, and—sometimes—carrots. I would buy apples and carrots and cheese, pack a lunch, put it with my flute in the knapsack, and head up the valley. Beyond the last houses, where the sand walls became more precipitous, there was no place to walk except in the streambed. A few poplars and small firs sprung from the rocky soil, but mainly a thorny scrub grew. Several caverns had been cut into the sandstone, and I could see inside, past the locked iron gates, huge casks of wine, and massive tables and chairs, constructed out of cut logs. A new wine cavern was being cut into the left bank, and fronting it was a hideous terrace of concrete, molded to imitate flagstone. The terrace had a cartoon fakeness—like something Fred Flintstone might frequent. A coy, curving arch surmounted the entrance terrace, and I could imagine it lit by electric bulbs on a summer night, saying something like TSANKO'S TAVERNA and backed by a wall of amplified Gypsy music. But fortunately the construction was not finished yet, and there were no tourists in November, anyway. None of the caves would open again until April.

The sand walls mounted up three or four hundred feet, squeezing into the valley and falling back again in a series of irregular ridges. It was possible to scale a couple of the ravines in between the ridges, where streams in the spring wore step-like chutes of rock, but the way was not safe. I took that route one morning and reached the top with an inkling that I had been stupid to try it. At the head of the valley, where the walls broke up into wedges and fingers (despite the nickname, they looked nowhere, from any angle, like pyramids), it was easier to find a way up.

The Melnik sandstone was similar in consistency, if not in composition, to the rock of the Badlands in South Dakota, which is to say, rotten. The stone came away in my hands, and dissolved readily into a clatter of pieces the size and general appearance of chick peas. It was easy to see why wind and rain had eaten out the cilia-edged valley in which Melnik was built; it was harder to understand why these incontinent walls had endured. But of course, they would not endure. The process of erosion was continuing at a rapid pace, made more rapid by people like me, who climbed over the rocks and sent showers of chick peas into the poplars and firs a hundred feet below. Within a few centuries, the sides of the valley would have receded so much that Magda's café would first feel the winter sun at half past eight.

I would spend the days up on these hills, wandering from ridge to ridge along sheep paths that crowded each other like corduroy wales, or sitting on the lip of the north wall and watching the few inhabitants of Melnik appear and disappear on the streambed, like ants in a sand colony pressed between panes of glass. Or I would just lie on the outcroppings of harder rock that poked occasionally through the grass and that would, in five hundred years or so, stand alone, like the Buicks on the spikes beyond the head of the valley, and I would soak up the sun and the heat from the rock, which by now would be as luxurious as the warm bread in the morning had been. To the south, an inviting path led into woods of fir and pine, but a sign said, in three languages, that this was the beginning of the border zone and that I was likely to be shot if I succumbed to the temptations of an arboreal stroll.

I would return to Melnik as the sun began to tan, and sunlight would already have fled from the valley by the time I entered it.

Eggs appeared in the cheese store by 4:00 p.m., and I would buy a few to take up to the hostel. The couple who ran the hostel were always there when I returned, and I would knock on their door, along the right side of the bare front hall.

The man was much older than the woman, with a hairy, frowning face—unyielding brows and a pugnacious snub nose. The woman appeared to be in her early twenties, and was cheerful, with long hair, an oval open face, and delightful gray-blue eyes. Their room was tiny, about a hundred square feet, with a four-poster, a combination desk and dining table, an iron stove, and a television crammed into it. I would pay for the night while my eyes drifted, uncontrollably, to the woman—she dressed like an American, casually, in jeans and sweaters. She looked bright and hopeful. The television was always on. I wondered where they had room to sit while eating.

I would boil the eggs in the dormitory and write letters, until the evening chill became too much to bear. Then I would escape to Konstantin's for dinner. There were two or three other places to eat in Melnik, even during the off season, but I never saw anyone in them. Konstantin's seemed to be the place where the villagers went. I had found it by accident: the windowless, yard-thick stone walls—they were the foundation of a nineteenth-century merchant's home—absorbed the music and conversation so well that even when the tavern was full, and the noise inside close to deafening, only a murmur escaped beneath the thick oak door.

The waitress, a rangy blond named Anna, kept a large fire going in a hearth of boulders with a coppery flue, and I would sit near it until I was warm, then yield my place to someone else who had recently come in. Every night, the same band played: three village residents who performed old Bulgarian folksongs with microphones and electric guitars. They dressed in short rust jackets with lapels cut at strange angles that were intended to look hip and instead looked like marching-band uniforms. Their music was terrible—really horrendous—but everyone knew them and was, I think, glad to have them up there, by the door into the kitchen, twanging through the old songs. Occasionally Konstantin, a rather fat, powerful, heavy-boned man, would stand at the door to the kitchen, with his arms crossed, and listen to them with slitted eyes, smiling faintly.

At Konstantin's, as elsewhere, the language barrier proved almost impenetrable. Only the band's lead singer, Dimcho, could speak a foreign language—a stumbling, telegraphic form of English. Sometimes, during the band breaks, I would talk with him, but it was difficult to move over the treacherous terrain that his English laid before me. And in any case, he was a shy, nervous man and not usually in the mood to talk. So more often I would drink the stultifying wine, eat one of the three dinner plates that Konstantin offered, and write. Eventually the wine and the warmth would overtake me, and I would doze. Unlike the lobbies of Balkanturist hotels, Konstantin's looked benevolently on sleepers. Several of the regulars would drop off every night, and it was pleasant to contemplate their slumped forms, feet stuck out in the aisle, breathing quietly. It made the tavern feel like home.

As for myself, I never slept for long before being wakened by the band launching into another ghastly rendition. Once I woke while Anna was clearing my table. I kept my head down—I was still only half conscious—and I could see her hands sliding away the plates and utensils carefully, as delicately as if she were lifting soap bubbles. She was trying not to disturb me, and her kindness went to my heart. It had been so long since anyone had cared whether I slept or not.

Another time, the power went out (a frequent occurrence in Bulgaria). Perhaps because I was a foreigner, or perhaps because she knew that I wrote each evening at my table, Anna brought the first candle from the kitchen to me. The same odd feeling of intense gratitude came over me—I was beginning to realize how vulnerable I had grown during these months of solitude, how emotionally defenseless.

Every night at quarter past ten, the band packed up and Anna stopped putting wood on the fire. People would begin to drift out, while the door, opening and closing, let in cold air. Konstantin would come out of the kitchen at 10:25 and hang his apron on a hook next to the door.

The stars, by then, were an armful of brilliant, powdered ice and the air bitter. The trees, absolutely still, groaned as they cooled. Numb as I was, I would linger on the path at a point where I could see the yellow lights of the town and the misty arch of the Milky Way. The sounds of the two or three houses nearby would drift to me, through closed shutters around which splinters of light shone: kitchen noises—running water, plates knocking—tired voices of children, a snippet of excitement that could have come only from a television set. Dimcho had told me that 350 people lived in Melnik—a mere eighteen fewer than in 1963. And I had seen a good number of children during the daytime sliding down the banisters of the school porch, kicking sand at each other in the streambed, playing and fighting in the ruins of the Byzantine House that straddled a spur of rock over the town. So the town did renew itself, on into the future. *Nagel's*, so far, was wrong.

Yet it was hard for me to believe that there were even as many people as Dimcho had said. Where were they all? I counted no more than threescore houses, and many of them appeared to be summer houses, showing no life or light. Even the houses that *were* inhabited seemed just barely so. Exactly as Melnik huddled in one corner of an area that once held thousands of people, so the Melnikans seemed to live in the corners of their houses—most of the shutters of every house never opened, even when the sun was high and strong. From 20,000 people, from the capital of the Turkish district, down to this: a few yellow lights and a murmuring in the darkness. Melnik did not spin much of a web to hold off oblivion, or to keep back the walls of sand that seemed, when the night was coldest and the stars outnumbered the villagers twenty to one, to be on the verge of collapsing inward, of flowing together like two hands clapping, to bury the town under the sand of a million hourglasses.

At last I would return to the hostel. Sometimes, as I passed through the hall to the dormitory, I would hear from behind the right-hand door the sound of violent lovemaking. I wondered, as I slipped into bed, what life could be like for that woman, what it was like to live in a shrinking shell when you were young and bright. With her long brown hair and frank, smiling eyes, she looked like a Radcliffe student of the seventies, like a Cantabrigian. How did she fill her days, here, among empty houses? How could she be happy? I would fall asleep with questions and doubts still in my mind—the urban creature's amazement at rural life.

.

I arrived at Konstantin's one night to find Anna sweeping the floor furiously and the three band members, already wearing their Sergeant Peppery uniforms, dusting the shelves in the bar. Someone had put thick red candles in bowls around the room. Two tables near the fire had been pushed together and covered with a handsome red cloth. The fire was high, and a large stack of wood next to it promised to keep it that way.

I asked Dimcho what was going on. He stood up, with a green rag in his hand, shaking dust from his ruffled shirt front.

"Big tonight. Big big. Polsk—Polsk MinisterofTourism. He come here."

"Really! Why is he coming here?"

Dimcho shrugged. "Here good. He visit Melnik. Big visit. He go round Bulgaria. He learn tourist stuff. He tell Polsks. Polsks learn tourist stuff."

"The Polish Minister of Tourism is in Bulgaria to get ideas for tourist development in Poland?"

"Da, da."

Egad. Balkanturist was probably organizing his trip. Poor guy. "And he saw Melnik today?"

"Da. Now eat here Polsk. Polsk eat Konstantin."

"Why isn't he eating at the Balkanturist hotel?"

Dimcho snorted. "Why? Konstantin best in Melnik! Who eat Big Hotel?!" Dimcho never called it anything but Big Hotel—a reasonable name, since the hotel's size was the first thing that anyone would notice. "Big Hotel new—not Melnik. He want eat Melnik. He eat here nine."

"Am I allowed to stay while he eats here?"

Dimcho looked surprised. "Oh, da, da! By nature. Noproblem."

This was a stroke of luck. I had been interested in the relationship between Melnik and its tourist trade, and now I would be able to see a little tourism in action: Melnik putting on its best face for a representative of the hordes.

Most of the tables were still empty this early in the evening. I sat in my usual place. (There were seats closer to the table of honor, but it was better not to switch: most of the customers had their regular tables, and I would have risked looking up in the middle of my meal at the hurt expression of a displaced Melnikan.) Anna interrupted her sweeping for a few seconds to fetch me a carafe of wine, although I hadn't asked. For this special night she had on a clean white dress, with traditional Bulgarian folk designs on the bodice, and a rose in her hair. Konstantin appeared from time to time in the kitchen doorway, and he was in his finest, too. He'd even shaved.

Shortly before 9:00, with the tavern half full, Dimcho and his two cohorts plugged in their guitars and started fiddling with the amplifier. They usually did this earlier and started playing by 8:00, but tonight they were saving their voices for the Guest. Dimcho dealt with the electrical equipment as if it had been designed for creatures vastly more intelligent and dextrous than himself. He twiddled knobs with an expression that said, "Well, I wonder what *this* will do." He reminded me of times back in high school, when there was always one kid who, for some obscure reason, was thought by the teachers to know how to run the audio-visual equipment and who was unfailingly incompetent at it. Dimcho's feedback threatened at times to drone us right out of the tavern. The Melnikans grimaced and smiled. I think they looked on the noise as an inseparable part of the equipment setup. At last Dimcho had the arrangement he wanted. He stopped bothering the equipment and settled, with the guitarists, into a cluster in the vicinity of the kitchen door, whence he occasionally looked out, nervously, toward the front door. Tonight was a big night for him.

Meanwhile, Anna was stocking the big table by the fire. She brought out several carafes of purple Melnik wine. Then a bottle of Bulgaria's best grape brandy, Euxinograde *grozdova*. Baskets of bread. A bottle of *Troyanski slivova*. Butter on petite disks of copper. Then a surprise: dishes of hazelnuts, Brazil nuts, and almonds.

Then a bigger surprise: wedges of three or four different kinds of cheese on a wooden platter. And finally, a shock: an enormous bowl of oranges, grapes, peaches, pomegranates, and bananas. Every eye in the room followed the fruit bowl to its place at the center of the table.

The reaction may sound exaggerated, but neither I nor, doubtless, anyone else in Konstantin's that night had seen anything more exotic than a shriveled grape since the harvest at the end of October. Peaches had disappeared in September, pomegranates and oranges were not native to Bulgaria and were rarely seen even in the summer, and bananas—well, bananas were unheard of. The last time I had seen a banana was in Budapest, which is far and away the best supplied city in the East Bloc—and the line for those bananas, which had appeared one day without warning, at a couple of booths in the makeshift market on Fehérvari Street, had stretched for a block.

The two little stores in Melnik were indicative of what people ate in the winter in small Bulgarian towns—apples, carrots, and onions. Occasionally pears. One kind of cheese. This was not, as in Romania, a case of a food shortage or of mismanagement—it was an understandable lack of variety in an area where the roads were difficult and there were not enough people to justify carting in a lot of different foods from other places. I had bicycled the road to Melnik and knew that it was a tortuous route for a supply truck. Melnik ate what Melnik made, and the town had plenty of whatever it did have. The choices in winter were naturally few. And now, in Konstantin's, there were *four* different kinds of cheese on the same table, and fruit that pulsated in the firelight like a mirage of summer. My shock, I think, was as great as the Melnikans'.

Shortly past 9:00, Anna ran to the door, and suddenly eight men were standing there. Everyone turned to look.

The men were all about the same height and weight, and were dressed in identical homburgs and straight-cut, knee-length overcoats—the Politburo uniform. They moved portentously, like a council of ancients in a Wagner opera. Konstantin came forward in a suspiciously clean apron and shook their hands, ducking his head, while Anna struggled with the heavy coats. Dimcho trotted past me and shook a couple of hands also, which prompted a look of surprise from Konstantin. Some introductions were made. I could feel the excitement of the other people in the room. Melnik did not often have such important visitors.

Konstantin ushered the eight men to their table, and they sat down. They were all rather large, although not as large as Konstantin, and in late middle age. All the other customers were watching, waiting for something. The eight men looked around at the cozy, spelean room, and smiled. Everybody smiled back. Then Anna took up the bottle of *slivova* and poured generous portions into the eight glasses. The men toasted one another. They started to eat the nuts. Konstantin bowed and scraped his way back into the kitchen, and Dimcho picked up his microphone, signaling enthusiastically to the two guitarists. The other Melnikans, released from their welcome, turned back to their own conversations. But everybody kept an eye on the center table.

Anna came out of the kitchen with bowls of *tarator*, a cucumber and yoghurt soup. Normally, there were only three dishes you could buy at Konstantin's, and they were similar: *kebabches*, lamb kebab, or lumps of meat like oniony hamburgers. All three came with the same accompaniment: french fries and a pickled mixture of cabbage and peppers. If you really felt like being fancy, you could order the combination plate, which consisted of one *kebabche*, one meat lump, and a small kebab, also accompanied by french fries and pickled cabbage and peppers. If you felt like being fancier than that, you had to go somewhere else—probably Balkanturist. Maybe to another town.

But the bananas had been a signal that unusual things were to be expected tonight, so Anna's entrance with the *tarator* was greeted not with surprise but with an aah of recognition. *Gyuvech*, a complicated vegetable dish served in earthenware bowls, followed the *tarator* and hardly elicited a comment. By the time the steaks and *kebabches* and kidney-bean stews came out, no one was paying much attention.

Except to the fruit. *Gyuvech* and *tarator* could be made with frozen vegetables, and dried kidney beans lasted all winter. One could not usually get these things at Konstantin's, but one could make them at home. The fresh fruit, however, was a mystery. It smacked of important connections, which made it intriguing. And, of course, everyone wanted some for themselves.

During one of his breaks, Dimcho sat with me for a couple of minutes. He was excited. "They happy, right?"

"They certainly look happy."

I was being polite. Actually, the guests looked unimpressed. I had the feeling that they ate this well or better, every day.

"Only two Polsks. Sex Bulgarsks."

"Who are the Bulgarsks?"

"That one, and that one, and—"

"No, I mean, what are their names, or their positions? How important are they?"

Dimcho shrugged. "Bigguys. From Sofia. I don't know." A pause. "Fatguy is Polsk MinisterofTourism."

"*Which* fat guy?"

"Him." He pointed. "With—uh, with—what that called?"

"That's a banana."

"*Da.* Him fatguy with barana."

Speaking of bananas, they were disappearing faster than anything else. Some of them lay on the table, half eaten.

"Dimcho, where did this fruit come from? Has Konstantin been saving it somewhere?"

"No. Konstantin? No. I don't know. Konstantin no have baranas."

"You helped set up, right?"

"*Da.*"

"Tell me"—I tried to keep the urgency out of my voice—"is there any more fruit in the kitchen? Or is that all of it?"

Dimcho shot me an understanding glance. He nodded his head sadly. "That all, I think." He grabbed a french fry and popped it in his mouth. "No stuff in kitchen."

By 10:30 the eight fatguys were mostly done. A couple of them still picked at the fruit and nuts. The bowls were nearly empty, but bananas and oranges that had hardly been touched were still scattered between the plates. A dense haze of cigarette smoke hung in the air. One of the fatguys was asleep. The rest slumped back in their chairs and talked on, slowly and dreamily, while they knocked back raspberry liqueur.

The sounds of Konstantin cleaning came from the kitchen door. Most of the Melnikans had gone home. Dimcho sidled to the end of a song on a last quavering moan, while his lead guitarist aimed for a note far down on the neck and missed. Dimcho put down his microphone. But then the guests made a mistake: since they thought he was done for the night, they applauded. The Poles nodded their heads and the Bulgarians shook theirs in formal approval. The Melnikans had never applauded Dimcho, since they heard him every night (and probably for more immediate reasons), and he wasn't accustomed to it. With an expression of pleasure, he turned around and picked up the microphone again for one last number. The eyes of the guests clouded over.

Dimcho's final song was a beaut, one of the most aimless and monotonous in his repertoire. He sang it leaning forward on his toes, with his eyes bugging straight out in front of him, fixed on some musical landscape far away that none of the rest of us could either see or comprehend. The guests sat through it in abstracted silence. I thought: Listen, listen. Pay no attention to the fruit and the cheese. Dimcho is Konstantin's. At the end, the men did not repeat their mistake. But they were polite: they clapped once or twice, not too perfunctorily, and then stood up.

They shook Dimcho's hand, which he acknowledged with a delighted smile. They woke up their sleeping partner. Anna went to fetch their coats and hats. Konstantin stepped out to wish them good night, and they thanked him, with the air, somewhat, of giving old clothes to a servant. They were sluggish with satiety as they filed out in their straight, stiff coats, a row of pillars of the Soviet system. A rush of cold air came in from outside, and they were gone.

The latch came down on the door and Dimcho reached the guests' littered table at about the same moment. He had forgotten, this time, to put down his microphone, and he almost yanked the wire out of the amplifier as he sat down. The two guitar players struggled out of their straps and followed him. Konstantin hurried into the kitchen and returned with a new carafe of wine, which he placed in the middle of the table. He and Anna sat down as well. I realized, suddenly, that I was the only other person in the room. It was past 10:30, and Konstantin's was officially closed. I put Ibsen away and got up to go.

But Dimcho called to me: "Brian, you go? No go! Come, come! Eat!" He beckoned me to the table, holding half a banana in his hand.

Of course, I wanted to. But— "Is it all right? Konstantin doesn't mind?"

"What? No, no!" He nodded his head vigorously.

So I sat. Konstantin poured me a glass of wine, while Anna handed me a peach with a bite taken out of it. The two guitarists were divvying up a pomegranate. Konstantin had another orange and a cluster of grapes, which he shared with the rest of us. Dimcho held the only banana, and he seemed reluctant to let anyone else taste it. But there were enough nuts for everybody.

As I look back now, that evening seems strange. It's slightly unappetizing to think of the six of us working through the remains of that meal, like scavengers; especially after those self-satisfied, porcine guests! Yet I can remember my senstions then very clearly, and they had nothing to do with squeamishness. The Polish Minister of Tourism could not possibly have enjoyed his seven-course meal as intensely as I enjoyed the crumbs that he left behind him.

Was every spring in poor, starved Melnik this explosion of tastes? If so, then it seemed the long and empty winters were worthwhile. Melnik had known tremendous ups and downs in its history, and it still knew ups and downs every year, with the round of the seasons. The Melnikans seemed to take it all in stride, the way they accepted the feedback from Dimcho's amplifier. They seemed conscious only of the pleasure of being allowed a little piece of summer in November—as if they had stumbled upon a daffodil growing in a block of ice.

Soon it was time to go. The six of us cleared the table and helped Konstantin rearrange the room. Dimcho dropped handfuls of nuts into my pockets. Outside, by the door, he said again, "Polsks happy, right?"

"Yes, they looked *very* happy. They enjoyed the music, too."

Dimcho expanded before my eyes. "Oh yes? Yes?" He clapped his hands. "They do. You hear?"

"Yes, I heard."

A delighted smile spread over his face. He applauded himself again. "They do. They happy. Konstantin best place. Melnik best place!"

We shook hands and parted ways at the streambed.

I had come to Melnik wondering if I would find a dead village, if Melnik would be like Italy's San Gimignano, where the tourist bite had infected the civic blood so thoroughly that the town endured only to please—and to profit. San Gimignano was a slick and cynical place, where the tourists were continually—and not altogether politely—being reminded of their duty to spend money. You could find eight high-priced gelati stores on any given street, but God help you if you wanted to buy a loaf of bread. And since San Gimignano was so small, it seemed that there was no village life beneath the cosmopolitan, crafty tourist trade.

Melnik had its outward similarities to San Gimignano—it had those slick wine caves farther up the valley, and it had Balkanturist perched on its shoulder. But Melnik also had a spirit, a life, of its own. Men came into Magda's each morning with a thick rime of dirt on their boots, and I would see them later, shoring up some of the vineyard terraces on the slopes of the next valley, or digging a new drainage trench along the streambed above the town. At night Konstantin's would fill, the noise would grow deafening, and three or four people would fall asleep with their feet stuck out in the aisle. The village did not wither in the off season; it took its winters like a peasant town, with just a couple of vegetables and plenty of evenings together around a big fire. And it treated me with the respectful curiosity of a hamlet that saw strangers no more than twice a year.

Even the Balkanturist hotel failed to touch the town; because of its ridiculous size, it looked less like part of Melnik than like an apparition from another dimension. It was significant that the first man I met in Melnik directed me *away* from the Balkanturist hotel, and that the villagers did not crowd the Balkanturist restaurant at night, as they had done in Ruse, Pazardzhik, and Velingrad. The Melnikans collected in their own tavern and listened to a Melnik band. And so, when the Polish Minister of Tourism came to visit, he ate at Konstantin's.

.

I left Bulgaria on the following day under a cloudless sky. Between Melnik and the border I did not see a soul.

At some point during my stay in Melnik, Leonid Brezhnev had died in Moscow. I would have been interested to gauge the Bulgarian reaction to the news, since I had managed to learn so little about the people's real attitude toward the Soviets. But I didn't even learn of Brezhnev's death until I arrived in Greece. I took a room above a café in Sérrai, and the owner of the café told me. He was surprised that I didn't know.

The café owner and I sat at a table near the television set and drank retsina. He had spent some time, years ago, running a souvlaki place in Chicago, so he had no trouble translating the follow-up stories for me. When he found out I was from Massachusetts, he informed me that Michael Dukakis had regained the governorship of that state just a couple of days before. Of course, I hadn't heard about this in the Bloc. The Greeks were happy about the election because Dukakis had Greek ancestry. The café owner and I drank a toast to the political demise of former governor Edward King, and we began to talk more of Massachusetts than of the mysterious workings of the Kremlin.

The close, comfortable world of the West had reclaimed me.

HUNGARY

NOTES FROM BUDAPEST

February–March 1983 / January–March 1984

The café was a long, glass-fronted business with an impressive array
of fancy cakes lined up in the show windows. I had already stopped
once, to admire the cakes—many of them carved into complicated
replicas of houses, boats, trees, even whole village scenes, cleverly
done up with colored sugar frosting, chocolate squares, Life Savers,
grapes, and orange sections, and so on. At the time, there was a
score of other loafers and shoppers peering into the windows and
exclaiming with satisfaction at the ingenuity of the bakers. There
were, however, no prices on the cakes, and no one seemed to be
buying them. I had the feeling that it was a special occasion; perhaps
the cakes were the result of a contest. It was unfortunate, though,
that no one could or would buy them, because the little cakes offered
inside the café with the muddy horrible coffee were ugly and
unappetizing.

Eeeyouuch. I squeeze out a few more lines and then stop,
defeated by the stretch of blank page. I flip through what I've
written and experience that familiar sinking feeling: *some of this
ain't so hot.*

One p.m. Time to quit. Light pours through the windows
from a white February sky, and the parquet floor glows with it,
the white walls holding it between them like plates balancing an
electric charge. But the room is chilly. I should start a fire for
Zsóka.

Árpád begins to bang on his piano as I come out onto the landing. Another good reason to quit—I can't concentrate with that noise.

Down the stairs. In the light from the open back door, the hallway looks sadly dilapidated—the marble steps are cracked in dozens of places; the walls need cleaning and, here and there, new plaster; the gas, electric, and water meters, sprouting next to Árpád's door like gray fungus, threaten to fall clear out of the wall. It's hard to believe that this was a private home once, that this piss-colored hall was hung with pictures, or that red carpeting under brass rods once covered the marble stairs. Now it could only be what it is: a beat-up quadruplex, squeezed between the weedy slope of Castle Hill and a filthy six-story apartment house that was thrown up fifty years ago and should have been condemned forty years ago.

To the ground floor. One of the drunken woman's cats gives a shriek and bolts through the animal door, leaving it to TOK-*tok*-tok into silence. There is a wood cellar here, on the left. The light has been out for months. I take the basket into the darkness and feel my way over a scattering of logs to the pile, reach high to pull pieces off the top, trying not to bring the whole damn thing down on top of myself. I fill the basket and haul it up to the landing, between Árpád's and Zsóka's doors. The wood goes under a dirty marble slab, once a table for calling cards, fastened to the floor and therefore never looted during the wars and rebellions, now scarred and chipped, a convenient cover for the wood in case the roof leaks.

Down to the cellar, up with wood—nine, ten times. I work quickly, taking the steps two at a time. A morning of writing always slows my blood; I have to quicken it forcibly or I will doze through the afternoon on the couch with a book (my excuse, for the first fifteen minutes) wedged between my face and the armrest. And there's another reason to hurry: I don't want István, who works odd hours and is often home afternoons, to find me in the hallway. István and Éva live at the top of the stairs; Éva and Zsóka are sisters. István and Éva have three young daughters, money problems, and hardly enough room to move in their two-room garret apartment. I am supposed to be helping István learn English for his engineering exam, but I have been avoiding the task because István—an intense, introverted man who (for obscure reasons) has never been accepted by Éva and Zsóka's family—always gives me the impression he's about to spill his guts to me. It's the Nick Carraway syndrome: István's intimate revelations quiver on the horizon, and I don't want to hear them. I am afraid he will talk about his in-laws' rejection of him.

Back in the apartment, I build a fire in the great brick stove that dominates a corner of the bedroom. I have let the bricks get cold, which Mrs. Nagy tells me I'm not supposed to do, and it will be a couple of hours before they're warm again.

As I am bent over the hole, poking around recalcitrant sticks and wads of newspaper, a key turns in the front door. Zsóka is home already, and I meet her in the front hall as she comes in from the landing. She takes off her hat and gloves, her mouth twitching toward a smile, and I can see words turning in her gray eyes. She has news. What would release her from her editing job so early?

"You're home," I say, waiting for the words.

"Oh . . ." She stands on tiptoe and puts her hat and gloves on the high shelf, folds her coat around a hanger. "You haven't heard? Guess what's come out. Just now."

"I can't guess. What?"

The corners of her mouth curl up and over like an ocean wave, making a mischievous smile: "Yuri Andropov is dead." Two beats. Then a tired shrug, and a laugh like the scurrying of a small animal. "Can you believe it?!"

•

Zsóka and I have been invited to a costume party for Fasching at her friend Aniko's apartment in Pest. Zsóka wants us to do something clever, but we haven't enough material for that, not to mention the imagination. We keep saying we'll figure it out later, but the intervening days are gone, the party is tonight, and we have settled on nothing. We are at the point of going in our street clothes and earning the disapprobation of everyone there.

But at the last minute Zsóka digs through the closet and comes up with two Iraqi smocks, given to her by an engineering friend who worked there before the war. We don handfuls of heavy jewelry (with which Zsóka, fortunately, is well supplied), wrap towels around our heads, and we are Berbers. Or something like that. We burst out of the back door into the garden and run down the steep stairs, through the hall of the filthy apartment house, then down Hunyadi János Street, two shafts of color and a jangling of metal in the dark. Eliciting stares, we catch the #4 bus, packed as always, at Clark Ádám Square (Adam Clark, an English architect, built Budapest's beloved Chain Bridge: in Hungarian usage, surnames precede given names). The bus ride across the Chain Bridge to Pest and toward the Great Boulevard is the usual rough-and-tumble affair, the driver taking the corners with maniacal disregard of the laws of physics. In this chivalrous city, I have learned to ride the buses standing, so that the women will not wonder out loud, eyeing me balefully, why I do not get up for them; and I always stand in the back, facing backwards: the wild buckings of the vehicle are the most pronounced there and I have to hold on to the pole by the ticket machine for dear life, but there, at least, I am blessedly unable to see what the driver is doing. For I have been a bus driver myself, and it terrifies me the way the Budapest drivers fling their buses into traffic, through intersections, or into crowded bus stops. A waiting person who lost her footing would surely be killed; a Trabant puttering blithely across our path would be flattened as easily as a Sucrets box.

So through the rear window, Zsóka and I watch Roosevelt Square disappear, then József Attila and Népköztársaság (People's Republic) Avenues roll out from under us, past the lights of cafés and sweet shops, neon *szendvics* (pronounced "sandvitch") signs, late-night clothing stores and barber shops. The city is no different tonight. All the cafés are open, music penetrates the doors of the bus, and the sidewalks are filled with people; as we roar into November 7 Square, backward, I catch sight of an overcoated crowd heading for the Music Academy.

"The concerts haven't been canceled," I say.

Zsóka shrugs. "He wasn't around very long."

But when we get off at Szinyei Merse Street, we spot a black flag set in a bracket on the corner building. "Perhaps that will be all," Zsóka says hopefully, and we walk up the street, making metallic noises, between dirty Habsburg-style buildings embossed to look like constructions of massive stone blocks. There are no streetlights. Whole blocks here haven't been fixed since the war, and entire façades are falling off. Creosoted tree trunks hold up balconies.

Through a large doorway, into a filthy entrance—rusted broken mailboxes, smashed floor tiles—past the courtyard and up the exterior stairs from balcony to balcony, which run around the courtyard like scaffolding that someone has forgotten to dismantle. Third floor, left, toward the bang of rock music.

Aniko answers the door. She is wearing street clothes, holding a drink, and she laughs at the sight of two Berbers on her threshold. "Goodness, Zsóka, did I tell you it was a costume party? I'd forgotten! I changed my mind after I called you. No one else is in costume!"

Zsóka pales. Aniko laughs again. "You two look so funny!" Then she tries to make amends. "But really, you look very good, both of you. Better than anyone else here!"

Too late. Zsóka is angry. In the kitchen, while Aniko goes to tell the others that two Berbers have arrived, she asks, "Shall we go?" in the slow cadence that anger lends her voice. A burst of laughter comes through the door.

"No," I say. "Why don't we get drunk? I think Aniko is drunk already. She just forgot."

Zsóka shakes her head. "No. I don't understand why she did this."

So the evening begins badly. But Zsóka's embarrassment wanes after her first glass of cognac. She begins to notice what I, being less modest, saw immediately—namely, that Aniko was right: we *are* the best-looking couple at the party.

Aniko and her husband, Jenő, love to have parties, and they throw their money into them. The rock music blasts out of a system occupying almost an entire wall of their small living room. On the tables are bottles of imported Scotch, bourbon, brandy, gin, vermouth, vodka, kahlua, and Hungarian wines; cranberry juice, orange juice, ginger ale, Pepsi (which owns the Russian franchise), lime and lemon wedges. The glasses are crystal. Aniko and Jenő drag everybody out of their chairs to dance. Iraqi smocks, it turns out, are great for dancing, and Zsóka, with her second glass of cognac waiting for her on the mantelpiece, drops the last of her anger and swirls in the semidarkness, the smock billowing out from her slight frame, clapping her hands over her head and pounding her bare feet. Jenő, a fleshy bear, corners people and talks about his passion, basketball. Zsóka pours another cognac and says, "You must promise to get me home." Aniko asks me about my travels since 1983, when I last saw her, and immediately loses interest. A professor in a deep chair tests my Hungarian, and is very polite. Jenő dribbles an imaginary ball and throws hook shots into the fireplace.

It's a university crowd, and much of the conversation, out of deference to me, is in English or German. The biggest topic, even bigger than basketball or rock and roll, is Andropov.

"He died yesterday at four o'clock. They announced it in our office at noon today."

"They announced it in *all* the offices at noon. These things are so orchestrated, so dramatic—why do they insist on making such a formal thing of it, as if the gravitational constant had changed?"

"I imagine it's to forestall rumors—"

"Rumors! Pffft! What do they expect? Panic in the streets? I hardly had the time to learn how to spell his name!"

"The Russians are getting faster with all this practice. It took them five days to announce Stalin's death, and Brezhnev's last year was announced after thirty-six hours. Andropov gets only twenty hours. Do you suppose that is an insult?"

"Yes, just imagine—at this rate, they'll announce the death of the next one *before* he dies. Now, that's really insulting." (Laughter.)

"Well, it's getting ridiculous, don't you think? They're in and out now like economic ministers. Boom, boom. 'Say, who's the leader of Russia?' 'That depends, what day is it?' "

And I: "Won't there be any mourning period? All we saw on the way here was one black flag on a corner."

"Only one day, thank God. Tuesday, I think it is. All the cafés and cinemas will be closed, and no music will be played, but of course we have to go to work. All of the bad and none of the good."

Two simultaneously: "As usual." (Laughter.)

"But we can count our blessings—in Russia, the official mourning is for three days."

"Yes, but he's *their* leader, not ours."

"Something we have to keep reminding ourselves, to be sure."

"My question is, Who turned off the machine?" a chubby man with high black eyebrows and an ingenuous smile asks.

A weary answer: "Chernenko."

I ask, "What machine?"

"The kidney machine," the chubby man replies. "That's the way all the premiers die—Brezhnev, Andropov. They just turn off the machine," and he twists a dial in the air. "They look at the calendar, you see? And they say 'Hmm . . . Today is convenient: the Afghans are quiet, there are no Party congresses—nothing terribly important is happening this week,' and so they turn off the machine." He smiles charmingly and shrugs his shoulders.

"Either that or they have been refrigerating him for weeks," someone else says.

"I think things will get worse now." That is Zsóka.

"But that's what you said when Brezhnev died," I say. "You always say things are going to get worse."

She is a little hurt, and her eyes widen; she gestures dramatically with her cognac. "Well, they always do!"

"The interesting question is who will be next. It may *not* be worse if one of Andropov's men takes over."

"Who do you think it will be?" Someone is asking me, for some reason.

I answer with the sudden, groundless certainty that a bottle and a half of wine bestows: "Chernenko." A couple of nods.

But a thin man with a glum face disagrees. "Chernenko is too old, even for the Kremlin. He is seventy-two."

"Andropov was no spring chicken," I point out. "And Ronald Reagan is seventy-two."

"But Chernenko is senile."

Someone beats me to it: "So is Ronald Reagan."

Zsóka bets the man a bottle of champagne that Chernenko will be next, and he takes her up on it. I wonder if she is risking the price of a bottle just to back me up.

"If it *is* Chernenko, then there may be problems."

"He might not be happy with the way Hungary has been moving lately."

Ever since the Hungarian leader, János Kádár, began to decentralize the economy in 1968, this has been a ubiquitous Hungarian anxiety that seems to grow stronger with each passing year. How far will Moscow allow Hungary to go? Might it suddenly decide that Hungary has gone much too far? And what then?

The conversation goes on, moving into the kitchen, where food is being warmed in the oven: pastry filled with ham and onions, a strong horseradish sauce. On the side table, a tomato, pepper, radishes, and hot dog salad. A few jokes are told, of the disparaging Eastern European kind, none of them very good.

("Here's a riddle: What will Lenin Boulevard be named in ten years?"

"I don't know. What?"

"You don't know?! What's the matter, comrade, don't you have faith in our regime?")

More is said about the machine, and someone goes into a detailed description of the indignities of dialysis. Everyone, I sense, finds it pleasurable to speak in such an offhand manner about the deaths of kings. The Soviet leader is so powerful, it is impossible not to resent and fear him, and one cannot vote against him or print objections to his decisions; one can say he's senile, but one cannot yell it. One can only assert oneself in these weak ways— laughing at him in private when he cuts a poor figure, bandying his name about when, despite all his power, he is snuffed out and leaves his subjects one step closer to inheriting the earth.

The party moves back into the living room for more dancing. A neighbor comes up from below to complain timorously about the noise, and Aniko turns the stereo down marginally. The party is beginning to soar, as parties occasionally do. Both the dancing and the conversation have taken on lives of their own. But then Zsóka becomes sick. She weighs only 100 pounds, and she has drunk four glasses of cognac. She sits at the kitchen table with her eyes rolling, struggling to hold herself up. Jenő offers to help us get back to Hunyadi Street, but my Hungarian is good enough now to do simple things and I tell him not to worry.

I find a cab on Népköztársaság and lead it back to the doorway on Szinyei Merse Street. It is one of the more exotic phenomena of the past year or two: a privately owned taxi (they were made legal around 1981). The name and photograph of the driver adorn the sun visor, the back of the front seat, and the door of the glove compartment. The driver is an excitable man of thirty or so, who speaks a little German. He works during the day as a stonemason and started moonlighting six months ago. The photographs stem not from a regulation but from pride. All the way down Népköztársaság, onto József Attila Avenue (named after a proletarian poet-hero who martyred himself in 1937), around Roosevelt Square (past Budapest's only Chinese restaurant), across the Danube on the unlit Chain Bridge, and up Hunyadi János Street, while Zsóka leans on me, holding her head and apologizing, the cabdriver tells me how great it is to own a cab, to have the privilege of working thirteen hours a day to get a few extra forints. "Things are changing," he says, at the end, as I hand him the money. "Chernenko, Gromyko, Romanov—it doesn't matter who's next. The rules here—what you can earn, what you can have—will get looser no matter what. You know why? Because it works. Hungary has the most decentralized economy in the East Bloc. And Hungary is richer than any of the others. They won't make us change, because we export food to Poland and Romania. They *need* our system."

Optimism like the cabbie's is anathema to Zsóka, who thinks the material advances are trivial. For her, the important issues remain—official lies, restraints on free speech, restrictions on travel, privileges of the Party elite: injustice. And in any case, she is quick to point out, the economy has not been looking good of late. The turnaround was in '81–'82: inflation has been steep for the past three years; production has stagnated, in some cases regressed; the foreign debt is huge. The world recession has hit Hungary pretty hard. The economy, she will argue, may cycle through better and worse times, but politics endure, and the politics are bad.

But tonight, Zsóka is too weak to argue with the cabdriver. She hasn't even been listening to him. I carry her up the stairs, while the taxi takes off in a horrendous cloud of burnt oil and carbon monoxide. Someone has affixed a black flag to the corner of the filthy apartment house.

·

The word the Tennesseean linguist in Ravenna used in connection with Budapest was "jewel." Of all the cities of Europe, Budapest is my favorite: I am perpetually drawn to it; I daydream about it when I am away. But I can't agree that Budapest is a jewel. Salzburg is a jewel. Venice is a jewel. Budapest shines, but it shines like anthracite, like oil. Valuable, but not precious. Enthralling, but not seductive. Budapest shines like sweat.

Over two million people, or more than one-fifth of the total population of Hungary, live in Budapest. Every time there has been a disaster in Hungary—an invasion, a famine, a rebellion— people have left their ravaged villages and sought refuge in Budapest. Since Hungary's history is little more than a succession of disasters, it is only logical that the city should be so large, that it should so completely dominate the country's administrative and cultural life.

Budapest is also, almost incidentally, a gigantic industrial center. Important factories line both banks of the Danube in the northern third of the city, and the truly gargantuan Csepel iron and steel works take up hundreds of acres in the south. Special trains bring armies of workers each morning from the Western Station in Marx Square out to the surrounding factories. Meanwhile, 200,000 commuters drive or ride the Hungarian-made blue buses and yellow trolleys from the Budapest suburbs to their offices in town. Tourists swarm into the city each summer, filling every hotel and hostel bed, every camping slot, within a radius of ten miles. Tourism is one answer to the foreign debt, and the government has bent over backward to provide enough beds: new international hotels (Duna-Intercontinental, Atrium-Hyatt, Forum) have gone up along the Danube Quay, but the summer rooming shortage is still acute. Thousands of tourists find accommodations, through agencies, in private homes; others have no recourse but to leave town. And the newsreels before the movies in Hungarian cinemas say, "Tourism is up! But not enough; not enough."

That Budapest architecturally resembles Vienna is no great surprise: the Habsburgs built much of modern Budapest, particularly central Pest, at the middle and end of the last century. That Budapest is much dirtier than Vienna is even less surprising: the city's hundreds of thousands of little plastic generic cars (not to mention the wildly driven buses) follow no emission standards, and the citizens drive them until they fall apart in the road; tens of thousands of apartments in the city are still heated by wood or coal stoves; the industry that rings the city pollutes with what one can only call enthusiasm; and the government—the biggest landlord—is perpetually too strapped for money to spend it on cleaning anything other than cultural monuments such as the Opera House or the Royal Palace. Black grime covers everything, and the air smells perpetually of nonrenewable resources. A half hour's walk in Pest on a windless day can leave you weak in the knees.

The river defines the city. The Danube was one of the great natural boundaries of antiquity. At this place seventeen centuries ago, the Roman outposts in the Pannonian hills looked uneasily across the Danuvius toward the distant fires of the barbarians who roamed the great eastern plain. In the ninth century came the Magyars (Hungarians), archers and horsemen from the Ural Mountains who shortly owned the plain and terrorized their neighbors, jabbering an Altaic language of guttural sesquipedalians. The Magyars controlled *both* sides of the Danube, the first race in the region to do so, and they began to see their reflections in the river's divisive waters: since they straddled the river, they grew to consider themselves a bridge between East and West, linked to the East by their heritage and their language, linked to the West by their adopted Christianity, their adopted monarchy. As the centuries passed, the Magyars turned increasingly to the West. They were an outpost, they thought, of civilization, defending the old, soft West against the hard, nomadic tribes from which they themselves had sprung. So they set up a special buffer zone in Transylvania, filling that region with Szeklers and Saxons, who would act as frontier guards.

The Magyars' settlement along the Danube (still a boundary, still unbridged) quite naturally took the form of two towns: Buda on the hills on the west bank, Pest on the plain on the east. Buda grew earlier, because its hills protected it, so when Buda and Pest were administratively joined in 1873, twenty-five years after the first bridge across the Danube, the Chain Bridge, had been built, Pest was the junior partner. But the exposed position that had hampered Pest's growth in dangerous times aided it in prosperous ones. When the Habsburgs went on a building spree in the last decades of the nineteenth century, Pest had the space to expand, semicircularly, away from the river. By 1900, Old Pest had become the Inner City, and outside the old ruined city walls, beyond the Nagykörút (the Great Boulevard), stretched a vast area of six- and eight-story buildings, most bearing the Habsburg stamp: massive and meticulous, enclosing square courtyards, facing the streets with heavily embossed façades in neo-this or neo-that.

The Habsburgs were trying, both with the Ring in Vienna and with the Nagykörút in Budapest, to make their dual empire *look* like an empire; to give their two capitals the grandeur and historical weight of Rome or Constantinople. The task was impossible, yet the Habsburgs did surprisingly well, particularly so long as one is unaware of the true chronology of construction, because with knowledge comes a certain disappointment. There can be a feeling of emptiness about Vienna's Ring, in which the Gothic-style Town Hall, the Classical Greek-style Parliament, and the Renaissance-style Opera House are all about the same age. Budapest's façade is even more ambiguous, since the city was demolished in 1945 and heavily damaged in 1956. There are original buildings that pretend to be older than they are—such as the immense neo-Gothic Parliament on the east bank of the Danube. There are modern replicas of buildings destroyed in World War II that once were as old as they pretended to be—such as the houses on Castle Hill. And there are modern replicas of buildings destroyed in World War II that pretended even before the war to be older than they were, such as the Royal Palace. Moreover, at least Vienna enshrines a recognizably Austrian style of imitation. Budapest has few buildings in a Hungarian style, even an imitative one. There has been no Hungarian tradition of urban architecture on which to draw, since most of the Magyar cities from the Middle Ages on were built by the German immigrants who arrived after the Mongol and Turkish invasions. (Three-quarters of Hungary's urban population under Maria Theresa was German-speaking; Zsóka, like many Hungarians, has more German ancestors than Magyar ones.) The first attempts at evolving a Hungarian style did not come until the 1850s, after Hungary lost its war of independence against Austria. One such attempt was the Pesti Vigadó, a concert hall behind March 15 Square, which is supposed to be a mixture of Byzantine, Moorish, Romanesque, and Hungarian influences, but which looks simply like Romanesque Art Deco (if you can imagine that). Or at least its replica does, since the original was destroyed in World War II. Other attempts dot the city, reminding you that you are definitely *not* in Vienna. The style is called, vaguely, Hungarian Romantic, but this gave way quickly to another style, neither Hungarian nor Viennese: Art Nouveau. And unhappily, the Art Nouveau buildings in Budapest look like immense, gene-spliced vegetables transplanted from the Paris Métro.

One could argue that none of this confusion matters. The Royal Palace may have been built in the nineteenth instead of the seventeenth century, and it may have been rebuilt, from rubble, as late as 1980, but it is an impressive building nonetheless. The Danube reflects its dome and ranks of arched windows as faithfully as if it were three centuries old. Yet there lingers a feeling of dissatisfaction—the same dissatisfaction that one feels in connection with the embossed façades on the hundreds of buildings beyond the Nagykörút. The buildings look as if they were made of massive, well-cut stones. But at street level, on the corners, where thousands of people have kicked, or around the doors, where loading trucks have backed a little too far, the great "stones" are cracked, and the powder that slowly comes out of them is stucco. Everything in Budapest and Vienna, *everything*, is actually made of brick. When you are reminded of this, it's as if you'd found a scratch on fine glass. If only Budapest *were* a jewel, you think, like Salzburg or Venice. Diamonds cannot be scratched.

Every Sunday, Zsóka and I go to her parents' three-room flat, in a pleasant modern duplex on one of the Buda hills, and eat Sunday dinner. At 11:00 a.m., we catch the #2 bus at Clark Ádám Square and pay the four-cent fare, ride it through the tunnel under Castle Hill, and gradually out of the concrete apartment houses, onto quieter streets that grow steeper and more winding, passing older stone houses and then modern flats set behind trees and fences. If the weather is good, we see people out for Sunday walks; if it has just snowed, children with sleds or pieces of cardboard under their arms drag their parents behind them up the hills. We get off at the end of the line and continue up on foot along streets that no bus could navigate, sometimes taking staircases from one street to another. Where the Nagys live, each house has its eighth of an acre, its little built-in garage, and the yards, as in Bulgaria, are enclosed behind chain-link or concrete picket fences. Zsóka does not like the unfriendliness of the fences, their ugliness, but at least they keep the fierce little guard dogs—poodles and long-haired terriers—from challenging us in the streets.

Mrs. Nagy is an imposing woman, big-boned and vaguely regal. Her auburn hair is always arranged perfectly, and she carries her head tilted slightly back, as if determined not to see what is beneath her. Born into a comfortable Budapest family, she grew up accustomed to having her own way, and none of the hardships that have permeated her life since she turned eighteen and since the Second World War, in the form of a good-looking Hungarian officer, knocked on her parents' back door has diminished her initial confidence in herself. She is a private tutor of English and German, a job to which she is admirably suited, since she never allows pupils to disagree with her. She has a way of brushing aside opposition that is as relaxed as it is effective—she simply sweeps past objections with a full-toned laugh that leaves one bobbing in her wake, clinging to the flotsam and jetsam of one's convictions. When she compromises (as she does with the inevitable) she manages it so thoroughly that one wonders if she ever held a different opinion. She is essentially a cheerful person, and her pronouncements therefore dwell more on the good around her than on the bad. Even for the government, Mrs. Nagy often finds optimistic things to say—a capability that annoys Zsóka beyond description.

Mr. Nagy has a slight build, to which, over the years, he has managed to attach a fair amount of flesh. Where Mrs. Nagy is domineering, Mr. Nagy is subtle, even delicate. He does not say much, but he listens brilliantly. He was born in the Maros valley, not far from Bela Lugosi's native village, and he speaks English quite well, but with Lugosi's accent. As a result, on the few occasions when Mr. Nagy speaks, it is hard for me to concentrate on his words, because I always expect him, at long last, to say what is really on his mind: "I vaunt to sock yorr blaaud."

Zsóka inherited not only her small size but her pessimistic cast of mind from her father. Behind the attentive face and the thoughtful words, Mr. Nagy dwells in the silence of a mild but perpetual chagrin. Just as he catalogues, in his mind, his wife's eccentricities and her enthusiasms, he has catalogued both his country's misfortunes and his own. He was born to poor farming parents in 1920, the year that a new line was drawn between Hungary and Romania less than two kilometers east of his village. That line magically transformed more than half his blood relatives (his mother's large family) into Romanian citizens, or at least Romanian subjects, who before long found themselves out of work, out of land, out of a church, and out of a school. Mr. Nagy grew up among sickly chickens and pig droppings, to find himself the perfect age for the World War II sausage mill, and he was shipped precipitously off to the eastern front, where he fought and was taken prisoner, beaten, and very nearly starved to death. In 1945, he returned home to find that home didn't really exist anymore, not only the pigs and chickens having disappeared, but his parents as well, and he ended up in Budapest, with a lot of other refugees, where he nearly starved to death again. Later, he went to the University of Budapest and did well enough to become a professor of chemistry at the university, but just recently he was forcibly retired, and now he misses his beloved work, even though it was among ideologues. Worst of all, for the past two years Mr. Nagy has suffered increasingly from Parkinson's disease. Zsóka and Mrs. Nagy, both of whom are devoted to Mr. Nagy far more than they are to each other, find his deteriorating gait, his shaking hands and masklike face, nearly impossible to bear.

Hungary retains many of its traditions concerning male and female gallantry. When a couple goes out, for example, the man always walks at the left side of the woman (so that if he draws his sword to protect her, pulling it with his right hand from the sheath on his left hip, he will not cut her in half); similarly, the man must always allow the woman to enter a cinema, a private house, or an opera house first—but never a restaurant, café, or bar; he must let her exit before him from a subway, but not from a bus (from a bus, he should step down first, then turn and help her down after him). And so on. At the dinner table, the man always pours the wine. When Zsóka and I eat in her apartment, I pour the wine for her, and at the Nagys', Mr. Nagy pours the wine. Which would not bear mentioning, except for the fact that Mr. Nagy is gradually approaching the point where he will no longer be able to get the wine into the glasses. His hand shakes more each week, and as he pours, one must undulate one's glass to keep it under the oscillating arc of wine. Mrs. Nagy watches the operation intently, stopped in mid-sentence, willing her hands to stay in her lap. Zsóka looks down so that she will not see. I cannot intervene, because the guest does not pour. Each week, I dread the beginning of the meal.

The Bull's Blood wine is strong, almost black, and it benefits from much breathing, so there are always fruit flies in the bottle, or floating upside down on the surface in the wineglasses. Mrs.

Nagy is the only one at the table who can spoon out her flies without losing a shred of dignity. Zsóka and I do it clumsily. Mr. Nagy, who does not like to be helped, must leave the flies where they are and hope that the same number that he began with will remain at the end in the dregs. Every third Sunday or so, Mrs. Nagy makes a joke about protein and treats us to her marvelous laugh.

Sunday dinner at the Nagys' is always a caloric affair, convinced as Mrs. Nagy is that Zsóka cannot cook to save her life and therefore that we are in need of sustenance by week's end. We have potato soup or cabbage soup, pickles, horseradish, rice, a mound of roast pork, dessert, and coffee. There are plenty of interesting Hungarian recipes, but Sunday is the day for meat, and on visit after visit, Mrs. Nagy roasts us pork after pork. Pork grease drips off the roast and is spooned over the rice. The joint is half fat, and the Nagys, true Hungarians, eat it enthusiastically, sopping up the oil and grease with the rice, or with the butter-fried dough, sometimes mixing in sour cream. Zsóka eats less traditionally during the week, avoiding pork fat and butter, cooking with margarine, as the new breed of Hungarian doctors recommends, and she cannot eat much at her mother's table. One needs only to compare the bodies of parents and daughter: two fleshy presences at each end of the table, and a slight, boyish build facing me across the grease-stained linen.

Dessert is more varied—a heavy pudding with raisins and cream; lemony cheese pie with the thinnest of pastry, like brown Bible pages, top and bottom; a sweet mixture of ground walnuts and liqueur wrapped inside a butter cookie; pancakes rolled around sweetened poppy seeds or jam. With dessert always comes espresso, which the Hungarians make not as strong as the Italians but more bitter, like a steaming, dark shot of *gammeldansk*.

We carry our espresso back into the study and sit, Mr. Nagy behind his great wooden desk and the rest of us around the coffee table that has been made out of a ceremonial brass gong. Mrs. Nagy always begins our postprandial conversations the same way, leaning back in her armchair and placing her fingertips together by her lips: "Now tell us, Brian, what can we do for you?" She means to ask if there are favors I need done, but the way she asks it, in a measured, imposing voice, makes her sound like a doctor or psychiatrist who wants to know what the matter with me is, and I always answer, "Nothing, thank you; I'm fine."

Our duties as hostess and guest over, we are now free to go on to other things. Often we talk about music, as Mrs. Nagy has subscription tickets to the opera, the Budai Vigadó, and the Pesti Vigadó, and Zsóka and I go out nearly every night. Mrs. Nagy tends to talk about concerts which she had tickets for but forgot to attend (many), while Zsóka talks of concerts that she saw but didn't like (also many). Or we talk about the past. Mr. Nagy dwells lovingly on his years of teaching, especially his year at the University of Chicago, since he never loses sight of the fact that he is entertaining an American. Mrs. Nagy reaches further back, to talk about her childhood on Hunyadi Street, before the ugly apartment building went up, when the family house had a hillside garden and a clear view to the east. Or we talk about politics, which is problematic, because Zsóka and Mrs. Nagy disagree so violently. Zsóka's position is that one cannot compromise one's opinions about a bad government; Mrs. Nagy compromises effortlessly, even elegantly. Zsóka thinks that it is crucially important to bear witness against lies; Mrs. Nagy prefers to believe lies. Mr. Nagy abstains from the political discussions on the grounds that whichever side he takes will put the other side unfairly in the minority. Or we talk about family, the only subject on which Mrs. Nagy and Zsóka usually agree. To wit: Zsóka's younger brother, Pál, still has some growing up to do, and he's been unpleasantly sullen lately; Pál's wife, Márti, is quite pretty, but too forceful, not right for him; Zsóka's sister, Éva, cannot control her three children properly and would be wise not to have any more; Éva's husband, István, is probably a good enough father but, ohhhh, just a hopeless man, a creep; Zsóka's uncle Árpád is getting crazier every day, poor man.

Mr. Nagy never contributes to the conversation for long, in any case. The heavy meal in his stomach gets to him within a few minutes, and he has to push himself up from his desk and make his way awkwardly to the spare bed at the back of the study, where he lies down. Several minutes later, the room fills with his snoring, and he looks so much like a corpse, crumpled on the brass bed, that Zsóka and Mrs. Nagy stop frequently in their arguments to glance over at him in dismay. Sometimes Mrs. Nagy will say to me, in a voice that is shockingly unhappy compared to her usual cheerfulness, "I don't know what to do, Brian—he just gets worse and worse," and her face will take on, for long seconds, the regretful, defeated expression that I see so often on Zsóka and Mr. Nagy—and also, for that matter, on Éva and young Pál. During those moments of worry, Mrs. Nagy actually seems like a member of the family.

·

There is a note tacked to the door of Árpád's apartment: *I have gone out.* The note has been up for years, and naturally I have come to view it as a comment on his mental state.

Zsóka's Uncle Árpád is tall and cadaverously thin. He always wears black suits with a black beret. Tufts of white bristle that his razor has missed dot his face. Wetted blobs of toilet paper cover other spots, where he has shaved off both the beard and his skin. Árpád doesn't walk; he *vibrates* from place to place.

Árpád does not know how to deal with me. He knows that I am a guest in the house and so he is determined to make me feel welcome, but he has no idea how to do that. Whenever he sees me, he hobbles over and says *"Szervusz"* a dozen times or more and shakes my hand five or six times. Then he switches into German (he is convinced I am German, no matter how often Zsóka tells him otherwise) and says *"Guten Abend"* another dozen times. He always says *"Guten Abend,"* whether it's evening or not.

I have glimpsed the front room of his apartment, once or twice, as he came out on the landing. It's a huge, high-ceilinged room, with a line of windows: it used to be the dining room of the house. In the far corner is a 1930s piano; the rest of the room is taken up with wooden tables, ancient sofas, benches, discarded church pews. On every surface, and over much of the floor, are papers and books—in enormous stacks or jumbled and flung about, like tornado debris. "Árpád keeps *everything*," Zsóka says. "He has piles of used bus tickets in there, from twenty years ago.

I've seen them—in packets, with rubber bands. When I ask if he's going to throw them out, he says, 'I take care of them.' He has books I would like to read, but he can't bear to lend them to me. That wouldn't be taking care of them."

Árpád plays violin, French horn, cello, flute, and piano. On most days, the sounds of one or more of the instruments come floating through the locked doorway that separates Árpád's music room from Zsóka's bedroom (and my study). Years ago, Zsóka maneuvered her oak wardrobe into the doorway in a futile attempt to muffle the sound.

Árpád plays all of his instruments the way he moves and talks—nervously and repetitiously. One imagines that the notes are a pack of wild dogs, snapping, yipping, and straining to bolt in every direction. His piano playing is the worst of all. Árpád tries to *compose* on the piano—he has a strange young friend who encourages him. He mutters to us about the progress of his composition on the cracked stairs in the piss-colored back hall. Unfortunately, Árpád has been working on the same measure of the same piece for the past two years. The piece, so far, is very short: the first four measures are simple and melodic, a little cartoonish; then the fifth measure suddenly jumps out of the home key and crawls up, hitting the sixth measure, which is the one that has stymied Árpád for so long. Here, he abandons the melody entirely and plays a dissonant chord a dozen or more times very rapidly, almost spastically. It is usually the same chord. Not always. But regardless of what chord it is, Árpád is not satisfied, and he breaks it off; then he returns without pausing to the first measure of the piece, and plays to the sixth again—and derails again. This he does over and over, for perhaps an hour at a stretch. At the end of the day, if we are really tired, Zsóka and I can ignore it, but at other times, it is sheer torture. Leopold Mozart used to get his son Wolfgang out of bed mornings (or so the story goes) by playing an unresolved series of chords on the family's fortepiano. Young Wolfgang, unable to bear an unfinished harmonic progression, would leap out of bed and run to the fortepiano in order to play the resolving chord. Árpád has helped me to empathize with Mozart's anguish. I fantasize about breaking down Árpád's door and playing a resolving chord on his piano with a sledgehammer.

•

The Győri Ballet is in town for two performances. Zsóka has a friend, Ági, who was raised in Győr, a town in the northwest of Hungary, and who wants us to go to the ballet with her. Ági is a strong-boned and strong-willed woman with thick dark hair as straight as her manner. She has a degree in biochemistry, a two-year-old daughter, and maternity leave for one more year from her research post at the city hospital. When Ági wants Zsóka or me to do something, we usually do it. So we call up the ticket agencies, but they all say the same thing: the performances are sold out.

Sold-out performances mean nothing to Ági. "Let's go, anyway," she says. "We'll find some tickets. Brian will get them for us."

Whaat? I think. How am I going to do that?

The three of us get on the subway at Moscow Square and take it to the People's Stadium stop. The Győri Ballet is not performing in the usual place, which would be the Erkel Theater, but in the Sportcsarnok, the new Sports Hall. The reason is that there are too few seats in the Erkel. In the Sportcsarnok, a ballet or theater group can block off half of the arena and perform for the other half, which will hold a little over 6,000 people.

We reach the Sportcsarnok an hour before the ballet is to begin. The plaza is mobbed and no one has tickets. Everyone is hoping to coax tickets from other patrons when they arrive.

I ask Zsóka and Ági why the Győri Ballet is so uncommonly popular. As I have been in Budapest for some weeks, perhaps I should have known the answer: the man who leads the Győri Ballet used to work in Budapest; he was a brilliant young choreographer, but he would not toe the Party line or kowtow to the head of the ballet school, who was a Party member. The brilliant young man was thrown out of the Budapest ballet, went to Győr, and founded his own company, where he choreographs ballets that say vague things about repression. Everyone in Budapest remembers his expulsion, and the great majority of citizens, who paid scant attention to him before, now clamor by the tens of thousands to see his work whenever the Győri Ballet comes to Budapest.

Zsóka asks at a ticket window and is told to give up; Ági asks at another one and has no more luck. Hundreds of people are being turned away all around us; the tickets really are gone. There are no scalpers. There is no hope.

But Ági says, "Brian, go to one of the entrance guards and ask for three tickets."

"Me?!" I exclaim cravenly. "I can't even speak decent Hungarian!"

"Oh no, no," Zsóka interjects, alarmed. "Don't speak Hungarian! That will ruin it. Ask in English. Ask like a tourist."

Doubtful, I approach the stone-faced guard. Like a tourist? At the sound of my English, her expression falters. I say, "Three." I hold up three fingers and try to write Western all over my face (which, in this case, means looking forlorn, ingenuous, and confident of getting what I want—all at the same time). Magic. Another woman is summoned. She speaks a few words of English; she listens to my plea and says, "Wait," then disappears. She returns with an envelope, and out of the envelope she pulls three tickets. She will not take money. She smiles and tells me to enjoy the ballet. People all around me are still being turned away by the guards.

Zsóka and Ági bound to my side. For the first time this week, I feel as if I have been useful (I also feel guilty). "My treat," I say magnanimously. As it turns out, we have excellent places in the great domed hall, halfway up the concrete mount of benches. "Why on earth did that work?" I ask, after we are seated.

"They want tourists to come," Ági says.

"But she refused to take my money."

Ági waves it away. "The price of a ballet ticket is nothing compared to a hotel room. As long as you come, that's all that matters."

The ballet is somewhat bizarre. It is set to Strauss's tone poem *Don Juan*, which has been electronically (but not very successfully) modified. There are three parts, somehow interrelated, although we are not sure how: the first concerns the legend of Don Juan; the second is a version of *The Trial*; the third is a version of *Doctor Faustus*. The main character in all three parts is danced by the brilliant choreographer, who is perhaps a better choreographer than he is a dancer. Don Juan/Joseph K./Doctor Faustus spends a lot of time being tied down, confronting faceless, threatening intruders, running in place. A bit of Christ symbolism is thrown in for good measure, when Don Juan jams his sword into a cross and then impales himself on it. We are made to infer that the ballet means something, something about the lack of dignity, the lack of freedom. But *does* it mean anything? Are there any real ideas behind the running in place, the gruesome cross?

The performance ends in deafening applause. The huge stage below remains empty for a full minute, while thousands of people cheer. Then the brilliant choreographer walks out alone, stiffly, head down, his long black hair glistening with sweat under the spotlights. He moves to the center of the stage, and keeping his eyes on the floor, he raises two fists over his head and shakes them three times while the crowd goes wild. He turns and retreats from the stage, then comes out again and does exactly the same thing. At no point does he look at the audience or make anything resembling a bow. By the third time, I have decided I don't like him.

Zsóka, too, is annoyed. As sympathetic as she is to the brilliant choreographer's troubled career, she was looking forward to an evening of good ballet and she didn't get it. We leave the Sportcsarnok while the audience is still cheering and applauding rhythmically.

•

The house in which Zsóka lives on Hunyadi János Street was built by Mrs. Nagy's family in 1864, and Mrs. Nagy was raised in it, along with her half-mad younger brother, Árpád. The house follows the usual Hungarian style: square and stuccoed; yellow-beige like the sky before a summer storm; simple, without ornamentation other than a bit of stone carving around the front door. There were twelve big rooms divided unequally among three floors, with a front entrance on the ground floor and a back entrance on a landing halfway between the ground floor and the middle floor. French windows in the back opened onto a small garden, and the view from the front, down the slope toward Corvin Square and the Danube, made every morning worthwhile. A few years before the war, when Mrs. Nagy was eight, her father, a doctor with a small practice, had to sell the land below the house, and the river view was soon blocked by a six-story apartment building. The new building kept out the sounds of the street, which was getting busier all the time, but it also blocked the sunlight every day until noon. It even appropriated the old house's street address, and Mrs. Nagy's parents now had to go out their front door and straight into the back of the new building, then down a flight to the ugly little foyer to collect their mail from a box in a rank of thirty.

Then the war came, and the so-called Siege of Budapest at the end of the war, when the Germans took refuge in the Habsburg citadel in Buda and the Russians shelled them for weeks on end from the Pest plain. While 74 percent of Budapest was pounded into rubble by two foreign armies, the Nagys' house had a corner blown off and a few holes bored through its floors by bombs. But it survived, as did the family. The corner was fixed and the holes patched over in 1948, by some of the last freelance laborers to work in Hungary for the next twenty years.

For a few years, the family was allowed to stay in its own house, while thousands of refugees poured into Budapest and the living conditions became impossibly crowded. Many families had to share a single room; some had not even that. Mrs. Nagy and her parents took the upper two floors of their house (seven rooms), and Árpád, playing his musical instruments and living in his own world, took the ground floor (five rooms). Several political parties competed for power after the war, but the Communist Party, enjoying the support of a certain large nation to the east, steadily gained ground. By 1949, a Hungarian named Mátyás Rákosi, one of the Moscow Communists (who, as opposed to the "national" Communists, had spent the war years in Moscow, on Maxim Gorky Street), was in something like complete control of the country. A new, Soviet-style constitution was adopted in that year, and Rákosi—short, very fat, with a countenance suggesting illness—soon established himself as a leader that the Hungarians would not forget for a very long time.

Mrs. Nagy would normally have left the house when, in 1949, she married Pál Nagy, a young chemistry student from a southeast village. But unfortunately, there was nowhere for the young couple to move to. Pál had no family that could take them in, and the city as yet had hardly cleared the streets of debris, let alone repaired the buildings for habitation, since funds were going to more important things, like a monument to Stalin and an enormous new People's Republic Stadium. So Pál and Erzsébet (now Pálne) Nagy took the top floor of the old family house with the new corner behind the six-story heap, leaving Mrs. Nagy's parents on the middle floor and Árpád undisturbed, as he needed to be, on the ground floor.

A daughter was born on the top floor in 1950; she was named Erzsébet, although the Nagys always called her by the diminutive Zsóka. When Zsóka was too young to remember it, the ownership of the house was taken away from Mrs. Nagy's parents and assumed by the state. The family was lucky: it was allowed to remain in the house (some other families were being shipped out to the villages), provided that it pay a small rent for its rooms, but it could not have all the rooms. The state divided the house into four apartments: after all, thousands of people in the city were still without decent shelter, and the construction of new apartments was progressing more slowly than most people would have believed possible. The ground floor was divided in half; a quarrelsome, dirty couple moved into one half and a secretive little man who produced a lot of trash into the other. Árpád was moved to the small third floor, complaining bitterly in his quaking and repetitious way of speaking, while the Nagys moved in with Mrs. Nagy's parents on the middle floor. After Éva and Pál were born, the Nagys were a little short on space, with seven people in five rooms. But they were still better off than practically anybody else, and besides, they could do nothing. Árpád still played his piano, French horn, flute, violin, and cello on the third floor, while the quarrelsome couple was replaced by a drunken woman with three fearful cats. Meanwhile, the state never fixed anything, and the Nagys couldn't work on the house themselves, because the materials were not available to individuals. So the plaster came off the walls, the wood floors deteriorated, and the marble steps in the back hall that had been cracked during the war stayed that way.

When Zsóka was three, Josef Stalin died, and a "national" Communist by the name of Imre Nagy (no relation) became Premier of Hungary. Imre Nagy, a dedicated, idealistic man, set about dismantling Stalinism, which he considered a blight on the good name of Communism, but when Zsóka was five, the balance of power in the government shifted slightly and he was deposed.

When Zsóka was six and a half, a student demonstration across the river mushroomed first into a citywide protest and then into an armed insurrection. For a few days, people were being shot in the streets and buildings were being blown up by tanks, streetcars were overturned, bridges were blocked; the government fell and a new government under Imre Nagy replaced it. The insurrection came to an end after thirteen days, with the arrival of a few hundred Soviet tanks. Imre Nagy took refuge in the Yugoslavian embassy. A new government was proclaimed from the occupied Parliament building. The new government guaranteed Nagy safe conduct, and when he emerged from the embassy, he was arrested on the spot. When Zsóka was eight, he was executed.

By then, both of Mrs. Nagy's parents were dead. The young family of five now had the whole middle floor to themselves. Their luck had continued: the housing situation was still desperate, and the government, under the new leader, János Kádár, had established a goal for urban living space of ten square yards per person. But the Nagys already had more than that—about twenty-two square yards apiece. Nonetheless, the middle floor began to feel crowded as the three children grew. (The average American house, for a family of four, has over fifty square yards of floor space per person.) And the future was unclear—what would happen when the children were married? Where would they live then?

So when Kádár began to free up the economy after 1968, Mr. and Mrs. Nagy decided to work for a flat in one of the fast-growing suburbs up in the Buda hills. Mr. Nagy, who by now had been a professor at the university for over a decade, brought home a decent salary; Mrs. Nagy helped earn money, after Pál reached adolescence, by teaching English and German to children. In 1975, Mr. and Mrs. Nagy bought and moved into the upper floor of a duplex on a quiet street two miles from the Danube, with a built-in garage and a chain-link fence. Árpád, who was gradually getting worse as the years went by, was moved down to the larger rooms on the middle floor of the old house, and Éva moved to the top floor with her new husband, István. Young Pál got a job programming computers and actually landed an apartment behind the Déli train yards. Soon enough, he, too, was married, to a stylish woman named Márti, an interior decorator who could outtalk (and if the times had been different, probably outshoot) her husband. Zsóka remained unmarried. She had wanted more than anything to be an illustrator, but she hadn't won a place at the university's art school. In 1968, the opportunity to become a freelance illustrator did not exist, so Zsóka studied English and became a copy editor for a publisher of English technical books. She stayed on, alone, in the portion of the second floor that had not been given to Árpád. For a citizen of Budapest, she had a great deal of space: a small kitchen, a tiny bathroom (the two together had once been the master bathroom), and two large rooms, one opening through French windows to the little garden in the back and one at the front of the house with a big brick stove in the corner. The kitchen and bathroom were decrepit; but Zsóka's two big rooms still showed, in their parquet floors and trim, and even in some of the delicate wooden furniture that had survived so much, that the house, and the family, had known wealthier days.

·

Zsóka wants to see a certain rock opera that plays about once a month at the Erkel Theater. But the opera, A Próba (The Rehearsal), is always sold out, which leads me to believe that it has a political message. Even I, asking in English, have not been able to coax two tickets out of the black-wigged woman in the ticket booth. So one night, when Zsóka feels like attending something loud and *A Próba* has proven once more to be impossible, we pick a rock opera at random (half a dozen different ones are always playing in the city) out of the thick Budapest arts weekly, the *Pesti Műsor*, and hop on the #78 bus.

The production is called *Sztarcsinálók*, or *Starmakers*, and we know nothing about it. It's playing in a rundown theater off Lenin Boulevard, in which the seats are made out of plywood and the old red wallpaper has been kept in place with bright red duct tape. As soon as we get a look at the program, we know we're in for more political allegory. The characters are named Tiberius, Nero, Seneca, Juvenalis, and so on. There is even a Kyprios-Jezus. The libretto is printed in the program, and neither Zsóka nor I can make head or tail of it. There are apostrophes to Youth and to Hope; there are poems about the Senate and the Forum, about hemlock and Jesus Christ and show business and gangsterism.

The hall fills with people, mostly teenagers, and the curtain rises on Juvenalis, who, it turns out, will be our guide through the allegorical maze. Juvenalis is a boy with blue jeans, guitar, and a brown Afro, quite clearly the Spirit of Youth as it once manifested itself in the United States and has been imitated elsewhere ever since. He sings of a new beginning, and because he is so predictable, he palls quickly, but the rest of the opera is fun, in a foggy kind of way. It has something to do with Nero, dressed snazzily in white, coming to power as a reluctant tyrant, good at first, but coming to depend increasingly on his corps of henchmen, who wear black and actually carry around violin cases. Ultimately, Nero poisons almost all the cast, including the people who prodded him into power. The opera ends with Rome burning and Nero, still in white and quite elegant, flinging himself from the ramparts—not backward, behind the stage set, but forward, thrillingly, toward the audience. Then a blackout, and an epilogue by Juvenalis, looking like a refugee from *Godspell*, who tiresomely regales us, strumming beatifically, with his vision of a new spirit, which perhaps is meant to show that Youth never learns, it just sings songs.

Despite the play's implication that attempts at new beginnings (of which Hungary has had half a dozen since 1867) tend to result in Neros and burning Romes, the audience of teenagers catches on to the optimism of the last song and starts to sing the lines with Juvenalis, who encourages them. A few people begin to shout vaguely antiestablishment things above the singing, and others applaud. As Zsóka and I leave, the crowd is still singing, and the words follow us into the foyer: "Things are gonna change . . . You and I will make it better . . . the old times will be swept away," and so on.

We catch the #78 bus on Rákóczi Avenue, and the cafés and movie houses of the busy avenue stream by and diminish in the back window while we struggle to keep on our feet. Zsóka says that she didn't understand much of *Sztarcsinálók*, and wishes that we had someone there who knew what all the symbols meant. Zsóka is frequently taken with the sad conviction that everyone else knows what's going on and no one is telling her. My impression of *Sztarcsinálók* is that details are not going to improve our comprehension of it, but that the general message was clear enough. (Perhaps I would be more confused if I had understood more of the text.)

"Isn't the government disturbed by some of these shows?" I ask.

Zsóka laughs. "Disturbed? The government encourages it! This is all carefully planned. The government decided a few years ago that if it allowed this sort of thing, then people would think the situation was getting better. They would watch the shows and say, 'That was impossible under Rákosi.' Listen to my mother, that's just what she says! So they watch the shows and decipher all the meanings, and they are satisfied, they think they have struck at the government—then they go home and go to sleep. It is safe, and means nothing."

Zsóka watches the cables of the Erzsébet Bridge flicker by, the Danube below, winking, like Argus, its hundred silver eyes, and says, "So everyone sings at the end that things will change. But nothing will change." Perhaps not. At least, one presumes, not as long as Hungarian anger confines itself to rock operas with plots about ancient Rome.

•

Hidden meanings, hidden stories.

On the top of Gellért Hill, at the point where the cliff face of Buda draws so near to the Danube that there is room below only for a few lanes of traffic and a Turkish bath, there stands a huge statue of a woman in a belted robe, with her feet together, leaning forward as if to execute a swan dive into the water and holding a palm leaf high above her head. You can see her from almost any point in Budapest, and she is grandly lit at night (during the tourist months) so that she hangs above the Danube, always falling forward, like some colossal, confident angel. She is the Szabadság Szobor—the Freedom Statue, also called the Liberation Monument. Her plinth is adorned with bas-reliefs depicting the building of Socialist Society, and it is fronted, beneath her feet, by a bronze Soviet soldier holding a flag and a machine gun. The monument stands before the fortress (now, partly, a hotel) that the Habsburgs built on Gellért Hill after 1848, in order to keep an eye on the rebellious Hungarians; the same fortress in which the Nazis took their final stand in the Siege of Budapest of 1944–45. The Szabadság Szobor commemorates the end of that siege and the liberation of Budapest by the Russians. It's a must-see for all Russian tour groups and visiting dignitaries, so there are always fresh flowers laid at the foot of the plinth.

But the statue (minus the plinth and the bronze soldier) was actually made just before the siege, by the Hungarian sculptor Zsigmond Kisfaludy-Strobl, in honor of the son of Hungary's right-wing regent at the time, Admiral Miklós Horthy—whom the Soviets vilify as a Fascist (not without reason). Kisfaludy-Strobl managed to pass off his work, after the war, as a tribute to the Russians, and the Russians, desperately short not only of memorials but of workers and materials to *make* memorials, were only too glad to believe him, adding only the soldier (who fit right in, as Fascist art and Socialist-Realist art are so similar).

But it was unwise of the Russians to accept the work. Today, Hungarians regard the statue's origins with amusement, and when they look at her, pressing her palm leaf forward high above the Danube, they don't think of the greatness of the Soviets but of their foolishness—their foolish belief, stemming from a characteristic disregard of human nature, that the Hungarians would forget that the figure was designed and the metal poured in honor of Russia's most implacable enemies.

.

One Sunday, after dinner, Mrs. Nagy sits with Zsóka and me around the brass gong in her study and talks about her life during the war. Her large face is flushed from a couple of glasses of wine, and she never stops smiling; she laughs off and on as she speaks. Her expression—nostalgic, affectionate—could be that of a woman going over memories of summer camp.

"Our family lived for months in the basement of the house on Hunyadi Street. A Hungarian officer—oh, you know, a very good-looking man—came to our back door one day and told my mother that the house was going to be used to billet one hundred soldiers. Imagine, just like that! When was that? 1944? I can't quite remember. During the war, you know, calendars did not mean much, at least to young people. It seemed as if the war would go on forever . . .

"Until the good-looking officer showed up at our door, the war had not affected us much. My father was too old to be fighting, and of course Árpád was too ill in the head. Good Lord! Can you imagine Árpád as a soldier?! The poor thing wouldn't know what a gun was for! When the soldiers came to billet in the house, they took all the rooms, and we were forced to move into the basement. Have you been down there? No? Well, it's small and rather dark all the time. We slept on the coal pile, on blankets: it was softer than the floor. There wasn't much room, but we had to let Árpád have as much space as we could. He cannot stand to have people near him, you know—he has always been that way. Everything has to be just right for him, everything in its place, or he flies off the handle. So my parents wanted to bring down a bed for Árpád. The officer refused. What could my father say? 'I know the world is falling apart, but my son is still sick in the head'? No. So we slept on the coal. Then Árpád brought down his musical instruments, and he drove us crazy trying to keep us from touching them, although of course we had no intention of touching them. And it was almost unbearable when he pla—have you heard Árpád play, Brian?" Zsóka laughs. "Yes, now and then," I say. "Well, you know how impossible it is. Down there in that dark basement, with the cello and violin and flute—like a menagerie! I think Árpád would have tried to bring the piano down, except that it was too large to fit through the door into the hallway." Mrs. Nagy laughs delightedly. "So there was always something to be thankful for, you see!"

Mrs. Nagy holds her glass out to me for a refill, and I oblige. Zsóka is eating nuts and staring out the window. She is intimidated by her mother's loud voice, her breathless way of relating anecdotes, as if, from beginning to end, they are huge jokes; when Mrs. Nagy speaks at length, Zsóka's attention wanders.

"The soldiers didn't have much to do while they were with us; all the soldiers in Budapest were waiting for orders about where to go, and of course, the communications were in a terrible condition, and no one could decide where to send anybody, or they would send them out and bring them right back again. Also, the Hungarian government—this was when Horthy was still the regent—the Hungarian government did not really want to cooperate with Hitler; we were only in the war because otherwise Hitler would invade us. Many of the soldiers were kept in Budapest by design, I'm sure. Our troops in the East were being decimated by the Russians. The ones in our house were good young men, very civil, and of course nice to me, because I was eighteen and pretty. The officer, in particular, was *very* kind." At this, Mrs. Nagy looks pleased with herself, and Zsóka looks irritated. "That's what you always say!" Zsóka mutters. "Well, it's true!" Mrs. Nagy overrides her with her schoolteacher voice. "He was quite a gentleman!"

I know Zsóka. Her complaint is that Mrs. Nagy, with her comfortable belief in the old hierarchy, naturally remembers the soldiers as nice and the officers as *very* nice. Her assessments of people usually correspond neatly to their rank.

"Whenever bombing started, the soldiers would crowd into the basement with us, or into the basement of the block of flats in front. They sat all over the floor and smoked. They had to get used to Árpád, who was very nervous with them so near, but they were very patient with him . . .

"For a while, we were being bombed by both the Americans and the Russians. When the air raid sounded, people would try to figure out which way the planes were coming from; if they came in from Pest, they were Russian, and if they came over the hills, they were American. It was much worse to be bombed by the Americans, let me tell you."

"Oh?"

"The American bombs were smaller than the Russian bombs, but unfortunately, they always worked! The Russian bombs were enormous, but half the time they didn't go off." She laughs again. "So we already knew, you see, even before the war was over— American products were better than Russian! Ah, God—*so* many bombs!" Mrs. Nagy says this as one would say, "So many memories!"

"We would ask each other, 'Why are all the bombs falling on *us*? This is not our war!' But it is always that way, is it not? The Russians are fighting the Germans, and so Budapest is destroyed. Crazy! One of the Russian bombs came through our roof and landed on the steps in the back hall; then it rolled down the steps and banged into the back door. But it didn't explode, which was lucky for us, because it would have brought the house down. After that, everyone had to step over the bomb whenever they went out or came in. We had another unexploded bomb in the garden, also Russian, which was even bigger than the one on the stairs. A third bomb came through the roof and went through all three floors. It landed in the basement when all of us were down there with the soldiers. The soldiers in our house were German by that point— that was 1944, and Horthy, our regent, had been arrested by the Nazis. The German soldiers were not nearly as friendly as the Hungarians had been. It was very amusing to see all of them run out of the basement when the bomb came through the ceiling! But there was no explosion. It turned out to be a "flour" bomb— food dropped for the soldiers. Perhaps that was during the siege. I can't remember . . .

"There were actually quite many things during those times

that were not so bad. One bomb exploded right beside our house—that was an American bomb, of course. Along with taking that part of our house away, it also put this enormous hole in the garden. That hole turned out to be quite convenient, because we could throw all of the damage into it, the broken glass and stones that were lying everywhere. We also didn't have to spend any time digging to bury anybody—we would just throw the bodies into the hole and cover them with a little dirt. We even had a dead horse brought up from Fő Street, and that was thrown in. We had the biggest hole on the block! Finally, when the hole was full, all we had to do was smooth it over. All of those things are still buried next to the house.

"There were other positive things. We lost our water at the house soon after the bombing started. There was no water anywhere on Castle Hill, since the pumping stations had stopped running, and everyone had to go down to Corvin Square to fill up their bottles. That was all right for a while, when all we had to worry about were the air raids. But after the Russians had taken Pest and were trying to get the Germans out of the—you know, the citadel on Gellért Hill, then the Danube was a free-fire zone. When you ran down to get water, there were always soldiers shooting at each other over your head, and only the women would get water, because the men were more likely to be shot at. I'd run down with my bottle over my head, yelling, 'Voda, voda; wasser wasser!' " Here, Mrs. Nagy breaks down in a fit of laughter. I laugh along with her, although I am not sure what is so funny. Zsóka keeps her gaze on the tree outside the window. Mrs. Nagy catches her breath and resumes, wiping tears from her eyes.

"So we finally had the Liberation. In February 1945, the Germans left the citadel and the Russians came into Buda. First we'd had Hungarian soldiers in our house, then Germans, and now a troop of Russians. We kept getting them, because our house was in better shape than most—only one corner missing! When the Russian soldiers first came to our house, we had gotten Árpád to understand that the war was over, and he wanted to do something for the Russians, but of course the poor man had no idea what to do. Finally, he got out his flute and played for them. Some Bach.

But the Russians didn't like it, and they made him stop. Can you believe it? They were afraid of—of God knows what, that it was a trap or something. From such a pathetic man!

"They were like that in everything! The Germans were bad, but the Russians were worse. The Russians were the victors, you know, but they never *looked* like victors. They were always *sneaking* around and looking over their shoulders; they were a *terribly* cowardly and suspicious bunch, always thinking there was a trap. They called it the Liberation, but even *they* didn't expect the Hungarians to be happy about it! And we were afraid of them . . . The Russian soldiers stole everything, you know; they raped women all the time . . .

"And we still had a big Russian bomb inside the back door, just where you wipe your feet. We had tried to get the Hungarian soldiers to move it, and they had said, 'Oh, not us!' Then we asked the German soldiers to move it for us and they said, 'Oh, not us!' So when the Russians came, we demanded that they liberate us from the bomb in the back hall. Ha! Of course the Russians wouldn't do it, either. They just kept stepping over it, day after day. They always said, 'Why are you worried about it? It won't explode!' And we said, 'If it won't explode, why don't you move it?' But they would shrug. You know, the Russians are just impossible.

"Then one day it was gone. I came back from getting some bread and there was nothing in the hall. So I thanked the Russian officer, and his mouth fell open. 'The bomb is gone?!' he said. What a jerk he was—is that the word?"

"Could be."

"A jerk, then. I asked my parents about the bomb, but they didn't know how it had disappeared, either. No one seemed to know. Finally, one of the Russian soldiers told us: he had seen Árpád take the bomb away!" Mrs. Nagy dissolves into laughter again; then, gasping for air: " 'Árpád?!' I said. And it was *true*! Árpád had understood that no one wanted the bomb in the hall, but he'd never understood exactly what it *was*! So that morning he'd come with his friend—there was another man in the neighborhood who was also not right in the head—and the two of them just picked up the bomb as if it were a sack of potatoes and dropped it into a wheelbarrow!" Mrs. Nagy shrieks in delight, as her face turns a darker shade of rose. "And—and they took it out and buried it under the stairs beyond the garden! Can you believe it? It's still there! There's a Russian bomb under the stairs!" Mrs. Nagy breaks down completely. Her story is over.

Zsóka turns from the window, coming out of her reverie. "Why do you make that sound like such a good time?" She looks plaintively in my direction. "Why does she? I can't understand that."

Mrs. Nagy's laughing simmers down, and she replies more seriously, a bit annoyed herself, "Because people helped each other then, Zsóka. Shared their food. Protected each other. You had a feeling that things could never become too bad as long as that was true." She appeals to me. "Like going down for the water. Down in the streets, with the bottles on our heads, we couldn't tell where the shots were coming from. People in the houses all down the hill would stick their heads out of windows and tell us which way to go; or they'd tell us to wait, if the shooting was too bad for the moment. No one would do that now. People stopped helping each other after the war."

I wonder if Mrs. Nagy's nostalgia for the war is primarily a matter of age. She was young and pretty then. Living in the basement was an adventure. Good-looking gentlemen officers were kind to her, and young soldiers, especially the village boys, were probably a little awestruck. Then also, the period following the war was not much of an improvement. The Soviets stayed on, all of the parties other than the Communists were gradually suppressed, and by 1949, fat, violent, vulgar Rákosi, who called himself "Stalin's best disciple," was dictator. By then, indeed, few people *would* help anyone else. Sticking your head out the window under Rákosi meant having your brains blown out.

Also, Mrs. Nagy's memories of the war are not marred by the deaths of close relatives. One cousin whom she hardly knew died on the eastern front—that was all. Such is the advantage of having a small family, a halfwit brother, and a house ensconced behind a big apartment building. Mr. Nagy's account would no doubt be less offhand, since he would have to mention that both of his parents were killed, that his village ceased to exist, and that by the time of the liberation, he had scurvy and dysentery and weighed 110 pounds. But we cannot hear Mr. Nagy's account, even if he wanted to give it (which he probably doesn't): he lies spread-eagled on the brass bed, dead to the world, and his helpless snoring fills the room.

•

Zsóka, Stefánia, Ági, Sándor, and I are sitting at the table in Stefánia's tiny kitchen, drinking her mother's homemade wine, and engaging in two popular Hungarian pastimes—political speculation and rumormongering.

I am not contributing much to the conversation, but because I am present, everyone is speaking in English or German. Ági is finishing her account to Stefánia of the conditions she and Zsóka witnessed on their last smuggling trip to Transylvania (they take in material specially bound by a certain Western press to look like innocuous textbooks, but it is actually political, cultural, and social news of Hungary, which is contraband in Romania). Sándor (Ági's husband), who has heard it all before, is concentrating on the bottle of wine and a platter of bread slices smeared with duck lard, topped with raw onion and paprika.

"I cannot imagine getting through a winter there. Everything is rationed now—the gas, the electricity, the oil. There is hardly any wood to burn. No one has fuel for their cars, so the roads are empty. My grandmother has no heat in her house some days, and on the coldest days she has to go to another house. She spends the winter with rags tied around her feet, her neck, her hands—and some days she just sits, all day, under a cover. She doesn't leave it because she will lose her heat."

There is a noticeable difference of emphasis between Ági's and Zsóka's tales of Transylvania. Ági talks about physical discomfort—no heat, no food. Zsóka talks exclusively of the subtler things, of discrimination and cultural deprivation—no Hungarian magazines, no books, no news. Zsóka's emphasis accords both with her pride in Hungarian culture and with her concern about what makes living worthwhile, beyond food and comfort—the less clear considerations, such as self-respect. Ági is blunter than Zsóka: she looks at the world out of her wide-set, unblinking gray eyes and asks, "Is there enough to eat? Are there children? Do people smile?" The two of them agree on the misery of Transylvania, for their different reasons. They do not agree on Hungary. Ági is pleased with the economic progress (although she, like everyone, is worried about the inflation of the past couple of years—meat prices were "adjusted" again recently by 20 percent), while Zsóka, both more idealistic than Ági and less susceptible to feeling satisfied, is not.

"So without heat and light, on top of the fact that they haven't any food—I think that if things do not get better soon, there will be a revolution there. There has to be. People simply cannot live like that." Ági speaks with her customary finality. Faced with her decisive chin, her unwavering gaze, I would not think of contradicting her.

But Zsóka is impervious to other people's confidence. "How can there be a revolution?" she exclaims. "What will they fight with? There is no chance for people to talk, to organize. Less chance all the time!" She shakes her head furiously, outfinalizing Ági. "No. Ceauşescu has been there for twenty years—he will be there for twenty years more. He will die old and happy and in his bed. Like Stalin." Her face darkens. "Like Rákosi."

Zsóka does not always make for cheerful company. Into the gloom that follows her words, the only sound is Sándor moistly dispatching a slice of duck-lard bread and washing it down with a gulp of wine. But Stefánia, a kittenish woman whom most men find irresistible, rescues the conversation with a juicy rumor: "While saying about Ceauşescu, you have heard the story about his son in the restaurant?"

Everyone has except me. Ági says testily that it's an old story.

"For Brian, then." Stefánia leans across the table, pulling strands of her black hair out of her face, and tells it with horror spread liberally over a substratum of morbid delight. "In the story, Ceauşescu's son went into a restaurant in Bucharest, with all his secret police and bodyguards. While he was eating, he saw a girl at another table whom he thought was quite attractive. Now, the son of the ruler of Rumania shall be able to have just what he wants, yes? And he wants this girl, this quite attractive girl. Nothing simpler! He claps the hands and orders his men to take everyone out of the restaurant except the girl. He is going to make love to her exactly there. But the girl has a boyfriend with her—and this boyfriend denies to go. Absolutely denies! So Ceauşescu's son claps the hands again, and his bodyguards beat the man to death. Exactly in the restaurant! This happened a year ago, maybe."

"My God," I say, satisfying Stefánia with my shock, "is that really true?"

She shrugs. "I have heard it."

Zsóka adds, "Ceauşescu and his family are completely outside the law in that country. It's a monarchy."

"But what about the girl?"

Zsóka and Stefánia look at each other, surprised I would ask. "Well, he raped her," Zsóka says. "Of course."

Sándor reaches between us to get another slice.

The talk shifts to a poignant subject: Ági has become increasingly convinced in the past few days that her own brother György has defected. György is younger than she is, and she feels protective toward him. He hadn't liked his job in Hungary and had not been able to find another one. He went on a group tour to West Germany with a thirty-day visa and did not come back. His visa ran out a couple of weeks ago. He has called several times, and has promised each time that he will come home soon. But Ági no longer believes him, and neither does György's wife, who has yet to figure out what to tell the two children. In speaking of the affair tonight, Ági shows a part of herself that I have not seen before. The mouth between the wide cheekbones and the strong chin trembles for a moment. When Stefánia asks how she is holding up, she suddenly cannot speak, she only shrugs—helpless, for once, in the face of her misfortune.

Sándor reenters the conversation to rescue his wife; he brings up Poland and Solidarity, and soon the talk is settled squarely on Jaruzelski, Walesa, and Gdansk. Sándor is taken with the ideas, and he relishes the words in his mouth: free trade unions, arbitration, a free press. "What we will have someday," he says, "is a real power among the workers to set their wages and working conditions. Every year, more freedom is given to the factories to run themselves." Sándor himself is an assistant manager at a factory that makes finished clothing. "We have our quota, and now they say to us, 'Make us this many of this and that many of that, and we don't care how you do it.' At the end, if we have a profit, the factory keeps it." His pale blue eyes shine enthusiastically. "There is nothing about Solidarity that should bother the Polish government—what is antisocialist about trade unions? If the work conditions were better there, Solidarity would not have to go on strike and there would be no trouble. Perhaps it won't be long before conditions in Hungary are good enough so that we will have more freedom of press."

Zsóka cannot resist mocking this attitude: "You mean they'll let us write what we want as soon as they're sure we'll want to write only good things. How kind of them!"

Zsóka considers Sándor weak and rather boring. But I like his innocent air. When he speaks, he usually says the obvious, but he gives the impression of having first thought of it only seconds before. It is as if he'd begun to make judgments only yesterday, about everything—his life, his friends, his country. His weakness, at least, seems fresh and kind. Ági and Sándor have worked out an effective relationship. Ági bulls forward, getting things done, and Sándor comes behind, polishing her results with his admiration.

Sándor takes more wine and lifts his glass almost to the hanging table lamp, causing purple-black butterflies of light to flutter on the white tablecloth. "To Poland!" he says. "May they have good fortune and a more just future!"

On several occasions, I have noticed a difference in Hungarian attitudes toward Poland and Romania. Both countries have attempted to free themselves somewhat from Moscow, and of the two, Romania has achieved the greater success. Yet when the Hungarians speak of Romania, they speak only of wretched internal affairs, of the stupidity of the Romanians and the tyranny of Ceaușescu. Of course, there is the Transylvanian issue, which will always be a reason for them to hate Romania; the Hungarians and the Poles have never disputed territory, because no common border exists between them. There are also religious grounds for the different attitudes: the Hungarians, as Roman Catholics, are touched by the singing of canticles in the Polish shipyards, the riots to prevent the removal of crosses from the Polish schools; but the Romanians, as Orthodox Christians, have suppressed the Catholic Church in the past. There are historical grounds: in the Middle Ages, Hungary and Poland shared a couple of kings; the great Polish general József Bem led the Hungarian Army in the 1848 revolution, and the Polish October of 1956 inspired the Hungarians to attempt a revolt of their own. But most importantly, the Polish struggle is a struggle for dignity—it comes from the people, who must fight the Polish government. The Romanian struggle is a struggle merely for power—it is fought by the Romanian government, at the expense of its people. The Soviets have treated the two disobediences of the Poles and the Romanians differently because they are perceptive enough to see that the former threatens to spread its contagion by example; the latter, if anything, discredits disobedience in the eyes of other East Bloc countries. I remember seeing once, tacked up on a wooden construction barrier in Pest, a badly reproduced picture of Lech Walesa—a mimeograph. When I walked past the same place the next day, the piece of paper had been torn down. The authorities in Hungary do not have to worry about anyone tacking up pictures of Nicolae Ceaușescu. Instead, people tell stories about how his son rapes women and kills their boyfriends.

The party breaks up, since Stefánia must be at a rehearsal early tomorrow morning. It is a fine night, with the March mists from the Danube hovering above the streets, making diffuse globes of the lamps and bright, liquid lines of the streetcar rails. Not a night to coop ourselves in a careening bus, so we walk south past the West Railroad Station, skirting the edge of Marx Square, then west toward the Margaret Bridge, into Saint Stephen Boulevard, named in honor of the first king and Christian of Hungary. Then south again, into Rosenberg Street, named in its turn after the American martyrs Julius and Ethel.

The juxtaposition of Karl Marx Square and Saint Stephen

Boulevard—the internationalist atheist and the national saint—is, I think, deliberately incongruous: it has the subtly iconoclastic edge that Eastern European wit allows itself. And certainly Rosenberg Street is not without its sly humor: it leads directly to the back door of the American embassy. We circle around to the front, into Freedom Square, where the American flag hangs solemnly from a pole cocked above a second-floor balcony; I can't help laughing again at the cheerful mockery in the names: the well-lit façade of the American embassy, proudly fronting on the grass and mixed trees of Freedom Square, and then around the back, on every dark corner, like a suppressed memory, signs that say ROSENBERG.

From Freedom Square we head west to the Danube bank and south again, along the narrow stone quay. The Chain Bridge is lit tonight, the hundreds of yellow lamps along its suspension cables pinpricking its graceful outlines, making it into an enormous, glorious toy, a tiara. Sándor and Zsóka clap their hands. "It's so beautiful!" Zsóka says. The Chain Bridge is the sentimental favorite among the monuments of Budapest, partly because it *is* beautiful, with its squat stone towers that resemble triumphal arches and its iron gas lamps, and partly because it was the first bridge to connect Buda and Pest, and so make the two separate towns a unity. In this city, where so many things stand for other things, the Chain Bridge has come to symbolize Budapest's strength. When the bridge was finished in 1849, the first people to march across it were Austrian troops, coming to quell the Hungarian War of Independence. To weaken the city's resistance, the Austrians tried twice to blow up the beautiful new bridge, but failed both times, succeeding only in killing the colonel in charge of the demolition. Unfortunately, explosives were far more sophisticated ninety-five years later, and the Nazis, retreating from the Red Army into Buda, had no trouble dropping the Chain Bridge into the Danube. All of the other bridges were blown up as well, but the first to be rebuilt was the Chain Bridge, which opened again for its hundredth anniversary in 1949. The bridge was not disturbed again until 1956, when Soviet tanks, trying like the Austrians to split the city, blockaded both of its ends during the Hungarian uprising.

Not only the bridge, but all the city monuments are lit tonight—

the neo-Gothic Parliament on the Pest embankment, the Mátyás Church on Castle Hill, the Freedom Statue (built for the Fascists) raising its palm frond high into mist over Gellért Hill. The lights are not usually seen in March, since there are not enough tourists around to justify their cost. We cross the Chain Bridge into Buda and climb Castle Hill on the far side, taking the long, covered, pitch-dark stairs up to the Fisherman's Bastion to catch the best view of the city, lit like a spray of candles and admiring itself in the Danube.

"What day is it?" I ask, leaning over the stone parapet between the ridiculous neo-Romanesque towers of the Bastion. The lights reflect off the moisture in the air, creating above the monuments canopies of gold and bronze.

"March 14," Ági says. Her profile is black against the spotlit stones of the Fisherman's Bastion.

"Why are the lights on tonight?"

The cheeks of her silhouette tense—is she smiling? She crosses her arms and hugs herself to ward off the cold air. "Well, I think March 14 is Marx's birthday." She laughs. "But they might also be on for tomorrow. The Russians are not sure they want us celebrating March 15, but . . ." Her voice trails off.

"They let us play guessing games here, too," Zsóka says.

"What is March 15?" I ask.

"Our National Day," Ági says. "It used to be our most important holiday. It dates from the Revolution of 1848. You have heard of Petőfi Sándor?"

"Yes."

"Petőfi was one of our greatest poets—he died very young." Ági says the latter in a way to suggest that it proves the former. "He wrote the *Nemzeti Dal*—the National Song—in 1848 to incite the Magyars against the Austrians, who had ruled Hungary for two centuries. It is the most famous of all Hungarian poems:

> *Rise, Magyar, your country calls you!*
> *The time has come, now or never!*
> *Shall we be slaves or free?*
> *This is the question—choose!*

> By the God of the Magyars
> We swear,
> We swear, that we will no longer be slaves!

Petőfi admired the French Revolution, and he wanted to make a sensation such as the singing of the *Marseillaise* in Paris. So he wrote the *Nemzeti Dal* and recited it before thousands of people outside the National Museum, on March 15, 1848. He was twenty-five years old. The people rose up, and when the Austrians would not accept their demands, they made the War of Independence."

Zsóka: "Only *we* could lose our war and still call it the War of Independence."

Ági adds, "We lost that war because of the Russians, you know."

"No, I didn't."

"Kossuth Lajos and his armies were beating the Austrians. We would have won the war. But Franz Josef asked the Tsar for help. The Russian Army was much larger than ours—we had no chance. The Hungarian armies fell back into Transylvania and were destroyed there. Petőfi Sándor was killed by a Russian soldier in the battle of Segesvár. Kossuth had to flee; the other Hungarian leaders were hanged in Arad."

Ági smiles crookedly. "And now the Soviets call that war the Bourgeois Revolution of 1848. They took away our National Holiday and put April 4 in its place; they call it Liberation Day. That is the day the Russians took over Hungary from the Nazis."

Zsóka sighs and looks out over the city. "Perhaps they put on the lights for March 15 to make us feel good. But that is all. Tomorrow is just an ordinary day. Flags will be up, but we will have to go to work, all the same."

So even in the lights there are hidden meanings. National Holidays, the Revolution of 1848, Petőfi Sándor—you really have to do your research in this town. If you don't know who built the Freedom Statue, and for whom, then you can't understand why the Hungarians smile ruefully whenever they look up at it. If you don't know that the brilliant choreographer from Győr was kicked out of Budapest by Party members, then you cannot understand why his company draws 10,000 people, and why, instead of bowing to the audience, he shakes his fist at it. It seems incongruous to stand here, with the city spread like a sequined satin dress below us, and to talk about dates, historical references, the veiled intentions of cynical leaders. Incongruous and sad. Unlike Zsóka, who I think enjoys the guessing in spite of herself, I am not attuned to the secret pleasure of symbols.

Suddenly, simultaneously, all the lights go out. Some master switch has been thrown, and the Parliament, the bridge, the church, statue, and bastion have leapt back into darkness. Only the mercury streetlights, the sodium lamps along the boulevards, and the Red Star on top of the Parliament remain on. Zsóka peers at her watch. "Ten o'clock, exactly," she says. "Game's over."

At 3:00 p.m. on October 23, 1956, an organization of students in Budapest held a demonstration in March 15 Square, in front of the Petőfi Monument. There had been no plans, no intentions, for a big affair; it was to be simply a peaceful demonstration against the government of Ernő Gerő, the hated man who had been Mátyás Rákosi's closest advisor. But the organizers were in for a surprise: 25,000 people attended.

A well-known actor stood on the monument and read Petőfi's anti-Habsburg poem, "Arise, Magyar." Leaflets were handed out, listing the fourteen student demands, which closely paralleled the twelve demands that Petőfi presented on March 15, 1848. Among others: new free elections, a free press, removal of foreign troops from Hungarian soil, reinstatement of the National Holiday, March 15, and the national day of mourning, October 6 (for the thirteen officers executed in Arad, 1849), recasting of Soviet-Hungarian friendship on a basis of equality, reform of the agricultural system, release of political prisoners, immediate removal of the Stalin statue at the entrance to the City Park.

The crowd then marched through the main boulevards of Pest, carrying banners and the tricolor Hungarian flag. At the West Railroad Station, in Karl Marx Square, thousands of workers happened to be returning from the factories in the north of Budapest just as the procession was passing. As Marx would have liked, the workers joined the students and marched with them up Saint Stephen Boulevard, across the Margaret Bridge to Buda. The march ended at József Bem Square, which had a double symbolism: Bem was a Polish general, and one of the purposes of today's demonstration was to declare Hungarian solidarity with the Poles, who currently were protesting, under their leader Gomulka, the policies of the Soviet Union; moreover, it was József Bem who had led the Hungarian forces against the Austrians in 1848–49 (he had been called "Father Bem" by his soldiers, who loved him).

At 5:00 p.m. in József Bem Square, two hundred yards north of the house on Hunyadi János Street, 60,000 people had amassed. The head of the Hungarian Writers Union spoke, expressing support. People in the apartments overlooking the square tore the Communist emblem out of their Hungarian flags and hung the mutilated standards from their windows. (In the crowd below, with a tricolor ribbon on her lapel, stood Mrs. Nagy, thirty years old; holding her right hand was Zsóka, six, and on her left was little Éva, three; Pál had been in her womb five months.) At the close of the rally, the crowd sang the old National Anthem.

Now what? There were no leaders, no plans. No one had expected things to go this far. The only political figure to whom the demonstrators thought they could turn was Imre Nagy, the popular "national" Communist who had been deposed the previous year by Rákosi and Gerő. Nagy was living, without power, some-where in Budapest—few knew where. So the crowd marched back across the Danube, growing as it went (Mrs. Nagy was tired and went home), from the Margaret Bridge, down the Széchenyi Quay, to the Parliament building, where it was hoped that Imre Nagy could be made to appear, and to speak, and to tell the demonstra-tors what they should do next. By 7:00 p.m., outside the Parliament in Kossuth Square (yet another symbol: Lajos Kossuth had been the political leader of the 1848 revolution), 200,000 people stood. In the grassy, quarter-mile-long square, in the dusk, there was literally no room to move.

Shortly after 7:00, as it did every night, the Red Star on the top of the Parliament dome went on; the crowd shouted, and, after a minute, it went off again. The crowd roared for Nagy, and a barely audible voice from a Parliament balcony said he was coming. Minutes went by, while the sky grew dark. Then suddenly all the lights in the square were turned off. But the people did not panic or disperse. They lit thousands of pamphlets and held the tiny torches above their heads. Finally, Nagy appeared on the balcony.

Nagy had hated Stalinism, but he was a fervent Communist, and he did not believe, at least not at that moment, that an insurrection was the answer. His first word on the balcony, shouted weakly over the sea of heads (he had no microphone), was *"Elvtársak!"*—"Comrades!"—and the crowd roared back, "No more comrades! We are Hungarians!" Nagy made a speech—an unsatisfying, supplicatory speech that did nothing but irritate the crowd. Nagy was surprised and almost left the balcony. But then he turned back and raised his hand for silence. He wanted to appease the crowd. So he began to sing the old National Anthem, and the huge mass of people joined him, singing it for the second time that day. When it was over and Nagy had gone, the people began to drift out of the square, into the darkness, to go home. Perhaps a strike would follow, or another demonstration tomorrow. No one knew exactly, since no one had planned for this. Most believed that the whole thing would just peter out.

But events were being transformed even while Nagy spoke. In another part of the city, a crowd of people had been massed outside the Radio Station since late afternoon. A delegation of students was trying to gain permission to read their demands on the air, but the security police (known as the AVO) had barred the gates. The government tried to dupe the demonstrators into believing that their demands were going on the air. Then Party leader Ernő Gerő broadcast a provoking, insulting speech. The student delegation was finally allowed into the building, but then it failed to return. Treachery was suspected. The crowd was getting angrier as fast as it was getting bigger. After demands for the return of the delegation were ignored, the crowd began to press against the gates. The members of the AVO had been instructed to hold the radio building at all costs. First they turned fire hoses on the crowd, then tear gas. But the protestors would not disperse, and some time between nine and ten o'clock that evening, the AVO opened fire with automatic weapons. The crowd fell back, shedding corpses. By midnight, the protestors, whom the AVO had transformed into insurgents, had gotten guns of their own and were firing back. Many of the guns had come from sympathetic soldiers and army officers, and here and there, in the bloody street fighting, one could see Hungarians still in their army uniforms shooting at the AVO.

The "siege of Radio Budapest" was to continue for the next twelve hours, ending with the storming of the building and the massacre of the AVO men inside (and the discovery of the bodies of the delegation members). By the morning of the twenty-fourth, with dead and wounded lying from curb to curb of Bródy Sándor Street, the situation had polarized. If there was still any way to turn back, it was going to be hard to find, and virtually no one who was in the streets was looking for it.

•

Mrs. Nagy on 1956:
"Even then the Russians were cowards. What did they have to be afraid of? There were 10 million of us and 200 million of them. But when they came back into Budapest and crushed everything, they kept only on the main streets at night, even in their tanks! I remembered them in 1945, sneaking around like criminals—and it was just the same in 1956. The tanks ran from little boys with Molotov cocktails. They fired on unarmed women and children. At night, they fired at lights in the apartments and killed people in their homes.

"The white soldiers were mainly Belorussian. They had been told they would be fighting the American Army. Can you imagine?! They kept asking us, 'Where are the Americans?' The fighting was over before any of them realized that the American Army wasn't just beyond the first Buda hills.

"But most of the soldiers were Asians. You know, I had never seen an Asian before. The Russians had taken soldiers from Mongolia and brought them to Hungary to kill Hungarians. The Mongol invasion all over again! But these Mongols knew nothing of Europe—they'd been told only that we were the enemy. How could they know? We weren't even human to them. Some of the Mongols, after the fighting, hunted for crocodiles in the Danube. They thought it was the Nile! Because, you see, the Suez Crisis was going on at the same time.

"I stayed in the house nearly all the time. Zsóka was only six, and I was pregnant. It wasn't so bad here, because most of the fighting in the beginning was over in Pest and the bridges were closed by Russian tanks. But when the Russians came back on November 4, we'd had a week, you know, of being left to ourselves, and I was caught out on Castle Hill—we were beginning to think it was safer—I was caught by some tanks. My mother and I were on the winding road that goes up from Attila Street, and the tanks were coming down from the palace. My mother was a very old woman, and she could not walk well. The tanks just came upon us. I was calling to the tanks, 'Wait, wait! Wait for us to get off the road!' But the tanks kept coming; just rolling, like big, silent animals—they were going to push us off the hill. We were at the bend in the road, and there was no room; we had to climb over the wall—even my mother! We slipped down the slope there into a bush." Mrs. Nagy is laughing again. She repeats her plea to the tanks, shaking her head affectionately: " 'Wait, wait! Go back!' Oh, but they didn't go back. They pushed us right off the hill. Imagine! Two old women!"

•

At the head of the two-mile-long, tree-lined People's Republic Avenue, lies Hősök Tere—Heroes' Square—a spacious bit of flatness flanked by the Szépmüvészeti and the Műcsarnok Museums. The black-and-white paving is laid out in a pattern of chains of nested rectangles. A tall, fluted column rising from the center of the square, topped by the Archangel Gabriel, and a semicircular colonnade at the back were erected in 1896 for the millenary celebration of the arrival of the Magyars in Hungary. At the base of the high column, mounted on magnificent bronze horses, are a bronze Árpád (the chieftain who led his tribes westward through the Carpathians into the Hungarian plain in A.D. 896) and his bronze lieutenants. In the colonnade at the back, between the pillars, stand fourteen statues, the most important of which represent: Saint Stephen, the first king and first Christian of Hungary, crowned with the Pope's approval in A.D. 1000, the man who linked Hungary (formerly a state of seminomadic pagans from the Urals) irrevocably to the West; Béla IV, the visionary king and tireless builder who founded Buda after the devastating Mongol invasion of 1241–42, and who settled the Saxons as border guards and burghers in Transylvania; János Hunyadi, the son of a Vlach boyar who became one of Christendom's greatest champions against the Turks, whose victory over them at Belgrade in 1456 we still celebrate (although we don't know it) whenever we ring church bells at noon, and whose castle, the Vajdahunyad, now in Romania, has been lovingly replicated on an island in Budapest's City Park, immediately behind Hősök Tere; Hunyadi's son, King Mátyás, or Matthias Corvinus, the Renaissance king, now called Hungary's only truly national king after the end of the Árpád dynasty, even though he was half Romanian; Ferenc Rákóczi II, a wealthy prince who led the Hungarians in a rebellion against the Habsburgs in 1703 and was defeated only after eight years of fighting against impossible odds, and whose battle march, a rousing tune in the Gypsy vein, was banned afterward by the Habsburgs, because every time the Hungarians heard it they would grab their pitchforks and head for the nearest Austrian outpost; and Lajos Kossuth, the brilliant and ruthless political leader of the 1848 Revolution, who, like Rákóczi, ended up in defeat, in exile, imploring a deaf world to come to the aid of his countrymen.

The unacknowledged presence of one and a half Romanians among this company of Hungarian heroes is not the only incongruity—the Communists have added their own. The millenary monument predates the Communists by half a century, and so these are national heroes, not socialist ones. The Stalinists never considered dismantling the monument, but I suspect they were trying to counteract its pronounced royalism when they built adjacent to it two large edifices housing the Trade Union Center and the Hungarian Building Workers' Trade Union. They also renamed the boulevard that abuts Hősök Tere after György Dózsa, a Szekler mercenary who was delegated by a papal aspirant in

1514 to lead a mass of starving peasants on a crusade against the
Turks, but who turned his ragtail army against the Hungarian
landowners instead. Needless to say, he was defeated, and the
King, showing the firmness if not the taste of which most of the
men commemorated in Hősök Tere would have approved, had
Dózsa roasted alive on a throne of iron and forced his supporters
to eat him before they were hanged. In my guide to Budapest,
printed in Hungary, the statues in the colonnade of Hősök Tere
are mentioned but not identified, while György Dózsa, the Trade
Union buildings, and the simple slab monument to the Hungarian
Unknown Soldier that faces the millenary column are each re-
spectfully described.

One thing that the guides do *not* describe or refer to is the
Stalin statue, which was erected in 1951 near the millenary
monument, perhaps as another attempt to alter the reactionary
tone of the square, or at least to add one more hero to the collection
already guarding the City Park. The Stalin statue was Rákosi's own
idea, and it was an embarrassment from the beginning: the
government, presiding over a vast acreage of rubble that it had
scarcely begun to clean up, demolished one of Budapest's very
few intact churches in order to make space for the statue. On a
crass, fifty-foot-high pedestal, the Stalinists erected an equally
crass, twenty-five-foot-high representation of the man, wearing
heavy boots and grinning. The inscription on the pedestal read
To the Great Stalin, from the Thankful Hungarian People. After Stalin
died, and particularly after the 20th Congress, at which Khrushchev
denounced Stalin, it galled the Hungarians to have this monster
staring like an iron Godzilla down Gorkij Fasor Avenue. But Rákosi
remained committed to Stalinism, so the statue was not removed.

When the students drew up their demands on October 22,
1956, they included a call for the immediate removal of the Stalin
statue. And the following day, when Imre Nagy disappointed the
crowd outside the Parliament with his request that they all go
home, a few students realized that, out of all their demands, only
one could be accomplished with neither the downfall nor the
acquiescence of the government, but simply with blowtorches and
a hawser. A crowd of young people headed from the Parliament

building toward the City Park, someone brought a 10-ton truck, and within a few hours the only thing that stood on the immense pedestal of the memorial were Stalin's boots. The truck dragged the footless body, striking sparks, down the wide streets toward the center of the city and abandoned it at the most appropriate place: the intersection of Stalin Avenue and Lenin Boulevard. There, over the next few days, the insurgents devoted precious time and energy (in between their battles with Soviet tanks) to beating the statue to pieces with sledgehammers.

Mr. Nagy was present when the statue was ripped from its pedestal. And today in the Nagy duplex there is a new family heirloom, a little piece of triumph and revenge, hidden at the bottom of a drawer. It's an iron Cyrillic letter. Holes at the top and bottom show where the letter used to be riveted to the pedestal. Mrs. Nagy tells me it was part of the word "Thankful."

•

Zsóka harbors an aversion toward the Russians that goes deeper than politics, a dislike so visceral that it is unassailable. Most Hungarians I have met are the same way. After years of being told by teachers whom they detested that everything Russian was the best, they instinctively believe that everything Russian is the worst. They were taught that the Russians invented electricity, the telephone, flying, agriculture, the wheel. Now they refuse even to believe that Sputnik beat Explorer into space. They were taught that the West produced nothing of value. Now they revere the West without discrimination, approving of Ronald Reagan, eating *szendvics*, forming huge lines to see *The China Syndrome*, and scrambling to find enough hard currency to buy tickets for the Budapest production of *Cats*. Having retained the age-old Magyar idea that their little country divides East from West, Hungarians view the Russians simply as the latest barbarians from the East: Slavic savages following in the footsteps of the Mongols, who sacked Hungary in the thirteenth century, and the Turks, who sacked it in the sixteenth. Few Hungarians, actually, are antisocialist (the demands of 1956, for example, were consistent with socialism); nearly all are simply anti-Russian or, more precisely, anti-Soviet.

Zsóka, like all Hungarians, was required to take ten years of

Russian instruction in school. Her German, after two years of tutoring, is quite good. Her English, after three years (plus continuing practice in technical language), is nearly flawless. She has been studying French for the past four months, and she can already carry on a decent conversation. But her Russian stinks. She can barely read the simplest signs; she cannot put together a complete sentence. It is the same with István, who has learned to stumble along in English; with Éva, who speaks fair German; with Mrs. Nagy, who teaches German and English; with Mr. Nagy, who speaks German, English, French, and Italian. Even Árpád can feel his erratic way around German phrases. But hardly a word of Russian from any of them. When they need to call it up, they just look at each other, shrug their shoulders, and break into laughter.

·

Mrs. Nagy on Rákosi (for once, without humor): "OhmyGod, RÁKOSI! What a terrible man! I don't even want to *talk* about him."
(Silence.)
"Well . . . They said, you know, that deep down he hated the Hungarian people—from his imprisoning here, before the war. He'd started the Communist Party again, when it was illegal, and they threw him in prison. Of course, he spent the war in Moscow, having an easy time, and came back to head the Communist Party in 1945. They were nobodies, these ones who came back at the end of the war! They were people with grievances, people who had been humiliated. We had never heard of them. But the Russians were behind them, and they just sat in a room and said to each other, Okay, you will be head of police, you will be Minister of Agriculture, you will be First Secretary. They asked no one's permission. They told no one. Suddenly Rákosi was there, in power, no one quite knew how. Then there were show trials; people were afraid to defend the accused, and so they died, one after the other. Rákosi called it 'salami tactics.' He just kept slicing off pieces, until there was nothing left to slice."

·

Hunyadi János Street rises along the flank of Castle Hill in Buda, and it is a short walk from the house up the twisting covered staircases to the narrow, flattened top of the hill. So if I am not carting wood to wake me up after writing, I am often on the hill, walking on the wide cobblestone streets from one end of the plateau to the other, between the Baroque and Empire and Louis XVI façades (hiding Gothic interiors), gathering images: ornate iron window gratings, statues adorning each corner like pedestrians waiting for the lights, great dusty wooden doors flanked by carved granite slabs that read HISTORIC BUILDING. On fine days, crowds of Hungarians are out, too, especially on the walkways that follow the old ramparts and provide the views—old couples who are cheerful and fussy when you ask them to take your picture and teenagers with lovers or, failing that, with imitation Walkmans.

Having been the capital of Hungary since the thirteenth century, the Castle District is the oldest section of Budapest. But its antiquity, like the antiquity of most of the city (or most of Central Europe, for that matter), is something of a sham. At the end of the siege of Budapest, in February 1945, only one house was still standing on the hill; the painstaking reconstruction has taken decades, and the job is now nearly completed. This is more than you can say for any other part of the city, and there's a reason: Castle Hill, with its quaintness once more intact, is the city's principal tourist draw. I usually go north along the Tóth Árpád Promenade, named, like so many of Budapest's streets, after a poet. Turning right from Tóth Árpád onto Úri Street and passing the statue of András Hadik (an eighteenth-century hussar who once began a charge in Hungary and ended it in Berlin) brings me to Trinity Square, which marks the center of the Castle District. The square is named after a Baroque representation of the Trinity that occupies its middle: a stone obelisk studded with clouds and topped with Jesus, a Father figure, and a sunburst. Like every Trinity statue I have seen (the fiasco near Saint Stephen's in Vienna comes particularly to mind), the monument fails utterly to convey a sense even of respect, let alone awe, concerning its divine subject. The clouds look like whipped cream, the sunburst is cold and meretricious, and God, rather heretically, I would think, is fully realized in all His lack of splendor as an old man clutching a golden orb. Typical Age of Enlightenment stuff.

The real prize of Trinity Square is the Mátyás Church, a

delightful edifice in a mishmash of styles spanning six centuries, from Béla IV's mid-thirteenth-century foundation to a late-nine-teenth-century roof of faience-like colored tiles. But the church fights a perpetual battle with the ridiculous elements around it. Facing the north wall of the church is the new Hilton hotel, a huge affair with protruding columnar windows that make one think of a gangster in a zoot suit. On the other side of Mátyás, toward the river, stands an equestrian statue of Saint Stephen that sits atop a wedding-cake pedestal of stone, on the corners of which are columns embossed with spirals and zigzags and rosettes, and grinning, half-crazed lions that look like Felix the Cat. Then, between the statue and the bluff overlooking the Danube is the most ridiculous structure of all, like a matte painting from the Wizard of Oz—the neo-Romanesque Fisherman's Bastion. Stairs lead up to walkways topping a series of coy cloisters with Norman arches, stone portholes, and more embossed columns; the walkways meander along the edge of the cliff, between fleur-de-lis crenella-tions, culminating in round towers with conical witches' hats. The whole thing is made out of a white, porous stone that, from a distance, resembles dirty Styrofoam.

Like Budapest architecture as a whole, the area around the Mátyás Church, with its borrowed styles, is redolent of playacting. The Baroque is pure Habsburg, the Hilton is Boston Stolid, and the neo-Romanesque is Twentieth Century-Fox. To someone expecting Budapest to be a revelation, a jewel, this uncertain eclecticism can be disappointing.

But to redeem it all, one need only climb the stairs to the platforms of the Bastion, ignore the damn towers, and look east. Buda drops precipitously away, and the Danube dominates the view below like a bolt of shimmering cloth; beyond it, Pest stretches out infinitely into the haze of the city's breath. The enormous Parliament building on the far bank and the Chain Bridge to the south balance the cityscape like two treasures, a music box and a necklace, being weighed for their silver. On cold gray days, the view is streaks of brown and black, an austere watercolor. On sunny moist days, it is a pastel. At night, it is a stitching of stars on black sailcloth. At all times, counterbalancing the city's borrowed architecture, its history of foreign domination, the view is distinctly Budapest's own. No city confronts itself so dramatically across its water as does Budapest—here has been the drama of Nazis in Buda being shelled by Russians in Pest, of Mohammedans in Pest laying siege to Christians in Buda, of Romans at their outposts in the Pannonian hills looking east across the Danuvius and the swampy plain for signs of the barbarians. East has met West at this place, across this river, for two thousand years. It is solely because of this view, I think, that people call Budapest beautiful.

.

Mrs. Nagy on János Kádár:

"He works hard and he believes in what he is doing. He is a good man.

"You know, at first, he was hated; *everybody* mistrusted him. Kádár was put in by the Russians when they threw out Nagy's government in 1956. How could we trust him? He was alongside Nagy during the uprising—after the first day of the rioting, he replaced Gerő as First Secretary. And people were happy about that—Kádár had been imprisoned under Rákosi just as Nagy had been—a 'Titoist.' He had been tortured, too. The two of them were friends; Kádár had spent the war in Hungary, not in Moscow like Rákosi and Gerő; he was a nationalist. But when the Russians came, Kádár proclaimed a new government and Nagy was arrested. Kádár hanged Nagy later. How could you trust such a man?

"But, you know, the living here teaches you to do things you never thought possible. Sometimes you have to forget—and now Kádár is a very popular leader. And I will say, rightly so. He has done a lot of good for the country; he put in this new economic plan that made the industry less central; he let people have a little private land, little private stores . . . There was a phrase that Rákosi used: 'Who is not with us is against us.' Kádár changed that when he became leader; he says, 'Who is not against us is with us.' That is the best thing about Kádár—people are not afraid anymore. You can go to church, you can say what you think. If you leave the government alone, it will leave you alone. You don't know how rare it has been that way for Hungarians.

237 / H U N G A R Y

"So it is a little funny—when Kádár came in, no one wanted him. But now—now that he is old and may die soon, no one wants him to go. Hungarians are never satisfied!"

•

János Kádár's fingernails were torn out in a Hungarian prison during the 1950s. His interrogators urinated in his mouth. When Russian tanks closed in on the Parliament on November 4, 1956, Kádár was in the building. The Russians confronted him, this man who had stood by Nagy as First Secretary when Nagy, as Premier, had declared Hungary neutral and announced its withdrawal from the Warsaw Pact. They offered him the chance to betray the uprising to stay on as leader of Hungary. It is known that Kádár refused. It is *not* known what the Russians then offered him or, perhaps, threatened him with. But eventually, he accepted. From the occupied Parliament building, Kádár declared a new "revolutionary peasant-worker government" under a new party, the Hungarian Socialist Workers Party. A general strike followed that lasted for months. Two hundred thousand Hungarians fled the country. The new government was held in so much contempt, it was virtually powerless.

But nearly three decades have passed. Kádár lives in a little house in Buda, not far from the Nagy's duplex. He works long hours and doesn't take vacations. Unlike Rákosi, he is not a bon vivant or a socializer, so when his work is done, he goes home to his peasant wife, who still keeps chickens in the back yard. And John Dornberg, who used to be *Newsweek*'s bureau chief in Vienna, is of the opinion that János Kádár, in a free and open election, could win any office for which he decided to run in Hungary. Kádár, by his ascetic life as much as by his reforms, has convinced the Hungarians that he has his country's interests at heart.

In Budapest, one hears, now and then, a startling admission: Kádár might have had the country's best interests at heart even when he agreed to govern at the end of the uprising. The Russians had already arrived; nothing was going to make them go away. Kádár's plans for reform could be buried with him, or they could be pushed to the extent that Russian control allowed. The path of

the collaborator is always paved with seductive justifications, and
for that reason, collaboration brings contempt even when its value
is inarguable. Kádár took the contemptible path and simply outlived
the contempt.

.

Isteven's father died yesterday, of a massive stroke. István and
Éva have gone to István's hometown, Kiskunfélegyháza, to arrange
for the burial. The baby is with Mrs. Nagy, and Zsóka and I have
taken the other two daughters for the day.

Eszter, aged six, has been in a rotten mood all afternoon:
crying without producing tears, asking for things she doesn't want,
picking on Zsófi, aged three. Zsófi misses her parents and can
produce enough tears for both of them. Zsóka has tried to appease
them with the box of toys that she keeps under her writing desk
just for this purpose, but the girls know something is wrong and
refuse to be comforted. Dinner is a failure. I haven't often cooked
for children, and I didn't realize that my stew would be suspected
of harboring all kinds of disgusting things, such as worms or
mushrooms; that it would be murdered through dissection, every
last piece of onion or green pepper being held up for inspection.
The only other cookable food in the apartment is eggs, and eggs
apparently belong to the worm/mushroom category. However, we
do have bread, and half a jar of Bulgarian strawberry preserves,
so Zsóka and I eat the stew while Eszter and Zsófi finally settle
down with glasses of milk and one sticky-red slice in each hand.

At 10:00 p.m. there is a knock, and I find István out in the
hall. He is dressed in black and looks terrible, his skin white and
drawn behind the bushy beard. Zsóka's sister Éva is on the landing
above, with the baby, opening the door to their apartment. She
looks down, over her shoulder, and smiles nervously, appeasingly,
at me. I invite István in to collect the girls. Zsóka, from the kitchen
door, greets him gravely: "Szervusz." She is polite but clearly
uncomfortable. It occurs to me that in all the time I have lived
here, I have never seen István in Zsóka's apartment.

Zsófi is asleep, and Eszter, now that she finally has her father
back, demands both his hands, so while István coaxes Eszter up

the stairs, I carry Zsófi. István and Éva's apartment is minuscule, consisting of a kitchen in what would normally be the front hall, a small dining room, and, up four more steps, under the apex of the pyramidal roof, a single bedroom. The baby sleeps in the dining room, and the two girls sleep on a platform built over their parents' bed. Éva is preparing the crib for the baby, who is awake but quiet. I take Zsófi into the bedroom and lay her on her parent's bed.

In the dining room, István thanks me. He thanks me too fervently. He's picked up Eszter, a big girl, and her head is on his neck, her hands clasped around his opposite shoulder; she's quiet and thoughtful now. ("He's a good enough father, I suppose, but—" "But what?" "Oh, I can't explain.") He wants me to stay for coffee. There's that feeling again, that he is on the verge of unburdening himself, of drawing me farther into his life than I want to go. I can't help him, I want to say. I live in the enemy camp, but I don't understand it. My record as a peacemaker is dismal.

Éva puts coffee on for us, and István talks about a play he is directing for the amateur theater group to which he belongs. He talks slowly, searching for the English words in the air in front of him, trying to tell me *precisely* what his thoughts are on this play, on character motivation, on dramatic theory in general. He doesn't seem to expect me to contribute, so I speak only to correct him when he makes a mistake. After all, I'm supposed to be tutoring him in English once a week, although I haven't gotten together with him for the past month. (He failed his engineering exam the first time, which might not have happened if I'd helped him more: he must pass the exam if he wants to earn a decent salary.) Every time I correct a phrase, István winces, repeats the corrected version several times, and thanks me clumsily. He assures himself, through saying it to me, that he doesn't mind being corrected. Éva sips her coffee and looks very tired. She does not understand English.

István's monologue becomes increasingly self-congratulatory as he describes his disagreements, his tribulations, with actors, stage managers, and theater owners. Those who don't understand. He speaks to me as artist-to-artist, as one David to another in the land of the Philistines. I have to assume that he wants my approval, and I find it depressing that he cares. What earthly good is my opinion? Eszter has fallen asleep in his lap, hugging him. He is half of the world to her, and he wants approval from *me*. A male thing, perhaps. But I am not very good at male things.

Eventually, I am on the staircase outside the apartment. "If there's anything we can do to help again, anything at all, just let us know. We'll bring up some food tomorrow, so Éva doesn't have to cook if she's too busy."

István clasps my hand. "You don't have to go back to her right now. You can stay here longer." Just now, I told him "anything," but this is one way in which I am not willing to help. I want too much to escape.

Downstairs, Zsóka has gone to bed.

•

Zsóka is planning to go to Transylvania again, this Easter. There is a man in Ági's grandmother's village, a Magyar, whom she may marry. She has met him only once, but if she marries him, he will be allowed to move to Hungary. When he does, he will put a few of his belongings in Zsóka's apartment in order to establish cohabitation. After a year, they will get a divorce. Many Hungarians have done this. However, Zsóka, a Catholic with both feet and one hand outside the fold, is still not certain marriage means so little to her that she can go through with it. Her friends tell her that it is for a good cause, and she knows that; but no arguments can touch the residue of an upbringing, and Zsóka's persists in her reproachfully.

And something else bothers her: the idea of the divorce itself. She will be a divorcée, and regardless of the intentions behind the marriage, divorce makes her think of failure. Hungary has the highest divorce rate in Europe, and she views that statistic as a symptom of the pressures of living here, of the constraints that make people petty. Zsóka does not want to contribute to a statistic that seems to say Hungary is losing its fight against resignation. The man in Transylvania may have to marry someone else.

•

The most hated document in Hungarian history is the 1920 Treaty of Trianon, the post-Versailles agreement by which the boundaries of Hungary were redrawn, allegedly along ethnic lines. Hungarians of all classes, all ages, all political beliefs can agree on one thing—whatever evil Hungary may have done, or (the preferred notion) whatever evil it was forced to do by the Habsburgs during the 230 years of Austrian rule, it did not do anything evil enough to deserve Trianon.

Good or bad, Trianon must be accepted as a part of reality, but Hungary has never come to terms with it. Attitudes here have not changed much since the 1930s, when the national rallying cry in reference to Trianon was *"Nem, nem, soha"* ("No, no, never"). Consequently, Hungary has never come to terms with its neighbors, all of whom hold some part of the historical Hungary that was given to them by Trianon. And Hungary's neighbors view the Hungarians as a quarrelsome, unforgiving people, made narrow by their disappointments.

Some suggestive statistics:

The land area of Hungary before Trianon was 325,411 square kilometers; after Trianon, it was 92,963 square kilometers. The population before Trianon was 21 million; after Trianon, it was 7.6 million. Of the 13.4 million people lost to Romania, Yugoslavia, and Czechoslovakia, the majority were ethnic Romanians, Serbians, Czechs, and Slovaks. But 3.2 million were Magyars, which meant that *Hungaria irridenta* was nearly half the population of Hungary itself. Some of these Magyars lived in concentrated pockets just outside the new boundary lines. Trianon was just as much a punishment of Hungary as it was a correction of borders.

Ironically, Austria is the only neighbor that Hungary does not now resent, even though it was Austria that dragged Hungary kicking and screaming into World War I and the subsequent debacle in the first place. Austria is the West, and the West is forgiven all things by the citizens of the East. Concerning the rest of her neighbors, Hungary divides her rancor unevenly; the statistics make it easy to see why a hatred of Romania would loom the largest. Half a million Magyars were lost to Yugoslavia, 1 million to Czechoslovakia, 1.7 million to Romania; 62,000 square kilometers were lost to Yugoslavia, another 62,000 to Czechoslovakia, 103,000 to Romania. The land area lost to Romania alone is larger than all of present-day Hungary. (The unfairness of Trianon can be ascribed partly to the fact that Hungary, caught in its dual monarchy with Austria, was regarded at Versailles not as an occupied state but as an aggressor during World War I. The *particular* unfairness of the redrawn Hungarian-Romanian border is due, perhaps, to the fact that France led the Allies at the negotiations in Versailles, and France, for cultural and sentimental reasons, was a champion of Romania.)

But the Hungarians have another special reason to hate the Romanians. In March 1919, the government of Hungary resigned in protest when the Allies ordered it to evacuate more land in Transylvania so that the Romanians could take it. A man named Béla Kun, a Communist who had taken part in the Russian Revolution, came to power. He had apparently been promised help secretly from Russia, so as soon as he was in office, he declared a dictatorship of the proletariat and announced the nationalization of industry and agriculture, the confiscation of private property, and so on. (One of the ministers of Kun's government was none other than Mátyás Rákosi.) Then, on the strength of Russia's promise of military support, Kun attacked Romania in order to win back Transylvania. Russia promptly forgot its promise. The Hungarian Army, largely disarmed and dispersed in 1918 in order to weaken the country's image as an aggressor, was no match for the Romanians, who beat back the attack and marched into Budapest on August 3, while Kun fled to Vienna. From August 3 until November 14, the Hungarians suffered the indignity of an occupation by the very people whom they had controlled and despised in Transylvania for seven hundred years. During those three months of 1919, the Romanians looted the country meticulously, and when they left, at the insistence of the Allies, much of Hungary's portable goods went with them.

Four decades later, Zsóka and her classmates were being taught in school the same verse their parents had memorized:

Kis Magyarórszag, nem órszag;
Nagy Magyarórszag, menyórszag!

Which means: "Little Hungary—no country/Big Hungary—
heaven!" Zsóka recites it for me and laughs, a little embarrassed.
"Silly, isn't it?"

.

Last week Árpád trapped Zsóka and me in the back hall and
extricated a promise from us to come to his next concert. Although
he spoke in German, his voice quavered so much, and I was so
distracted by the violent tic that contorts his face two or three
times a second, that I couldn't understand a word he said; I didn't
know we had signed away one of our evenings until after we'd
said "Szervusz" twenty times and taken refuge in Zsóka's apartment.
It turns out that Árpád plays second flute in the Budapest Traffic
Control Council Orchestra. Not a very good orchestra, Zsóka says,
but the people are very kind to him.

So here we are, swelling the crowd on the second floor of the
Budapest Traffic Control Council's House of Culture, a bullet-
scarred casualty from either the war or the uprising, a couple of
blocks off November 7 Square. The audience consists of family
members and close friends, and I'm reminded pleasantly of all the
high-school concerts I abetted, through which my parents sat
stoically, managing to emerge with convincing smiles. Árpád sits
in the chamber orchestra as if in another world, his thin, pinched
face looking down, or at the ceiling, never at the conductor,
squinting, twitching. But as the Mozart careens along, barely under
control, Árpád lifts the flute to his mouth a split second before
each of his entrances and plays his part—only approximately, but
no more approximately than many of the other players. Quite a
feat, considering that he is almost totally deaf.

During the intermission, we try to tell him how much we are
enjoying ourselves. But he is even more agitated then usual, and
it is not clear that he understands. In fact, it is not quite clear that
he even recognizes us. It has been a trying time for him lately.
Some of the members of the family arranged, last year, for one
of Árpád's nephews to live with him. The idea was that the younger
man would help his ailing uncle, but it seems now that he agreed
to move in only because he wanted Árpád's spacious apartment.
So he has been trying to drive Árpád out by moving his belongings

around, hiding things, messing up his packets of bus tickets and old concert programs. Last month, he adopted a new tactic: he applied to have Árpád committed, as mentally incompetent. Mrs. Nagy has been forced to hire a lawyer, and it will be fought out in court. The family is worried that Árpád, because of the way he speaks, will appear worse to the court than he actually is. Zsóka has expressed a desire to throttle the nephew.

Árpád disappears into the warm-up room to prepare for the second half, and Zsóka and I go back to our chairs. Then the orchestra files on, for a hair-raising rendition of the "Jupiter" Symphony. Affectionate if not quite thunderous applause follows.

Árpád accompanies us home on the bus. Despite his recent troubles, he seems to be in a good mood. After all, he loves his music, and he tells Zsóka now that he was happy with the performance. For all his awkwardness Árpád is the only person I have seen who can stay on his feet in the bus without holding on to anything. He stands there, clutching the flute case to his chest, murmuring to Zsóka, and twitching, swaying back and forth little more than he would if he were standing on the sidewalk, while the bus does 0 to 40 in six seconds out of the bus stops.

·

The sign is big, right in front of my face, and unequivocal: MAI ELÖADASRA MINDEN JEGY ELKELT—"All tickets for today's performance sold out." But the ticket seller is new; she hasn't yet pegged me as a worthless resident. Feeling a bit guilty (I tell myself that this is for Zsóka; it's *Eugen Onyegin* tonight, her favorite opera), I put my mouth to the speaking tube and use German: "Excuse me, are there any tickets for today's performance?"

"Of course," she responds, and pulls out a wad. I pick two seats in the orchestra, eighth row, center.

The man behind me has looked at the sign, has looked over my shoulder at the tickets I am buying. As I leave the window, I hear him say to the woman, in German, "I would like two tickets for *Eugen Onyegin*, please." He says it with a heavy Hungarian accent. I can't bear to find out how he will fare and walk hurriedly away.

·

"Magazines!" The boy lets the door between the train cars slide shut behind him and sidles down the aisle. "Magazines here!" He holds up a publication showing a great glossy fashion picture. More are in a bag around his neck. "Magazines, four forints!"

About ten cents. I have nothing to read and the pictures might be interesting, so I reach into my pocket for change. But Zsóka stops me. "Don't buy it," she says. "It's a Russian magazine."

The boy approaches our seats. "Magazines?" No one is buying.

"They can never sell these things in Hungary," Zsóka says with some amusement. "Hungarian magazines are seven forints, and these are only four—but still they cannot sell them. They are the only magazines offered on the trains—I think they hope that people will have nothing else to read. And the boys fold the covers inside so that people might not notice what they are."

The matronly woman sitting on the bench facing us signals to the boy and holds out some coins. She takes the magazine and drops it into the shopping bag at her feet; she resumes her knitting. Zsóka looks at the woman, expressionless. "It's called *Girls and Women*," she says to me. "It's in Hungarian, but is made in Russia. The boys put a pretty picture on the outside. It has stories for children, and games; clothes and fashion, recipes; but it's mainly about how wonderful everything is in Russia: pictures of workers smiling, of revolutionary youth; everyone very happy. And talk all the time about World War II—the Russians never want us to forget that war."

The matronly woman knits assiduously. But she is aware that Zsóka is watching her; the other woman facing us is watching her, too. Finally, she puts the knitting down and extracts the magazine from her bag. She speaks to Zsóka; her smile is reassuring and a trifle uneasy—the smile of someone explaining a smoking gun and a dead husband to the police.

Zsóka translates for me: "She says she buys it only for the fairy tales inside. She has three young children, and she reads them stories at night." The woman goes on for several minutes. "Some of the stories are serials—her children want to know how the stories end, so she must buy the magazine for them . . . They are charming stories . . . Nothing political . . ." The woman waves a hand in exasperation. "She says three children are so expensive—she saves wherever she can. This magazine is cheaper than the others, so she buys it." Zsóka says all this with a sly smile, and the matronly woman, perhaps suspecting mockery, grows more defensive. She flips to a picture—"she says the photographs are actually quite nice; you don't have to read the text"—and shoves it under Zsóka's nose. Zsóka looks at me and grins. "They are cheerful pictures, she says—and only four forints." A shiny, square-jawed man in a fur coat smiles up at Zsóka, but she ignores him. She looks straight at the woman, over the photograph, and says with exaggerated politeness, "Yes, I'm sure they are quite nice." Zsóka's smile is a wall, and the woman knows she is being shut out. She shows the magazine to the woman next to her, hoping to get sympathy somewhere, but this woman, too, refuses to look. She doesn't even smile, but turns pointedly to stare out the window.

The mother of three hesitates between the two of them—complete strangers whose opprobrium she has earned by buying a ten-cent Russian magazine. Then she shrugs and deposits the magazine back into her shopping bag. She doesn't return to her knitting but stares blankly into the aisle, fingering the square of yarn in her lap. I sense that her feelings are hurt, that she is genuinely ashamed, that she is hoping we will forget the whole matter. She doesn't speak to us again.

•

"Zsóka, there's a note in the *Newsweek* you brought home that you'll love. It's called 'In Cold Type.'"

Some people want to ban the bomb. Some would outlaw handguns. In Romania, the government wants to restrict typewriters. In an effort to stamp out anti-government leaflets, President Nicolae Ceauşescu has signed a decree banning possession or use of typewriters by convicts or anybody else who poses "a danger to public order or state security." Beginning this month, Romanians must register their typewriters with police and submit samples of their machines' distinctive type prints. And anyone who wants to buy a new typewriter must get state permission.

"Can I see that?"

"Sure."

"Oh, this is terrible; just look at this!"

"I just did."

"No, but did you notice? *Newsweek* spells Rumania with an '*o*'! Terrible!"

•

A movie has been playing in Budapest for months, called *Ez Amerika—This Is America*. Zsóka and some of her friends have seen it. They insist that I see it, too. One of the cinemas near Zsóka's apartment is showing the film, so one Saturday morning, Zsóka, Ági, Éva, and I cross Castle Hill, descend to Attila Street, and cross the stretch of brown grass under spindly trees to Krisztina Körút.

We buy four of the last tickets to the 10:00 a.m. show and squeeze behind the others into a threadbare viewing room. In Hungary, one buys film tickets for specific seats, as in a concert or a play. But this morning the cinema is in a hurry to start the show and the lights are turned down almost immediately after the crowd is allowed in. This leaves three-quarters of us in the dark, still standing, trying vainly to see the letters and numbers on the backs of the chairs. Some people, exasperated, sit down at random, and other people, who can see better in the dark, complain when they find the first people sitting in their assigned seats. Arguments spring up everywhere, with half the people asking the other half to move, and the latter half telling the first half not to be so asinine. The noise of the arguments completely drowns out the short subject, which hardly matters, since half the screen is blocked by silhouettes of people gesticulating. Ushers run up and down with flashlights, shining them in people's eyes and adding to the confusion. *Ez Hungary*, I think to myself.

Fortunately, the arguments subside by the middle of the short subject (a dinky travelogue with pictures of ugly hotels and even uglier sunbathers—the perfect tonic for February blues). Then *Ez Amerika* begins, with rock music and English lyrics, shots of urban slums and neon lights whizzing past the window of an American automobile.

I thought the movie was Hungarian, but now I see that it was made by Americans. It is a freewheeling documentary about all the weird things that Americans do, with English narration that is almost, but not quite, intelligible under the louder Hungarian dubbing. (The effect is of one commentator shouting down another.) The movie is divided into segments, or set pieces, each of which limns a particular form of American insanity. There is a segment on a karate school for nuns, in which a phalanx of women in full habit goes "Haaaieeee!" and kicks the air with thirty legs, breaks boards (in slow motion) with hands that protrude from capacious black-and-white sleeves. Another segment concerns a protein research center, where the director and his family eat worms at every meal—worm salad, worm sandwiches, worm meat loaf, even worm juice trickling clear and green out of a blender. Loving shots of kids slurping down worms cause Zsóka and Éva to cover their eyes, while Ági and I look bravely on. Next we are shown a typical evening in the life of an urban headhunter: a strong man with a gun whose job it is to locate and bring in people who have skipped bail. The camera follows him as he breaks down an apartment door, drags his victim back in through the window from the fire escape, and proceeds to beat the man senseless. He ends his performance dramatically, by throwing the man, who is much smaller than he is, over the banister in the hallway, then walking calmly down to pick him up from the floor below and drag him out to the street by his collar. Other segments include a whorehouse for dogs, where thoughtful owners can buy their charges a good time; a drive-in church in California, where men wearing leisure suits and women wearing pantsuits can listen to the sermon from noise boxes that they have attached to the windows of their cars; a wedding in which the couple and the minister perform the ceremony while falling to earth from an airplane, and after which the bride and groom (the minister having graciously absented himself by pulling his rip cord before them) tear each other's clothes off and land naked, except for their parachute harnesses, in the desert, where they are greeted with champagne by a bevy of well-wishers, also naked. And so on.

Of course, except for the drive-in church, which I recognized as Orange Grove, California's Crystal Cathedral, I have not seen any of this before. My mouth has spent the last ninety minutes hanging open just as far as those of the Hungarians around me. And of course, I spend all the time it takes us to walk back to Hunyadi Street trying to convince Zsóka, Ági, and Éva that, although I am an American, I have never bought a whore for my dog, never seen a nun subdue a mugger with a karate chop, never eaten worms, and never attended a wedding reception in which the bride and groom fell out of the sky like a pair of plucked turtledoves.

.

Zsóka and I finally get our hands on tickets for *A Próba—The Rehearsal*. As I suspected, it is another political allegory. Dancers come onto the stage randomly, one by one, practicing steps, talking with each other, stretching their limbs, while the music grows. The rehearsal gradually coalesces and rigidifies until the randomness is gone and the dancers follow each other's steps, arm motions, head movements. It is a tortuous, painful dance, quite long, growing more and more frenzied, and ending in what seems to be exhaustion. Then, confusion—there are pressures outside the rehearsal; more mysterious men in long coats sneak around. One of the lead dancers in the rehearsal becomes troublesome. Somehow, incredibly, he ends up on a cross, where he is machine-gunned by the mysterious men in the long coats. A lot of dancing goes on, while he lies dead at the side of the stage. Then everything starts over again, the dancers entering one by one and practicing their steps while the music grows. A new man has replaced the lead dancer who was shot. The show ends after the rehearsal has again become ordered, the dancers following each other's steps, arm motions, head movements, exactly, like machines.

Like the Győri Ballet or *Sztarcsinálók*, there is something deeply unsatisfactory about *A Próba*, something deeper than its artistic limitations. On our way to the #78 bus, Zsóka puts it nicely: "We are allowed to point our fingers at the injustices here as long as we don't try to solve them. This government is like a man who owes money to another man and thinks it is sufficient merely to acknowledge the debt, never paying it." She looks up at me as we turn the corner onto Rákóczi Avenue; the sodium light sinks far into her angry eyes, and is lost in the gray. "And you know what? It works! People have their little houses at the Balaton and their Trabants, their private vegetable gardens with chain-link fences all around—all they need is two or three nights a year to go to a show like this and they feel better. They don't care if the debt is paid or not."

And from there to the bus stop at Blaha Lujza Square, Zsóka repeats her favorite English word: "Terrible . . . terrible . . . terrible."

.

A new museum has opened in Óbuda, and Zsóka and I go to see it. First we get lost in the industrial wastes north of Buda, but after asking directions four or five times, going back and forth along the great choking thoroughfares that connect the factories, we find the museum, an eighteenth-century manor at the top of a hill, overlooking a field being torn up for apartment buildings.

The museum's collection is small and eclectic: half modern art and half history and technology. Zsóka has little appreciation for modern art, so she leaves me poking my nose into movable brass-and-glass sculptures and paintings that might as well be upside down, and walks back through the whitewashed, vaulted corridors to the technology section. For some minutes I wander, not much more appreciative than Zsóka, but slightly more patient; then I search her out.

In the very back of the museum, I find her in a room full of old printing presses—big, frightening animals with stomachs of iron and spindly, lead-tipped intestines: older, more complex versions of the modern movable sculptures. Guarding the machines is an ancient man with metal teeth, as vigilant as Gollum, whose job it is to demonstrate their operation. Zsóka and I point and ask, are warned not to touch, watch the workings of the lead tips, listen to the metal teeth. The old man is taken with Zsóka, who has a wonderful way with people who, because of their jobs, must serve her—she wears gratitude beautifully. So before we go, he takes us to one of the simplest presses, no more than a rolling drum and a slab of metal with a well for the composed page. The old man inserts into the well a board with type that has already been carefully laid out, clips a large piece of rag paper to the drum, tells Zsóka with a wink to watch carefully, and twirls the long handle like a medieval soldier winding a catapult. The drum rolls forward and back. The man unclips the paper and hands it to Zsóka with a flourish.

Hungarian words in blue Gothic script. The paper says:

> *Rise, Magyar, your country calls you!*
> *The time has come, now or never!*
> *Shall we be slaves or free?*
> *This is the question—choose!*
> *By the God of the Hungarians,*
> *We swear,*
> *We swear that we will no longer be slaves!*
>
> *Until now have we been enslaved.*
> *Our ancestors are disgraced—*
> *They lived and died a free people,*
> *And cannot find rest in captive ground.*
> *By the God of the Hungarians,*
> *We swear,*
> *We swear that we will no longer be slaves!*

•

"Have you heard?" Zsóka comes in with a Hungarian newspaper in her hands. "Helmut Kohl has won in West Germany."

I look up from the heavy Hungarian grammar book. ("*A magyar parasztok vidámok, boldogok, és gazdagok*": "The Hungarian peasants are merry, happy, and wealthy.") "I know," I say, probably with the kind of weary look that Zsóka wears so often. "I heard it this morning on the Vienna radio."

Zsóka takes a chair and pitches the newspaper into a wastebasket. "This is very good for Ronald Reagan, isn't it?"

"I'm afraid so."

"I think Reagan fixed the election."

"Huh?"

"This was an important election for Reagan, yes? So he fixed it. Through the CIA. He forced the West Germans to take Kohl over Schmidt."

"Well, no, I can't believe that. The relationship between the U.S. and West Europe isn't the same as the one between the Soviets and Eastern Europe. Washington can't just force West Germany to do what it wants."

Pause.

"And I wish you wouldn't look at me all the time like I'm incredibly naïve."

•

When I cycled through Hungary for the first time, back when not only former Budapest Ambassador Yuri Andropov was still alive but Leonid Brezhnev as well, I stayed for two days in a motel outside the town of Esztergom, a day's ride north of Budapest. The assistant manager of the motel was an endearing man in his thirties who would not book a room for me until *The Life of Emile Zola*, currently on the television, was over, and then he did it with tears in his eyes, since he had just seen Zola buried. After he learned I was an American, he barraged me with questions about life there—Did I have a car? A big house? Did I carry a gun? How did I dare walk on the streets without one? He was particularly worried about safety in America because he would be on a group tour to America the following summer and he was planning to defect. We discussed which cities might be the best ones to defect in. I had to admit to him that I'd never considered the problem before. He thought Washington was a bad idea, because the Hungarian embassy there might try to kill him. I opined that surely he wasn't important enough.

I suggested New York City or Los Angeles. (We had to restrict ourselves to cities included in his tour.) But he shook his head. He wanted to defect—and to live—in a city where there were no blacks. He was worried about getting shot by a black man. "Oh, these black people," he said, pouting his mustache worriedly, "I have heard—all they do is *poof poof* with the gun. They walk around and *poof poof*. Just like that." I asked him why he wanted to go to America if he thought he might be killed. "Because you know how much money I make working at this motel? Nothing, that's how much; 4,300 forints." (That was about $110.) "A week?" I asked. "A *month*!" I was suitably unimpressed. "I can't change to another job," he said. "Why not?" "I was trained for this job. No one can go back to training school. The other jobs, they're taken by people who had a different training." (I think now of Zsóka, doodling on the backs of her napkins and in the margins of books; delaying, every morning, the moment when she has to go to work.) "Why didn't you train for something else?" "I was young—I didn't know what I wanted."

"And now you want to defect."

"Americans make so much more money. I want to make more money in America." But everything was more expensive in America, too, I pointed out. A loaf of bread cost a dollar in the States, whereas in Hungary it sold for a fraction of that. He waved the argument aside. "How much does an assistant motel manager make in America?" he demanded. "We will compare this." He whipped out a pocket calculator. I ventured what I thought was a low estimate: $12,000 a year. He punched it in. "Hmm . . . okay . . . $12,000 . . . That would be $1,000 a month . . . or $230.76 a week, counting fifty-two weeks . . . Right. Now . . . How much does a liter of milk cost in America?" He was poised over the keypad.

"We-ell, we don't sell it by the liter. I think it's about a dollar for a half gallon."

The calculator lowered an inch. "But how big is a half gallon?"

"Let's see . . . The way I remember it is, a kilo is 2.2 pounds, and a pint's a pound the world round. I'm pretty sure a cubic centimeter of water weighs one gram, and a liter is a cubic decimeter, or a thousand cubic centimeters, so a liter of water would weigh one kilogram. Or 2.2 pounds. And since a pint's a pound, a liter equals 2.2 pints. Four pints to a half gallon, so a liter is a quarter of 2.2, or . . . uhh, .55 half gallons. A half gallon's a buck in America, so a liter of milk would cost 55 cents."

The calculator had lowered a few more inches. "You sure about all that?"

"No." The calculator dropped. "Actually, the pint's-a-pound rule might apply to British Imperial Pints, and I'm talking about

U.S. Customary Pints." The motel man rolled his eyes. "But it's probably pretty close," I ventured.

He returned to his keypad. "Well, okay . . . a liter of milk is 55 cents . . . An assistant motel manager in America makes $230.76 each week . . . so he could buy 419.58 liters of milk each week. Now, in Hungary, the assistant motel manager makes 4,300 forints a month . . . that's 51,600 forints each year, or . . . 992.31 forints each week . . . and a liter of milk costs 7 forints, so we divide 992.31 by 7 . . . and . . . he can buy 141.76 liters of milk each week . . . I thought so! . . . Now we divide 419.58 by 141.76 and we get . . . 2.96. Ha! 2.96! The American assistant motel manager can buy 2.96 times as much milk as the Hungarian!" He looked shocked; he'd expected American wealth, but not this much. He punched more keys. "Or to view it another way—in a forty-hour work week, the American earns 419.58 liters of milk . . . that's 10.49 liters of milk every hour . . . The Hungarian earns only 141.76 liters of milk in forty-two hours, or only 3.38 liters every hour . . . So *per hour*, the American earns . . . let's see . . . earns 3.1 times more milk than the Hungarian! . . . Or another way to look at it: the Hungarian earns one liter of milk in 17.75 minutes . . . but the American earns one liter of milk every 5.72 minutes . . ." This last statistic did it—he slammed down the calculator. "Every six minutes!" he informed the ceiling loudly. I could hear Christmas Eve anticipation in his voice. All the riches of America— its streets of gold, its two-ton cars, its houses averaging 2,000 square feet of floor space, and its swanky whorehouses for dogs— were encapsulated in that one enchanting idea: in America, even a lowly assistant motel manager could earn a liter of milk in under six minutes.

"But," I pointed out dystopianly, "you'll have to part with 15 percent of that milk in federal income tax, another 5 percent in state tax, and another 7 percent in social security. A single day of college education for one of your kids will cost you a *hundred* liters of milk. And if the milk ever gives you salmonella, God help you with the medical bills."

"The people in the villages live very well," Zsóka says, by way of preparation, as we come to the bottom of the Castle Hill stairs and continue down, under the trees, to Attila Street. "Much better than we in the city." I have heard this before. The citizens of Budapest often talk, a bit jealously, about the wealth of the villages.

We pass a new vegetable store on Attila Street. György and Eszter, who run it with their three children, work exhausting hours, but they are always in the best of spirits. As well they should be—they own the store. Small private shops were made legal in 1981, along with bars, restaurants, and taxicabs. And following the private cabbies who festoon the interiors of their cabs with photographs of themselves, György and Eszter have had large stencils in their likenesses painted on the front windows. Beneath their three-quarter faces (the stenciler has lifted their chins, invested them with a subtly heroic character) are green, cursive letters: *Eszter's and György's Vegetable Store*. Although it is a few minutes out of my way, I often shop here; not to make a political gesture, but because György's good cheer always gives me a lift.

At the South Railroad Station, Ági is waiting for us. (Sándor is home with their two-year-old for the weekend.) Three slate-gray trains, interwar vintage, are backed up against the stops, loading. We find the one going to Győr and get on. After a few minutes, the doors slam shut, the linkages shriek, and the train jolts into motion. Zsóka turns to me and says, "But they work very hard for it." "What?" I say. "The people in the villages," she says. And such is the agreement among the city folk on this wisdom that Ági, who didn't hear Zsóka's first remarks, takes up the thread instantly. "Oh yes," she says happily. "They *are* rich. But they work seven days a week."

Zsóka works only five days a week. Her salary is pretty average: 5,100 forints, or about $130, a month. With extra work, going over book proofs in the evenings, she raises that to about $170. (A private doctor in Budapest can make twelve times that amount.) The basic necessities are cheap. Zsóka's rent is $16 a month. A kilo of bread costs 15 cents. A bus ride is 4 cents. But as one moves away from this most basic level, affordability drops rapidly. A pound of meat or cheese costs a dollar. A pair of shoes, $20 to $25. A dress, $30; a suit, $60. For anything that is not food or clothing, the prices are daunting. Zsóka's black-and-white television set cost her nearly a month's salary. A Trabant, the cheapest car available, would cost her more than a year's salary. A small house, over a decade's salary. Worst of all, she would need the money all at once: it is impossible to buy on credit in Hungary.

For a while in the seventies, such luxury items were gradually becoming more affordable. But for the last three years (it is 1983), inflation has been running at 15 percent and salaries have hardly gone up at all. Zsóka's hasn't budged. The city dwellers are feeling the squeeze.

At the station in Győr, we are met by Ági's brother Béla, a slight, serious man with acne scars on his cheeks. He escorts us out to a new beige Trabant. "My family just bought it," he says, proudly patting the plastic hood. "The waiting list for these is five years long now."

Five years! Despite the cost, can so many Hungarians put up all that money? Or is there a waiting list simply because East Germany doesn't manufacture Trabants very quickly? Béla doesn't know. He's happy just to have the car.

We all squeeze in, and the little Trabant blubbers into life. At the first hill, the poor thing whines and slows to a crawl. "Hungary is a small country," Béla says to me ruefully. "We don't need very fast cars."

The sun is going down when we arrive at the village near Győr in which Ági's and Béla's parents live. Chain-link fences line the dirt streets; behind them stand solid stone houses. The parents (a stout, strong peasant mother and a smaller, frailer father) come out and kiss each of us on both cheeks. I forget my Hungarian, and instead of saying "Good evening," I say "Good night," and everyone laughs. Ági bounds delightedly into the house.

The mother is named Margit, and the father, György. They live in a typical village house—square, single-storied, under a pyramidal roof of tiles. There is a large cluttered kitchen, a smaller, cluttered dining room, two bedrooms, and a cramped, ambiguous space piled nearly to the ceiling with bedding. Both bedrooms and the dining room are filled with solid, dark, wooden furniture. Hangings, photographs, clocks, and curtains cover most of the wall space. The beds are immense, the bloated mattresses swelling in the middle like pitcher's mounds. A television set babbles at the end of the master bed, and Ági's father returns to it as soon as the introductions are over.

The house sits on about a quarter-acre lot. Built onto the back is a garage filled with agricultural tools. Sticking out from the garage is the stable, where the cow is kept. Next to the stable is the chicken coop, and behind the chicken coop is the pigpen. Between coop, stable, and pen—everywhere, in fact, except where the driveway is—lies the garden, which, since it is mid-March, is beginning to show sprouts of the earliest vegetables. Trellises for grapevines have been put up wherever they do not block sunlight from the garden—over the chicken coop, above the stone paving that skirts the stable, across the driveway. The whole lot is enclosed by fruit trees, which stand on all four sides, just inside the fence.

The family also owns a plot of land that lies just outside the village, about fifty yards away. Ági takes us there. The plot is not large—something around an acre—but every square foot of it is used. Half has been prepared for grain; the other half is an apple-tree nursery. Ági explains that the tree nursery is unusual, the result of a daring decision by her father. As the produce market frees up, more and more villagers are making use of whatever land they have. For borders and small pieces of unused land, apple trees are popular, because they bear heavily and are fairly hardy; but people don't want to start from seed, so they buy her father's young trees.

"When I first brought Sándor to meet my parents," Ági says, "we all had dinner together. Afterward, my father took me aside and said, 'He seems like a pleasant-enough fellow, but he doesn't know anything about apple trees.' "

Through a screen of beeches, we can see a very large field. In the distance, a tractor charges like a bull, head down, flipping the soil. Ági says that her family owned part of the field until the fifties, but that the whole thing now is a cooperative. Her father used to work in the cooperative, spending evenings and weekends on his own plot, but he retired from it two years ago. Now he is weakening, and Ági's mother does most of the work with the garden, the grain, and the young trees, while her father feeds the animals and trains the vines.

By the time we return to the house, dinner is ready, and the economics of this rich village life begin to be apparent. Baskets on the table hold bread that was made from wheat grown in the family plot. The wine in the bottles comes from the grapes that grew last year above the driveway. The two pig's feet in the big pot of broth originated in the pen behind the chicken coop. The chicken comes from the coop itself. The cheese and sour-cream sauce for the chicken come from the cow in the stable. The peppers and tomatoes in the pickled salad were grown in the garden behind the pigpen. The sliced apples were picked last November from the trees by the front gate. The yoghurt for dessert also came from the cow, and the strawberries in the preserves in the yoghurt came from the garden next to the chicken coop. As we eat, all Zsóka and I can say, somewhat inadequately, is *"Nagyon finom"*— "Very fine." The food in the stores in Budapest, especially the bread and preserves, is nothing like this.

Ági's mother never sits down, as she is kept busy bringing platters in and taking empty dishes out. Now and then she relaxes long enough to nibble, standing, on a pig crackling that she fishes out of a big metal bowl on the china chest. Béla complains to his mother about the broth, and then about the sauce, and although I met him only hours ago, I can barely restrain myself from kicking him under the table.

Dinner conversation is mainly gossip, in Hungarian, about people in the village. No one brings up politics. No one mentions young György, who still hasn't returned from West Germany.

Over dessert, I am asked about my travels. (Both of the parents speak only Hungarian, so Béla translates the harder stuff for me.) When I am asked how long I have been away from home, I try to figure it out from my departure date: March 19, 1982.

"But today is March 19!" Ági exclaims.

"It is?" (Sometimes I forget my own birthday.) "Well, tonight is my first anniversary, then." And I am duly congratulated.

Later, Ági, Zsóka, and I take a walk around the village's poorly lit streets. Ági tells us that her mother makes most of her own and her husband's clothes. The curtains and the tower of bedding in the ambiguous space were also made by her mother. Moreover, only a fraction of what her parents grow is consumed at home. Much produce from the garden ends up at the market in Budapest. Her father also rents out their machinery to other families in the village, and sometimes, in the spring, they sell piglets, or a calf, if they haven't enough grass to raise it themselves. With the money they have saved up, Ági's parents bought the apartment that Béla is now living in. Just recently, they paid for the Trabant. Ági views her family as evidence that things are getting better. People have food now, and clothes, and even a car to drive on Sundays. What else could they want?

"And there is nothing unusual about my family," Ági says. "Many of the families in this village are doing just as well." In the darkness beyond the feeble lamplight, I can see other well-kept houses, other trellises, other chicken coops.

One and a half million families—over half the population of Hungary—keep private gardens and animals in their yards (even János Kádár has his chickens). Together, this horde of tiny plots, worked during hours off from the cooperative farm with hoes and bare hands, produces one-third of all the beef and dairy cattle in Hungary, two-fifths of all the vegetables, one half of the pigs, one half of the fruit and wine, and nearly three-quarters of the poultry.

I think of the prices in Budapest, where the people would like to eat meat every other day but can't afford it, where a mediocre pair of pants costs a week's wages. Or the quality of the goods there, which may be high for the East Bloc but can't approach the food, the bedding, or the furniture of Ági's parents. I see now how people in Budapest could talk a little ruefully about village money. Still, I don't think the city dwellers are being fair when they say that the villagers live better. Certainly, they eat better. But the amount of work that went into our meal tonight, or into the sturdy clothing of Ági's parents or the impressive production statistics, is rather appalling. It's too easy for the urbanites to point to the results of rural industry and say that the life is good, and then to add, offhandedly, that the work is hard. The work *is* the life. The food may be beyond them, but people in Budapest could make their own clothes and quilts, too, if they wanted to. Instead, they moonlight for more of the forints that fall so pitifully short in the stores. Only the really industrious ones attain farmers' hours: those who drive private taxis every night after a full day's work, or those who spend fifteen hours a day in a vegetable store that used to be their living room.

We pass the silhouette of a half-finished house. Along the side of the lane, building material has been stacked. Farther back, in the yard, I can see a small cement mixer, designed to be turned by hand. Two trowels lie on a board set on two stacks of blocks. The walls that are already up look sturdy, if not precisely straight. An amateur job.

Perhaps the most telling statistic: fully 60 percent of Hungary's new housing is put up privately, by the landowner, friends, and neighbors. Virtually all the bungalows—the eagerly sought bungalows—on Lakes Balaton and Velence are put up on weekends, in off-hours, by people learning the trade as they go along.

What to think of all this industry, this tireless tending, Candide-style, of little gardens? Surely that depends on who you are. Americans, I think, are inclined to see hard domestic work as both a source and a symptom of optimism; source, because it causes the Hungarians' material prosperity to rise, and symptom, because people don't often work for the future unless they believe in it. But this attitude presumptively yokes the quality of life to material prosperity; Americans tend not only to ignore questions concerning the purpose or "meaning" of life (beyond the accumulation of wealth) but to deride such questions whenever they arise. The unique material success of our 200-year history has bestowed on us the unique conviction that we already *know* the meaning of life, which is simply to be American, to stay on the track we laid down in 1787. We have lost the awareness of the value of moral questioning and striving that Eastern Europeans, with their disastrous recent histories, still share.

By contrast, many Hungarians find cause for worry in their country's prosperity. "Selfishness and self-centeredness have grown to impressive proportions in our days," wrote Lajos Konya in the introductory article of a debate on Hungarian life. "More and more people have no other aim than to create a comfortable little existence for themselves, if possible, with a car." Konya wrote for the government, so his argument was cast in the usual socialist terms of morality, but Hungarians who dislike and defy the government say similar things, for different reasons. The Hungarian revolutions—1848 and 1956—loom larger in Hungarian minds than the American Revolution does in ours, partly because theirs were more recent, partly because they failed, and partly because Hungarians live under a government that pays constant lip service to revolutionary values. For Hungarian intellectuals, prosperity is not only not *enough*, it is not even *good*, to the extent that it lulls people into accepting the present society, with all its political shortcomings. This is Zsóka's opinion. What good is more leisure time to read when you can't read whatever you want? What good is a car when you can't drive it the sixty miles from Budapest to Vienna? The government, meanwhile, is caught in a bind, because it lauds revolutionary change even though it is fundamentally conservative. (Zsóka: "You shouldn't think I favor capitalism. If I lived in the West, I would be a socialist. The issue is not capitalism vs. Communism but opportunism vs. integrity. The same kind of people, selfish people, rise to the top in both systems. The Communists here are not idealists, they just want to live in bigger houses.")

There is only one thing that people like Zsóka and the government can agree on: prosperity encourages complacency, and complacency is counter to the Hungarian spirit. But can complacency be counter to the Hungarian spirit if so many Hungarians are growing complacent? Less than thirty years ago, Hungarians tried to take their fate in their hands and the Soviets stepped on them. Ten years before that, a postwar constitutional government died before it was born. For the thirty years before that, Hungary was ruled by a quasi-Fascist dictator, Admiral Horthy, and for the 230 years before *that*, the country was an abject vassal of the Austrian Empire. How much denial can people endure before they draw their heads into their shells and call their shells the world? An American might see optimism behind the villagers' work, but perhaps the real backdrop is resignation.

We turn another corner and find ourselves back on Ági's parents' lane. Lights are on in the dining room. "Oh dear, I think we have kept them up," Ági says. "They won't be pleased."

But when she opens the door, there is a happy shout of greeting, and as Zsóka and I come in, Ági's mother hands each of us a glass. Béla disappears into the kitchen and returns with a bottle of champagne.

"What's the occasion?" I inquire, as he fills my glass.

"Don't you remember?" he asks, surprised. "This is your first anniversary! *Egéségedre! Bon voyage!*"

The champagne is the only thing I consume at that house which was bought, not made.

·

In a red-velvet room in the National Museum, in a glass case flanked by two guards, lie the holy crown, scepter, and orb of the Hungarian state, which were sent (so the legend says) by Pope Sylvester II to Saint Stephen in A.D. 1000 to mark both Stephen's conversion to Christianity and his assumption of Hungarian (and with it, European) royalty. These objects are immensely important to the Hungarian people, who perceive in the curious bent cross and enameled bands of the ancient crown some mystical affirmation of Hungary's Catholicism and its legitimate statehood. In tandem with this odd iconography has arisen the so-called myth of Saint Stephen: the idea that Hungary is burdened with a divine mission to protect the West from the incursions of the East. Saint Stephen was an Easterner, a Uralic nomad who in taking the crown chose the West. And since A.D. 1000, Hungary has defended Catholicism against Orthodoxy, civilization against the Mongols, Christians against the Turks. Just as Hungary took the brunt of the Turkish advance in the sixteenth and seventeenth centuries, enabling Vienna (the Hungarians would say) to stop the Muslims at its gates, so it suffered Soviet occupation so that Austria might be neutral. The sense of doom that shrouds all talk of 1956 stems from the belief that Hungary was only fulfilling, yet again, its ordained role: to suffer, in this case, for freedom, and to be abandoned by the free societies for which it suffered.

This idea of suffering might sound familiar. "The Russians fight the Germans and so Budapest is destroyed!" said Mrs. Nagy. After his death in *Sztarcsinálók*, Nero was wrapped in a white shroud. The brilliant choreographer from Győr, dancing Don Juan in the huge Sports Hall, was impaled by his own sword on a cross. The lead dancer in *A Próba* was crucified before being machine-gunned. And in the Hungarian schools, after the Treaty of Trianon, the children once recited:

> *I believe in one God,*
> *I believe in the fatherland,*
> *I believe in Hungary's resurrection.*

Nothing has changed, not the Hungarians' grievance or its Christian trappings. Only faith in the resurrection has been lost.

.

On a frigid Sunday morning, when the sheets of ice on the streets reflect a sunless sky of dead white, Zsóka and I walk to Moszkva Square and wait for one of the electric trolleys. Gypsy women and their little boys are selling flowers and bracelets in front of the ticket machines. The Gypsies of Budapest, influenced, perhaps, by the Hungarians, are the most reserved I have ever encountered—they are almost shy. The heavily bundled boys tug on the coats of passersby and point them to their mothers' carts. "You don't want any flowers?" I ask Zsóka, and she turns, considers the line of swarthy, colorful women for a moment, almost in a daze. "No, I guess not," she says distantly.

She has been sleeping badly. Every night, I wake to hear her crying out and turning, always turning, from one side to the other. Some nights, she gets up three or four times and goes into the kitchen or the bathroom for a few minutes before creeping back across the floor and into bed, to wait for more sleep to come. In the morning, she goes off to work with her eyes barely open.

The trolley arrives—three cars end-to-end, like a row of yellow beetles—and we climb aboard, I remembering, for once, to follow Hungarian etiquette and hand Zsóka up first. The doors hiss shut, we punch our yellow tickets, and the trolley ascends gently and slowly into the hills. The city is quiet this morning, as it is only on the coldest of days. The Trabants won't start in the cold, so the streets are empty. The acrid smell of thousands of wood, coal, and gas stoves pervades even the trolley.

The only other person in our car is an elderly woman holding three white lilies. She stares out the window, and her reflection stares sadly back, as if a ghost were pressing its face to the glass, envious of our warmth inside. The woman gets off at the same stop we do. Another flower seller has set up next to the trolley stop, a jovial man with roses, lilies, tulips, and long-needle pine boughs. Zsóka considers again, and perhaps she thinks of the woman with the lilies, who has already disappeared through the gate. "Perhaps I *will* have some flowers." We buy two roses and a soft tail of pine; then we go into the cemetery.

It's an enormous place, one of the largest in the city, and it takes us some time to reach Mr. Nagy's grave. We turn from the gravel path onto one of the hundreds of narrow dirt tracks that form a close grid, and we go up, under bare willow trees, stepping over frozen roots. The tombstones, all of them new in this quarter, are crowded together unmercifully. Many of them carry photographs of the deceased, and all Zsóka will say, as we turn from one path to the next, walking among the markers like cold-dulled beasts forcing a way through underbrush, is "I think that is terrible—the photographs; isn't it enough that they are dead, that we cannot forget?"

On the side of a low hill, we come to it: a polished slab of black marble. It is grander than I had expected, larger than any of the markers around it. But the slab does not say *Nagy Pál*. It says *Karinthy Tamás*. I look at Zsóka questioningly.

"Tamás was a good friend of my father; he also worked at the university. My mother already had a place in her family plot, but there was no room there for my father. Tamás already owned this grave, and he had room for one more, because he had intended to marry and never did. That was very lucky for my

father; all the space has been sold in this cemetery for years now."
Zsóka draws her gloved hand over the surface of the slab, and it
comes away dirty. "Tamás died a few years ago. When my father
died in November, it was already terribly cold—they had to dig
up the ground with cutting machines. But they couldn't put his
name on the stone; if it is too cold, the chisel will crack the stone.
So we have to wait until the spring for his name."

Tamás's name is large and in the middle of the slab. Looking
at it now, I don't see where there is room for Mr. Nagy's name. It
will have to be smaller and over to one side—like an afterthought.
Perhaps that is the penalty for having lived longer than Tamás,
or perhaps Tamás gets top billing because he owned the place
first. In either case, it seems an unjust end for Mr. Nagy, this
melancholy man whom I knew so little. A helpless pawn on the
eastern front, an orphaned villager seeking a life with thousands
of other refugees in the crowded capital, an academic whose career
was held back by enemies, finally an ailing retiree in a small duplex
who knew too well that his wife bemoaned his deterioration and
who could see reflected in his daughter's eyes his own sense of the
tenuousness of happiness, of life itself—couldn't he have had his
own grave marker, or at least one with room for his too common
name? Did he have to scrounge for this final, deep place, exactly
as he had scrounged for a room after the war, in the half-destroyed
city where he had known no one? Even here, in the one club that
we all get to join, he is on the outside looking in—like the blank-
eyed ghost in the trolley window.

"We had to wait three weeks before he could be buried. The
state is always behind in the burials, especially in the winter. They
have to freeze the bodies so that they will keep until the grave is
ready." Zsóka says this while taking off her gloves. She kneels by
the slab and starts to wipe away the dust and the finely powdered
tree bark. Her gloves are too small to do much cleaning, and I
help with a large handkerchief. But we are just pushing the dirt
around. Finally, we take handfuls of snow and rub them on the
marble, working our way slowly across the big slab. The cold
marble and the snow wake a burning in my fingers which gradually
becomes a numbness. We keep working—kneeling, reaching across.

The black deepens, and we see our faces in the stone, looking up out of the grave. When all the dirt is gone, I take off one of my shirts and dry the whole slab with it. Zsóka puts the roses in the cup embedded in the marble and curls around them, like an encircling arm, the pine bough. We step back, and the marker looks much better, clean and shining like a fresh promise. Beside me, Zsóka is crying. I ignore her, because I know that is what she wants.

Later, waiting for the trolley, Zsóka says, "After the first stroke, he could move only his eyes. They came to take him to the hospital, and my mother and I were there—they carried him out of the house, with his eyes open; three big men. And then in the hospital he just lay there. He couldn't even move his head. But his eyes were the same. That was the worst part. I knew he was still in there, behind his eyes. He was looking out, but he couldn't speak. How terrible that must have been—to be trapped! I knew he wanted to tell me something. He would catch me with his eyes and beg me to understand. Then after a few days he had the second stroke, and he was dead." Zsóka shrugs. "I don't know. I think he wanted to tell me why."

" 'Why'?"

"Why such a thing would happen. *How* such a thing could happen to such a good man, such a kind man. I—I cannot understand that."

Zsóka means it. Her face, her voice show that she genuinely does not understand; moreover, that she believes there *is* an explanation and that other, mysterious people know it, but that none of them has bothered to tell her, just as these same distant, knowledgeable people never tell her what the symbols mean in the political allegories on television, in the theater, in the books. And now, by the trolley tracks, she says it—exactly what she exclaims when she feels the political art of her countrymen leaving her behind: "What does it all *mean?*" She is asking me. I have no answer, nothing, to give her.

Another funeral is going on behind us. Having seen it on the way out, I know that the casket and the mourners share a concrete pavilion just inside the cemetery gate. Two tripods emit thin flames that tremble and throw out threads of oily black smoke. The priest stands on a rostrum, a heavy coat over his vestments, and reads from a pocket-sized book. Now it has begun to snow, in the niggardly manner of very cold days, and even from outside the gate I can hear each hiss as a flake falls into one flame or the other. Then a different hiss—the trolley doors opening.

•

Another Sunday morning, closer to spring, in the Mátyás Church on Castle Hill. Zsóka and I arrived late and all the pews were filled, so we are standing in the back, on the stairs below the rose window. Light tainted by the colorful glass spills through the south windows and makes an Oriental rug of the stone floor, decorates the black Sunday coats with epaulets, but the cavernous interior is still, as always, somehow dark. The murals and geometrical designs that cover the dusky red walls are obscured by the darkness and the incense smoke. The old organ is still under restoration, and the pipes and fittings, the worm-eaten wooden casements lie like stacks of corpses under shrouds to the right and left of the nave. The temporary organ wheezes Haydn from one of the chapels in the north aisle, and the choir, singing from the loft on the west wall where the real organ belongs, is having trouble keeping time with it. Everyone is looking forward to the return of the old organ, but each week the piles of tubes look the same; the fine brick-red dust on the shrouds is undisturbed.

This 700-year-old building, perched thrillingly on its bluff over the Danube, is another of the symbols of Budapest. Its official name is the Church of Our Great Lady, but no one calls it that, as the Great Lady is not nationalist enough. The Hungarians prefer a more Magyar name, the "Mátyás Templom"—the name derives from King Matthias Corvinus, the Renaissance king who had the church splendidly rebuilt in 1470.

Like any good symbol, the Mátyás Church has about it elements that call aspects of the city and the nation to mind. Each time Hungary has been ravaged, rebuilt, or modified, so has the church. When the Turks occupied Hungary from 1541 to 1686, they converted the Mátyás Church into their principal mosque. They found it with murals on the walls commemorating János Hunyadi's great victory over them at Belgrade in 1456. Not surprisingly, they destroyed the murals, replacing them with a quotation from the Koran: "Behold, Allah commands truth and good deeds." When the Habsburgs took Buda from the Turks in 1686, both the city and the Hungarians' esteem were badly damaged—as was the church. The line from the Koran was obliterated and new Turk-bashing murals were put in. In the eighteenth century, when Viennese Baroque construction was changing the face of the city, Viennese Baroque touches were added to the church, and in the middle of the nineteenth century, when even greater Habsburg building projects were under way in Pest, the church was completely reconstructed. Today, people may call it the Mátyás Church, but it bears marks of each of the centuries after Matthias as well.

The congregation starts into the Hymn of Preparation as the sacraments are brought to the Holy Table. None of us has a hymn book, and the people sing uncertainly from memory, waiting for others to come up with the words. I hum along; Zsóka, who thinks you shouldn't sing to God unless you believe in Him, only listens. The organ sounds as if it should be accompanied by a monkey in a little bellhop's uniform.

The Mátyás Church remains a synecdoche of the city, a mishmash of influences. It boasts a cockeyed front, with a Gothic rose window in the middle (made of fragments of the glass blown out during World War II), a squat, square, Romanesque tower on the left, and a tall spire on the right. The spire is itself asymmetrical, with an extra rib of stone that shoots up one side. No two of the façade's arches match: they range from pure Gothic below to a rounded Oriental Venetian–St. Marks style above. The building is capped by a roof of colored tiles that might have been inspired by French work, while the murals inside are a mixture of turn-of-the-century Victorian pomp and some fairly inspired medieval fakery, all against an Oriental background of arabesques.

The shackled chaos of the Mátyás Church is no less appealing than the ordered confusion of Budapest; both have the scarred and patched, curiously attractive face of a fighter. If the Chain Bridge symbolizes Budapest's unity, then the Mátyás Church embodies its history. The bridge reflects the city's strength; the church is a monument to the city's suffering. What place better than a church?

The communion draws to a close. Men and women come away from the rail and find their places again in the pews, as the acolytes clear the Holy Table. The man in front of me stifles a yawn and his wife kicks him softly in the leg. The organ feebly groans through the Communion Hymn, and the congregation groans feebly back at it. Then the benedictory prayer is recited by the fleshy priest, with his hands, like pale basswood leaves, nestling palms in front of him.

In most countries, this would be the end of the service. But in Hungary there remains a final observance. The organ starts up again, and the people begin to sing the National Anthem. Even I know the words to this one, and I join in. Zsóka, too, sings.

Isten, áldd meg a magyart—

The National Anthem has always been viewed askance by the Communist government, partly because it is, of course, nationalist, and partly because it mentions God. (The entire song, in fact, is a prayer.) But there is, I think, a more important reason: the anthem, for the Hungarians, is wrenchingly sad, almost despairing. And despair, especially nationalist despair, does not belong in the optimistic, progressive atmosphere of a people's democracy. On the infrequent occasions that the National Anthem is played during a public ceremony, it is flanked on either side, like a prisoner escorted by two guards, by the Russian anthem and the Internationale. Only in church is it sung without an escort.

But whenever Hungarians sing the anthem, they put their hearts into it. For the first time this Sunday morning, the congregation manages to drown out the dreadful little organ:

I-sten, áldd meg a ma-gyart—

Not an interjection ("God bless the Magyar") but a plea— "Please, God, bless the Magyar people," sung quietly.

Jó ked-vel bö - ség — gel

"Give them joy and plenty."

Nyújts fe - lé - je vé-dö kart, Ha küzd el - len - ség — gel

A modulation down from the first line, the singing growing louder: "Extend over them a protective hand, if they are fighting the enemy."

Bal-sors a - kit ré-gen tép

A shift of key here, into G minor, and a poignant line: "To those whom misfortune for so long has ravaged—"

Hozz re-a vig esz-ten - döt—

Back into B♭ major, still crescendoing, and striking the hopeful major third: "Bring, God, happy years—"

And then, characteristically, a reason is given *why* God should be kind to them (the Hungarians not believing in happiness as a natural state). Full forte, reaching up:

Meg bün-höd-te már e nép a' múl-tat sjö - ven—döt.

This last line, descending from a wail on the highest note of the anthem down the long, dying scale, sums up the particular melancholy of the Hungarians: "This nation has already atoned for its past and future sins."

An arresting idea. And it has hints, beneath its sadness, of defiance, of arrogance, even of accusation. What does a nation need to have suffered, I wonder, to believe that it has atoned for all *future* sins?

The temporary organ plays the concluding measures and dies out. There is a small silence, while the multicolored incense hangs motionless in front of the windows. Then the postlude begins and the congregation dissolves into a hubbub of heads turning, shoulders taking on coats. Zsóka and I go out, at the head of the throng, through the south porch into the wintry sunshine. Zsóka is pensive. The National Anthem wakes longings in her that she cannot express, that possess her thoughts with the blank muteness of the incense we are leaving behind us. So we walk across Trinity Square without speaking, past the tortured statue of God on His cloud, and up Trinity Street, between the destroyed and restored Baroque and medieval buildings, the Mátyás Church with its lopsided visage of a losing fighter receding behind us.

Budapest, Carrara, Boston; February 1984–August 1985

ACKNOWLEDGMENTS

I would like to thank Abigail and Stephan Thernstrom for their encouragement, and for invaluable help in getting the manuscript off my desk and into an editor's office; Dick Margolis, for wise criticism; Peter Todorov, for information on Bulgaria and the Bulgarian language; Stefania Jha, for her patience in checking my Hungarian orthography; Blanche Gregory, for everything; Margaret Stetz, for teaching me how to write; Bill Newlin, for some fancy pencil work; and Steve Wasserman, for rather amazing persistence.

I would like to give special thanks to Jonathan Cohler and Patrick Kenealy, for a quiet place to work at night for thirteen months, and all a writer needs: light, coffee, a bathroom, and someone to talk to at 3 a.m.